INVESTIGATING THE BIOLOGICAL
FOUNDATIONS OF HUMAN MORALITY

Edited by

James P. Hurd

Symposium Series
Volume 37

The Edwin Mellen Press
Lewiston/Queenston/Lampeter

Library of Congress Cataloging-in-Publication Data

Investigating the biological foundations of human morality / James P.
Hurd.
     p.   cm. -- (Symposium series ; vol. 37)
    Includes bibliographical references and index.
    ISBN 0-7734-8843-X
    1. Ethics, Evolutionary. 2. Human evolution--Moral and ethical
aspects. 3. Sociobiology--Philosophy. I. Hurd, James P., 1941-
. II. Series: Symposium series (Edwin Mellen Press) ; v. 37.
BJ1311.I58 1996
171'.7--dc20   95-41538
                                                CIP

This is volume 37 in the continuing series
Symposium Series
Volume 37 ISBN 0-7734-8843-X
SS Series ISBN 0-88946-989-X

A CIP catalog record for this book is available from the British Library.

Copyright © 1996 The Edwin Mellen Press

All rights reserved. For information contact

The Edwin Mellen Press
Box 450
Lewiston, New York
USA 14092-0450

The Edwin Mellen Press
Box 67
Queenston, Ontario
CANADA L0S 1L0

The Edwin Mellen Press, Ltd.
Lampeter, Dyfed, Wales
UNITED KINGDOM SA48 7DY

Printed in the United States of America

The licentious tell men of orderly lives that they stray from nature's path, while they themselves follow it; as people in a ship think those move who are on the shore ... We must have a fixed point in order to judge. The harbor decides for those who are in a ship; but where shall we find a harbor for morality?

Pascal, *Pensee*, 383

TABLE OF CONTENTS

Preface

We see two trends in recent studies of social behavior: the accelerating ability to specify genetic predispositions for certain behaviors (alcoholism, aggression, etc.), and the breakdown of social consensus about what is moral or immoral (sexual behavior, abortion, etc.). These trends reinforce the interest in investigating the biological underpinnings of human morality. The impetus for this volume was the Conference on Biology and Morality at Bethel College, St. Paul, in March, 1992. Some of the conference participants contributed to this volume.

Morality means the human propensity to judge some behaviors as good, admirable, and worthy of reward, and other behaviors as bad, worthy of punishment. It includes both the rules about behavior that particular societies have developed and also a discussion of the behaviors themselves.

The central question of this volume is: *To what extent is evolutionary biology a necessary and sufficient explanation for human morality?* Biologists, psychologists, anthropologists, theologians and philosophers address this question from the perspective of their disciplines, and also from an interdisciplinary perspective. Four main issues are addressed:

1. Is human moral behavior unique? To what extent can it be explained using models of animal behavior?

2. Does biology provide us only with a description of how morality has evolved, or can it also provide us with a prescription for what morality should be? If the latter, do we seek to prescribe moral behavior as that behavior which our biology has programmed, or should morality be a culturally-designed strategy to combat, or compensate for, biological propensities?

3. Can morality be adequately explained by a demonstration of natural selection operating at the individual level, or are we forced to consider natural selection operating at the level of the group or species?

4. To what extent can humans make autonomous moral choices (i.e., choices that are not predetermined by their biology or environment)?

In Chapter 1, **William Irons** (Department of Anthropology, Northwestern University) finds sociobiology a necessary and sufficient explanation for the rise of morality, without recourse to other explanations. He doubts whether there can be any moral universals, pointing out that individual cultures have developed different moralities. Moral sentiments are explained as enhancing cooperation. Both the desire to punish wrongdoers, and also the moral aggression carried out against those who would undermine cooperation, are evolved checks against exploitation by cheaters who take advantage of the moral sentiments. He insists that moral beliefs and behaviors can be explained as the result of natural selection operating on individuals, rather than on groups or on species.

In Chapter 2, **Linda Mealey** (Department of Psychology, College of St. Benedict, St. Joseph, Minnesota) explains how natural selection might have produced specific cognitive mechanisms for human behaviors in response to specific environmental challenges. The human brain has a modular structure, where specific modules (such as areas for language perception and production) have evolved cumulatively in response to important adaptive challenges humans have faced in the past. She hypothesizes that moral behavior as well emanates from a specialized cognitive mechanism. A research design is presented that would test the hypothesis that a specific cognitive mechanism allows individuals to recognize cheaters and people of high status.

In Chapter 3, **Carole Young** (Department of Psychology, Bethel College, St. Paul, Minnesota) mediates a "dialogue" between B. F. Skinner and Richard Alexander in order to examine the behaviorism tradition of psychology in the light of sociobiology. Both theorists employ the concept of human selection of certain behavioral repertoires, including behavior we would classify as moral. She criticizes Alexander's idea that moral behavior can be explained as an anticipation of future reward. Rather, behavior should be seen as a response to a history of *past* rewards. The success or failure of stimulus-response experiments through operant conditioning, however, must still be explained within the constraints of natural selection.

In Chapter 4, **Garrett Paul** (Department of Religion, Gustavus Adolphus College, St. Peter, Minnesota) notes that biology and ethics have been polarized along several dichotomies: nature/history; determinism/ voluntarism; fact/value. He proposes several possibilities for re-connecting these two disciplines in areas such as natural law traditions, process philosophy and theology, and the doctrine of creation in Christianity. We need to understand our biology in order to formulate rules for our behavior. But our moral behavior is neither free from, nor determined by, our biology. Rather, we *respond* to our biological inclinations. Paul argues that we are the arbiters, and we can decide whether we should follow our biological impulses or resist them.

In Chapter 5, **Gregg Johnson** (Department of Biology, Bethel College, St. Paul, Minnesota) notes a high incidence of extended altruism in humans, altruism that goes beyond a biologically-adaptive behavior that increases the reproductive success of the altruistic individual. This extended altruism positions our species well to respond to novel environments and new challenges, since it has the effect of preserving a variety of genetic traits that may be adaptive in the future. Extended altruism, while adaptive for the species, is maladaptive for the individual. Thus, we need an explanation for it that goes beyond natural selection acting on the individual.

In Chapter 6, **Jeff Schloss** (Department of Biology, Westmont College, Santa Barbara, California) argues that biology is a necessary, relevant, but *not* a sufficient explanation of morality. He suggests that sociobiologists are highly skilled at re-classifying many seemingly "altruistic" acts as enlightened selfishness (e.g., kin selection or reciprocal altruism). They do this because the theory itself demands it. However, it is epistemologically very difficult to classify human behavioral phenotypes, and it is logically impossible to demonstrate the *non*existence of true altruism. He notes that some sociobiologists slip into discussing *motives* for moral behavior, even though natural selection cannot act on motives; it can only act on the behavior itself. He makes a sociobiological analysis of some of the statements of Jesus. For example, Jesus warns that even "Gentiles and sinners" share with friends and family; therefore this behavior is not particularly praiseworthy. Rather, the disciple is urged to share with strangers and even enemies. Schloss notes that people usually affirm these biblical moral norms, but at the same time are often reluctant to practice them. This is an observation consistent with sociobiological theory.

In Chapter 7, **Timothy Shaw** (Department of Biology, Bethel College, St. Paul, Minnesota) cites triune brain theory to argue that the brain has evolved in three successive stages: reptilian, paleomammalian, and neomammalian. In mammals, it is possible that these "brains" are simultaneously active, and that each of them might suggest a different response to one single stimulus. Shaw argues that the human brain is unique, where the human neocortex is the arbiter, allowing humans to choose how to respond to the stimulus. These structures provide the organism with the capacity for unique religious and moral behaviors. Religions often demand that an individual forego behaviors that would be satisfying to the earlier "brains" (indeed, these lower-brain behaviors are sometimes defined as "sin"). Instead, the individual is urged to choose behaviors that demand altruistic self-sacrifice for the good of the larger group. He argues that it is difficult to provide a sociobiological explanation for the evolution of these human behaviors.

In Chapter 8, **Elving Anderson** (Emeritus, Department of Genetics, University of Minnesota) and **Bruce Reichenbach** (Department of Philosophy, Augsburg College, St. Paul, Minnesota) argue that the brain mediates the impact of genes upon behavior. A symbiotic combination of biological and cultural evolution (including religion) has been essential for the development of altruism toward non-kin. Rapid advances in the neurosciences and the Human Genome Project will provide a critical test of some of the central hypotheses of sociobiology.

In Chapter 9, **Lucie Johnson** (Department of Psychology, Bethel College, St. Paul, Minnesota) outlines the intuitive moral systems of Sigmund Freud, E. O. Wilson, and Vladimir Lefebvre. She notes that, even though they deny transcendence, they use categories of good and evil when explaining human morality. Thus, they imply a moral "ought," although their theories do not allow for it. Freud explained positive morality as sublimation, or the workings of the superego. Wilson explained positive morality as adaptive, arising from the natural order. Lefebvre speculates that when humans make moral choices they conform to predictions generated by a simple binary mathematical model, as if the brain had an inner moral computer. Johnson observes that all three men were trying to understand, not why humans are capable of violence or evil, but why they are capable of exhibiting compassion and goodness.

In Chapter 10, **Gary Simpson** (Department of Systematic Theology, Luther Northwestern Theological Seminary, St. Paul, Minnesota) argues that biological explanations are insufficient to explain human moral behavior. Human behavior is always imbedded in a wider symbolic context that is inaccessible to biological or behavioristic explanations. He follows Pannenberg in arguing that theology should begin, not with God, but with empirical observations of human experience and behavior. Humans are capable of being centered "outside themselves;" thus they can reflect on their actions and consciously regulate them. Human uniqueness lies in this capacity for *exocentricity*, the ability to operate from outside of one's selfish center.

In Chapter 11, **Alfred Kracher** (Iowa State University) notes that to test sociobiological theory we need to focus on critical test cases where natural human appetites are in strong conflict with one another. In these cases, do humans choose the path of action that sociobiology predicts? He argues that biology dictates our behavior, but that humans can *transfer* their biologically-based behavior to new objects of their own choosing (as in the redirection of parental care to adopted children). He notes that people knew about human biological constraints, but often chose to transcend them, long before sociobiological theory was articulated. Thus he joins Paul, Gregg Johnson, and Shaw in arguing the role of human choice. Patterns of moral behavior are broadly determined biologically, but the *context* of the behavior is determined culturally, and the *object* of the behavior is chosen by the acting individual.

In Chapter 12, **James Fetzer** (Department of Philosophy, University of Minnesota, Duluth) argues that humans do not always behave morally, kin selection and reciprocal altruism are not invariably ethical, and any evolutionary approach to ethics is incomplete in itself. Fetzer, like Paul above, argues that morality cannot be merely a matter of individual taste. He suggests a biologically-based ethical imperative: the survival and reproduction of our species. He argues that this is ethical, if anything is. Theories of ethics based on evolution should be considered against the background of traditional conceptions of morality. Morality is still evolving in the human species; therefore, descriptions *of* morality do not automatically lead to prescriptions *for* morality.

Acknowledgments. Lucie Johnson, Tim Shaw, Roger Olson, Alan Padgett and Carole Young acted as an editorial committee and helped in the initial editing of some of the manuscripts. Jim Fetzer and Ron Harris gave helpful advice about the publishing process. Janine MacFarland handled much correspondence and editing of the bibliographies. Finally, I wish to thank each of the contributors to the volume for their patience and timely submissions.

James P. Hurd

Bethel College, St. Paul, Minnesota

August 29, 1995

Chapter 1   Morality as an Evolved Adaptation

William Irons

This paper presents a theory of the evolution of human morality by natural selection. By morality I mean the propensity of human beings to judge certain forms of behavior as good and deserving of admiration, encouragement and reward, and to judge other forms of behavior as bad, not to be repeated or imitated, and worthy of punishment. I also include in morality the systems of rules which particular societies develop to codify and systematize these judgments. These systems of rules are developed gradually over many generations and represent the judgment of many individuals about exactly what sorts of behaviors are right, what sorts are wrong and what rewards and punishments should accompany each form of behavior. Human beings have not only a propensity to judge various forms of behavior as morally right or wrong, but also a propensity to be sensitive to the judgments of their community about what is right and what is wrong and to be strongly influenced by the particular rules and codes of their own communities. This propensity to conformity to community standards is also a part of morality, and is an end product of evolution directed by natural selection.

The theory I present is a composite of my own thoughts and a number of theoretical statements by various authors (Alexander 1987; Boyd and Richerson 1991; Cronk 1994; Frank 1988; McShea 1990; Ruse 1986, 1990; Wilson 1978) who in recent years have been trying to develop a coherent theory of how moral judgments and moral values could arise in a creature shaped by natural selection. For the most part, I see the views of these theoreticians as complementary rather than in conflict with one another, and I think that combining them will produce a richer, more powerful theory. There are minor inconsistencies among the views I am trying to integrate, but I see much more in the way of basic agreement.

For the most part these theoreticians have attempted to construct a theory of how morality can arise by natural selection through the differential reproduction of individuals. I too have tried to build a theory that appeals only to individual selection. The logical alternative to this would be natural selection in the form of the differential survival and reproduction of groups (Wynne-Edwards 1962; D. S. Wilson 1980; M. J. Wade 1978). The majority opinion among evolutionary biologists is that adaptations can arise through group selection only under unusual and rare circumstances (Dawkins 1989; Williams 1966). The theory does not appeal to these unusual circumstances as the basis of the evolution of human morality, but rather is an attempt to construct a consistent testable theory based on individual selection.

Boyd and Richerson are a partial exception to this statement since they have theorized that culture history has been shaped in important ways by the differential survival of cultures (1985), but this is not an important exception, since the ideas I take from them for this essay do not logically or necessarily incorporate this idea of cultural group selection. (For a theory based on group selection see Richards 1986.)

Readers who are not especially familiar with the theory of natural selection as it applies to behavior will do well to read Dawkins, *The Selfish Gene* (1989), before reading this essay.

Basic theory: Human nature

Human beings are the products of evolution guided by natural selection and their psychological characteristics are as much an end product of this evolutionary process as are their anatomical structures (Darwin 1872). The human mind can be thought of as consisting of two parts: reasoning abilities and passions (McShea 1990). Under the heading of the passions belong all of the feelings, sensations of pleasure and pain, emotions, and motivations which one way or another move us to action. Reasoning abilities allow us to understand reality, whereas the passions provide us with the motivation to act. Reason is thus the servant of passion (Hume 1739). Reason alone would motivate us to do nothing. The motivation to act, the definition of goals for which we strive, comes from a vast array of emotions and feelings.

Our passions are not in harmony with one another and they do not always influence us equally; rather specific circumstances call specific passions to our consciousness. A hand accidentally placed on a hot stove creates pain and an irrepressible urge to remove the hand quickly. The smell of good food when we are hungry arouses the urge to eat. The sight of a shady spot by a cool stream when we are trudging down a long road under a scorching sun inspires the urge to sit quietly for a while in the cool shade. Each set of circumstances arouses a specific desire or urge which is temporarily thrust before our consciousness. When we are overwhelmed with one passion, the urge to remove a hand from a hot stove for example, we are temporarily unaware of other feelings and emotions that would move us to different actions in different circumstances. Our past experience affects our passions. A hungry Indian who smells a succulent curry dish will experience the urge to feast, but someone from Iowa who got sick on the only curry dish she ever ate will react differently. Many of these differences in experience are associated with cultural differences (Shweder 1990). A hungry Baptist from Georgia is likely to think of pork chops as a very desirable meal, whereas a fundamentalist Moslem from Iran will see it as an abomination. One will react with a watering mouth, the other with visceral disgust, perhaps even an urge to vomit.

Our reasoning abilities are similarly specific to some degree. The way we reason about the nature of inanimate objects is different from the way we reason about conscious fellow human beings (Cosmides and Tooby 1987). In trying to understand the nature of some novel inanimate object, we will be guided by a set of presumptions about the object which are different from those we would apply when trying to understand the behavior of other human beings. Both our passions and our reasoning abilities can be thought of as arranged in a hierarchy, with some being more general in scope than others.

Our most general reasoning ability is called to our consciousness when we make decisions that will affect our future in a very profound way. Both we and our Paleolithic ancestors have pondered periodically whether to leave one community and take up permanent residence in another distant community. The choice may affect our future opportunities to satisfy a wide range of passions: hunger, the pursuit of mates, our opportunities to gain in social status. As we ponder the choice we think of how it will affect our ability to satisfy each of these passions. The contemplated move may provide better opportunities to satisfy one passion, but poorer opportunities to satisfy another. Perhaps food will be more abundant, but our opportunities for high status will be more limited because we will enter the community as a stranger. We must then decide which is more important in the specific configuration of circumstances we face, or at least imagine we are facing.

When the potential migrant contemplates her choice, she is aware of each of her passions even though they are not immediately crying out for satisfaction. This condition of calm contemplation of each of her passion, feeling, and emotions in the light of the choice at hand is the condition that McShea (1990) refers to as calm passion. This is a condition in which we are aware of each of our passions, but because none is urging us to immediate action, we can accurately judge the relative importance of each over a period of many years. A person's age, gender, and other personal characteristics will influence the relative value assigned to each of the various passions. How the conditions anticipated in each community will affect the satisfaction of the total array of passions will then be considered at the basis of the decision. In this process, the understanding of reality produced by reasoning is not an end in itself; it is a servant of the passions that the decision maker wishes to satisfy as fully as possible.

The steps through which our passions lead us over a life course are numerous and we are not aware, most of the time, that they are leading toward reproduction. Each immediate goal is seen as an end in itself: eating when hungry; acquiring status, respect, and affection as community and family member; protecting ourselves from physical harm. Natural selection has not favored a full understanding of the overall plan of the life course. Such a broad understanding would be too difficult to arrive at and would be a distraction. It is better to see the satisfaction of each passion as a goal in itself and to pursue it undistracted by a knowledge of its place in a large life-course plan. The larger plan constructed by evolution, for most individuals, consists of growing up, acquiring the skills needed to be an effective adult in the community we live in, acquiring a mate, bearing children and nurturing those children to adulthood. For some, the overall plan may be different (to serve as a nurturing aunt or uncle without bearing children, for example). In moments of serious consideration of decisions that affect most aspects of our lives we sometimes have a glimpse of this larger plan, especially as we get older and have more experience to look back on. But such a broad awareness of the total life course is only rarely perceived and has relatively little influence on our actions.

Since our reasoning abilities and passions are widely shared among members of our species, "human nature" is a useful label for them. Our ability to reason and our passions are generated by our nervous and endocrine systems because, in the environments of past evolution, they conferred a reproductive advantage. This means that they led people to behave in ways that eventually resulted in either the successful bearing and rearing of children, or the assistance of genetic relatives in the bearing and rearing of children (Darwin 1871,1958; Hamilton 1964). In other words these feelings and passions caused human beings to pass their genes on to future generations either directly through their own reproduction or indirectly through the reproduction of relatives. Our species typical nature, our human nature, is a bundle of adaptations shaped by natural selection.

Moral sentiments

Our moral judgments are specific cases of decisions guided by reason in the pursuit of certain passions (Hume 1750; Wilson 1978; Ruse 1986). There are specific passions or feelings that lead us to moral decisions, that is, decisions about right and wrong, about which courses of action are admirable and to be rewarded and which are reprehensible and to be punished. Among contemporary evolutionary theoreticians, Robert Frank (1988) has been more explicit about the role of moral sentiments than any other. He argues explicitly that human beings possess certain sentiments that aid them to do what is best for the survival of their genes in a wide range of frequently recurring social situations. He describes these sentiments as solutions to the commitment problem. In doing so he argues against the common assumption among economists that human behavior is driven by the maximization of personal gain.

One of the examples he uses to illustrate this is the desire for revenge. He recounts (1988:12) the destructive results for the Hatfields and McCoys of their long enduring feud. He points out that a pure rationalizer of personal advantage among either the Hatfields or the McCoys would have recognized that vengeance would simply lead to more vengeance and that the way to maximize personal advantage would be to desist from seeking vengeance. This however, is a retrospective view. Looking to the future, a commitment to take revenge no matter what the cost can deter attack. If the Hatfields know that the McCoys are committed to avenge any killing of a McCoy no matter what the price, they will hesitate to kill McCoys. Consider the situation of a hypothetical neighboring groups, the Rational Maximizers who lack this commitment, and instead are known to react to each situation by maximizing their future personal advantages. Killing a Rational Maximizer when provoked is less of a problem than killing a McCoy. Given this the McCoys are safer among the Hatfields than the Rational Maximizers. However, the McCoys achieve their greater safety by being committed to behave irrationally (that is contrary to personal advantage) in certain situations. There is an element of paradox in this commitment. Because they are committed to seek revenge at all costs, the McCoys are less likely to seek revenge than are the Rational Maximizers. When the commitment serves its purpose, it is never necessary to act on it. But the commitment must be believable to do its job. An emotional makeup that bypasses any thought of personal advantage in a situation of inter-group killing and takes the form of an inflexible commitment to take revenge does the job best, and this is what evolution has planted in us according to Frank. Like most human passions it is flexible. Those of us who live comfortably in societies with police, courts, and prisons to punish killers can behave like Rational Maximizers without incurring great risks. However, where such law is absent, as among the Yanomamo (Chagnon 1992) or in the Appalachia of the recent past (Rice 1982; Richardson 1986: 73, 112) a commitment to take revenge at all costs is the best ticket to personal safety and that is what people in fact develop. It is relevant that throughout most of human evolution, people have experienced a situation like that of Appalachia or Yanomamoland rather than the comfortable law and order that this writer and most of his readers are familiar with.

Frank argues that human nature contains a number of potentials for commitments of the sort illustrated by the Hatfield and McCoy commitment to revenge. Among others he discusses are scrupulous honesty, a scrupulous commitment to fairness in bargaining, love, and moral outrage. Like all human emotions these are flexible. Most human beings have the capacity to develop these emotions, but whether we develop them or not depends on personal experience. A person is likely to develop scrupulous honesty in response to growing up in a small community where honesty is highly valued, and where dishonesty is easily detected and is severely punished through ridicule and ostracism. The person's honesty will not be that of a rational calculator who is honest so long as he detects that honesty will best serve his personal interests. Rather it will be a deep emotional commitment of the sort that would leave the individual feeling guilty and remorseful if he were to behave dishonestly whether caught or not. In fact the anticipation of this guilt and remorse is what keeps the individual honest, not a continual calculation of the relative risks and benefits of particular dishonest acts at one particular time. A similar individual growing up in a big city where people frequently interact with individuals they never will see again is less likely to develop the habit of scrupulous honesty in casual encounters with strangers. If he further finds that many people around him profit from dishonesty of one form or another and are generally admired for it, his chances of becoming scrupulously honest are even less. In a similar way, other moral sentiments are inherited as the potential to develop a number of different feelings, and a propensity to actually develop those which are most useful in the environment one experiences first hand. Each of these potentials for developing particular moral sentiments evolved and became a part of our human psyches because they, in one way or another, solved a commitment problem among ancestral populations. Those who developed inflexible commitments to revenge in lawless environments were less frequent victims of violence. Those who never went back on a promise and were ever ready to help a friend were more frequently chosen as allies in environments where allies were crucial to survival.

Proximate versus ultimate cause: More theory

The picture of morality presented by Frank is cast in terms of what evolutionary biologists call proximate mechanisms. Proximate mechanisms focus on actual psychological phenomena such as hunger, or a desire for revenge, or a commitment to honesty. The psychological phenomena are described as proximate because they carry out their functions over a short time period relative to the time needed for evolutionary change. They operate within the lifetime of individual organisms, and often within very short portions of that lifetime. They are called mechanisms to emphasize that they display design. The design is created by natural selection choosing, from the variants introduced by mutation, those forms that best accomplish some goal such as protecting that organism from a specific type of harm, or causing it to gain access to resources necessary for its survival and reproduction. Sometimes the expression "proximate cause" is also used to describe the way in which proximate mechanisms create a particular adaptive effect.

An alternate way of thinking about evolution is that which is labeled ultimate cause. Ultimate cause refers to the creation of adaptations over many generations by natural selection. Proximate cause is concerned with things that happen within an individual lifetime; ultimate cause is concerned with things that happen over many generations. Ultimate cause theory is usually cast in terms of logically derived propositions about what traits natural selection will favor in general.

The numbers of eggs which birds lay in a breeding season can serve to illustrate the nature of ultimate cause thinking. Often members of a particular avian species have a typical clutch size (number of eggs they lay at the beginning of a breeding season). Experimental data in many cases have been used to show that birds who lay more that the species-typical number of eggs, on average rear fewer offspring because they are less able to care for the larger number of hatchlings that result from a larger clutch of eggs. To care for its larger number of offspring, the avian parents must spend more time foraging for food, and must leave their nest unguarded for longer periods of time while foraging. The hatchlings are thus at greater risk from predators. They are also less likely to be adequately fed. The result is a higher death rate of hatchlings and fewer fledglings leaving the nest. Birds who lay fewer eggs may provide better than average care, but because they have fewer to start with they rear fewer despite the better care. The species-typical clutch size is usually the one which on average produces the largest number of fledglings and is therefore the fittest trait the trait most favored by natural selection (Lack 1954).

Dawkins (1989) describes optimal clutch size as the result of an optimal tradeoff between bearing and rearing. To reproduce, a bird must first bear offspring (lay eggs and incubate them till they hatch). Second it must rear its offspring, that is it must feed and protect the hatchlings until they are ready to leave the nest and live independently. There is an optimal tradeoff between bearing and rearing, if we assume the goal is to produce as many surviving, mature offspring as possible. As the number of eggs laid goes up, the burden of rearing goes up. That means that as each egg is added to a bird's clutch of eggs, the adequacy of its care for each hatchling goes down and the probability of survival is lowered. At some point the increasing death rate of hatchlings becomes high enough that adding eggs actually causes the number of baby birds reared to go down, even though the number the parent starts with has gone up. This tradeoff defines an optimal number of eggs to be laid at the beginning of each breeding season, and natural selection favors genes that tend to move their bearers toward producing this optimal number. This number is different for each species, being determined by the animal's way of making its living. This includes such factors as what kind of food the species typically gathers, how difficult it is to gather, and what sort of predator risks the animal must cope with to protect itself and its offspring. A host of such factors determines exactly what number is ideal for a particular species. In some species the optimal number is not fixed, but rather varies from year to year depending on the availability of food. In some such cases the animals develop the ability to track the availability of food and to adjust their clutch size up or down to meet the optimum under the current year's conditions (Lack 1954). The general proposition that clutch sizes are optimal in terms of the tradeoff between bearing and rearing is known as Lack's rule, after its author, David Lack. The rule is deduced logically and then evaluated against actual data on avian reproduction under a range of conditions to see whether it successfully predicts what in reality happens.

Altruism and selfishness

This same process of deriving logical propositions about what sorts of adaptations natural selection will produce and then testing them through observation has been applied to a wide range of questions. One of the questions that has been explored extensively has been the question of the conditions under which natural selection will favor altruistic behavior, and under which it will favor selfish behavior. This is obviously a discussion relevant to morality. In this theoretical discussion among evolutionary biologists, the words altruism and selfishness are given special meanings somewhat different from the meaning of these words in everyday language. Altruistic behavior is defined as behavior that lowers the actor's fitness and raises the fitness of another organism (or organisms). Selfish behavior is defined as behavior that has the opposite effect; that is, it raises the actor's fitness and lowers the fitness of another organism (or organisms).

Fitness also has a special technical meaning in this discussion. Fitness is a measure of the organism's success in bearing and rearing offspring. It is usually not measured by the number of offspring born, but rather the number successfully reared. The issue is usually how successful an organism with a particular trait is at producing adult progeny compared to organisms with alternate traits. If one trait consistently causes its bearers to rear more surviving offspring than bearers of an alternate trait, then the trait causing the higher rate of reproduction is the fitter trait. The trait leading to a higher rate of reproduction is by definition the one favored by natural selection.

(This meaning of fitness is sometimes called Darwinian or classical fitness; it measures only success in bearing and rearing offspring. Inclusive fitness is a distinct concept that measures an organism's effect on the reproduction of genes both through bearing and rearing offspring and through helping relatives to bear and rear offspring. Throughout this discussion, fitness refers to classical, not inclusive fitness.)

Evolutionary biologists have concluded that there are two situations in which natural selection at the individual level will favor altruism. One is when the beneficiary of the altruism is a genetic relative of the altruist (Hamilton 1964), and the other is when the beneficiary can be depended on to reciprocate acts of altruism (Trivers 1971).

Between genetically related individuals, altruism is favored whenever the altruist ends up reproducing more of its genes as a result of the altruism. This is the gist of Hamilton's 1964 classic theoretical paper on kin altruism. When an individual altruistically aids a relative, its own fitness (the number of its surviving offspring) is lowered, but the relative's fitness is raised. For most organisms its offspring carry a higher portion of its genes than do most of its other relatives. Nieces and nephews carry one-quarter of one's genes, children half. Thus lowering the production of children to aid a sibling in producing nieces and nephews, will be favored by natural selection only when the gain is more than twice its loss. An act that cost an altruist one child, on average over the life course, will be favored if its average effect is a gain of three or more nieces and nephews (one child represents half of a copy of the actor's genes, while three nieces or nephews represent three quarters of the actor's genes). Thus altruism is only favored when the cost to the altruist is less than the gain to the beneficiary. Also the ratio of gain to loss necessary to make altruism pay increases as the portion of genes shared among relatives decreases. Thus the expected adaptation in flexible organisms such as human beings is one of discriminate altruism. We should be willing to sacrifice for the benefit of relatives in some situations, but not others. Our willingness to sacrifice should be greatest for close relatives and greatest when the costs to us are low and the benefits to the relatives high. There is empirical support for these theoretical expectations for both animals and human beings (Alcock 1989; Borgerhoff Mulder 1991; Cronk 1991; Gray 1985; Irons 1991).

However, kin altruism cannot explain human morality. Human morality often causes behaviors that are altruistic among unrelated individuals. The only way that individual selection can favor these behaviors is through reciprocity. Thus the ultimate cause theories of reciprocity (Trivers 1971; Axelrod and Hamilton 1981; Axelrod 1984) must serve as the basis of any ultimate cause theory of morality. The primary difficulty limiting the establishment of reciprocity or reciprocal altruism is the possibility of being cheated (Trivers 1971). If individual A aids individual B in expectation of reciprocal aid, B can often gain the most by not reciprocating. A necessary condition for the establishment of reciprocal altruism is somehow arriving at a situation where reciprocation is probable. Theoreticians have specified several conditions that make reciprocation more likely. One condition is a high probability of future interaction between altruist and beneficiary (Axelrod and Hamilton 1981). Another is the ability and propensity of individuals with good memories and powers of observation to study the behavioral propensities of other individuals in a wide range of situations and altruistically aid only those who are likely to reciprocate (Alexander 1987). A third condition is created when individuals use punishments to discourage failure to reciprocate (Alexander 1987; Boyd and Richerson 1992; Trivers 1971).

Game theory analyses of reciprocity

Axelrod and Hamilton use game theory, specifically the game of Prisoner's Dilemma, to elucidate the effect of probable future interaction on the probability of reciprocation. Game theory is based on the assumption that the choices people make in playing games and in real life are parallel in many ways, and that we therefore can understand real life decisions by analyzing logically how players might strive to win hypothetical games. Prisoner's dilemma is a classical example of such a game. In its original form, it was illustrated by the choices facing two criminals who cooperated in committing a crime, bank robbery, and were then arrested and offered the opportunity to turn state's evidence in return for a lighter sentence. The criminals agreed beforehand that if either one of them were caught, he would not give the authorities any information that might harm the other. The state's attorney has enough information to convict them of a minor offense such as possession of an unregistered firearm, but not enough to convict them of the more serious crime of bank robbery. The punishment for possession of an unregistered weapon is one year in jail. The punishment for bank robbery is ten years. The deal offered each criminal by the state's attorney is a suspended sentence, that is, zero years in jail, in return for turning state's evidence with consequence that his companion will spend ten years in jail. Each must therefore decide whether to stick to his agreement with his companion in crime, or turn state's evidence. The outcome for each depends on what his companion does as well as what he does himself. If he turns state's evidence and his companion does the same they will each get five years in jail, a reduced sentence because of their willingness to cooperate. If he turns state's evidence and his companion does not, he will spend zero years in jail, and his companion will spend ten. If he sticks to the original agreement, and his companion does too, they will each get one year in jail, the punishment for the lesser offense of possessing an unregistered fire arm. If he sticks to the original agreement and his companion turns state's evidence, he will spend ten years in jail. Thus if he turns state's evidence, he will spend somewhere between zero and five years in jail. If he does not turn state's evidence, the range of outcomes is one to ten years. If there is no future interaction with his companion in crime to be considered, then clearly the better choice is to break his agreement with his companion and provide evidence. On the other hand if we look at the average outcome for the two criminals, the best choice is for both to stick to the original agreement. Then they each get one year in jail, a total of two years to be served by the two of them. If one gives evidence, one serves zero years and the other ten for an average of five between them. If they both give evidence, they each serve five years. Thus the average outcome for the group of two criminals is better if they stick to their agreement. Sticking to the agreement yields the best outcome for the group as a whole, but from the point of view of each individual thinking about only his own welfare, giving evidence yields the best result. If the criminals place their own welfare above that of the group as a whole (the pair of criminals), they will give evidence.

There are many situations in real life that mimic this situation where the outcome that is best for the group is at odds with the single individual weighing, only his or her own advantage. It is also clear that morality, as we usually conceive of it, often requires that an individual do what is best for the group. Consider the situation when a fire occurs in a crowded theater. The best outcome for the crowd as a whole is obtained if all the audience leaves in an orderly fashion without running or pushing. However, if the crowd is leaving in an orderly fashion, any individual who breaks ranks and shoves others out of the way and rushes for the door, will be at less risk from the fire than if she continues in an orderly fashion. On the other hand, once several individuals begin to shove and run, any individual that does not do the same is at a disadvantage.

Game theorists usually study the game of Prisoner's Dilemma as an abstract game in which outcomes, or payoffs, are expressed as points. See diagram 1 for a payoff matrix for the game of Prisoner's Dilemma in abstract form. The choices in this abstract form are described as cooperating or defecting. In the classic form of the game, cooperating is the equivalent of sticking to the agreement between robbers not to provide evidence. Defecting is the equivalent of giving evidence to the state's attorney. In the example of the theater fire, cooperating would consist of leaving in an orderly fashion; defecting would consist of shoving and running. If two players play this game one time and know nothing about how the other will play, the best strategy for each is simply to defect. Consider the payoffs to Player A. If B cooperates, A gets 5 points for defecting and 3 points for cooperating. If B defects, A gets 1 point for defecting and 0 for cooperating. Whatever Player B chooses, Player A's payoff is higher if he defects than if he cooperates.

Diagram 1: Prisoner's dilemma payoff matrix

	Player B cooperates	**Player B defects**
Player A cooperates	Both players get the reward payoff	B gets temptation payoff A gets sucker's payoff
Player A defects	A gets the temptation payoff B gets the sucker's payoff	Both players get the punishment payoff

Temptation payoff = 5   Punishment payoff = 1

Reward payoff   = 3   Sucker's payoff   = 0

However, if the game is played several times with the same player, the situation changes. This modified version of Prisoners Dilemma is called Iterated Prisoner's Dilemma. If A defects on the first move, B is likely to defect in response on the second move. On the other hand the response to cooperation on one move is likely to be cooperation by the other player on later moves. If two players interact for several moves, they can hope to get a series of Rewards each worth 3 points. However, if one defects when the other player cooperates, one is likely to get a "Temptation" payoff worth 5 points, followed by a series of "Punishment" payoffs worth 1 point each. If the series of interactions is at all long, it may pay to cooperate.

To test this possibility, Axelrod (1984) conducted two tournaments in which game theorists could submit strategies for playing Prisoner's Dilemma and the strategies would be assigned to hypothetical players who would use their strategy in playing a series of games of Prisoner's Dilemma with other hypothetical individuals. Each player would be matched in the tournament with a sequence of players. This sequence of players would each use one of the submitted strategies so that each player would be matched with one player representing each of the strategies included in the tournament, including players following one's own strategy. The score for the entire sequence of games would be tallied to see which strategy did best. The most successful strategy was a strategy named Tit for Tat submitted by a well-known psychologist, Anatol Rapoport. Tit for Tat is defined by two rules: (1) on the first move with a new player, cooperate, and (2) on all subsequent plays with this player do what he did on the previous move.

When a "Tit for Tat" player plays with another Tit for Tat player, (see the payoff matrix, Diagram 1), then each gets a series of Rewards worth 3 points. If a Tit for Tat player plays with another player who always defects, Tit for Tat gets a Sucker's Payoff worth 0 points followed by a series of Punishments, each worth 1 point. "Always Defect" does slightly better, with a Temptation payoff worth 5 points followed by a series of 1 point Punishments. If the sequence of plays with each player is long, Tit for Tat will come out ahead if it plays first another Tit for Tat player and then an Always Defect player. If each strategy is matched with the other and itself for a series of 10 plays, Tit for Tat will get 30 points when it plays itself and 9 points when it plays Always Defect. Always Defect will get 14 points when it plays Tit for Tat and 10 points when it plays itself. Tit for Tat's total will be 39 and Always Defect's total will be 24. Of course the total set of strategies in Axelrod's tournament create a much more complex situation than this simple example, but nevertheless the results in the tournament were the same as in the simple example above: Tit for Tat was more successful than all the other strategies.

The general conclusion relevant to morality is that with repeated interaction between the same individuals, it is easier to establish reciprocity. Human beings evolved in small communities in which the same individuals interacted with each other repeatedly over their lifetimes. Thus conditions were present during human evolution that favored a discriminate type of reciprocal altruism of the sort modeled by Tit for Tat. However, later theoretical thinking has identified further conditions and strategies that can assist in the establishment of altruism. In the theoretical thinking presented here, the establishment of altruism means: create a situation where interacting individuals who cooperate with one another will maximize their individual gains.

Indirect reciprocity

In his 1987 book, *The Biology of Moral Systems*, Alexander explored the consequences of what he labeled indirect reciprocity. Indirect reciprocity as Alexander conceived it occurs when the individuals in a population observe the other members of the population interacting with each other. Individual A sees individual B behave altruistically toward C, D, and E. A is altruistic to B on the assumption that B will be altruistic in return, because she has shown herself to be so when interacting with C, D, and E. On the other hand, if F is seen to behave selfishly toward C, D, and E, then A will also behave selfishly toward F on the assumption that F would defect in a Tit for Tat type of situation with A. In very simple terms, the basis of indirect reciprocity is to be nice to those who are nice and nasty to those who are nasty. Intuitively it does seem that human beings do have such a propensity, although it is hardly the only psychological propensity influencing our choice whether to be nasty or nice.

One could model this type of interaction formally by expanding Iterated Prisoners Dilemma to include this element of third-party observation. The new version of Tit for Tat, Indirect Tit for Tat that takes advantage of the information gained by third-party observation (Irons in press) would consist of the following rules: (1) cooperate on the first move in playing with another player about whom you know nothing; (2) if you know the other player (either from having played with him before or from having observed him playing with a third party), then use that information to decide how to play. Specifically, defect if the other player has ever been seen to get the Temptation payoff; otherwise, cooperate. This second rule allows one to distinguish between those who defect first and those who defect only in retaliation. Those who defect first will get the Temptation payoff; those who defect in retaliation will get the Punishment payoff. As a player of Indirect Tit for Tat, one need not hesitate about cooperating with those who defect in retaliation. If one cooperates with them they will cooperate in return. However, those who are willing to be the first to defect present a risk. This risk is best avoided by not cooperating with them.

This game, however, suggests some perverse possibilities. What if a player is first to defect with another player, but is not consistent so that he tricks you into getting the temptation payoff the first time you play with him and in the process ruins your reputation. One can think of ways to handle this situation that mimic real human interaction. Instead of defecting in playing with someone known to have received the temptation payoff in the past, one could simply avoid interacting with them at all. Alternately one could announce before defecting that one is defecting because the other individual on such and such a play defected first and got the temptation payoff. The rules would still be a realistic mimic of real situations if they allowed this. Still another option might be to respond to gaining the temptation payoff by mistake, by expressing contrition and either arrange to transfer the points gained to the victim (R. Boyd, personal communication). All of these are things that parallel familiar forms of human interaction and which could be ways to protect one's reputation in a complex set of interchanges where mistakes are possible.

However one chooses to think about potential reciprocity, Alexander's correctly suggests that indirect observation and reputation increase the ease of establishing cooperation. Of course, the use of indirect observation (observing people when they are interacting with third parties) opens up a number of other possibilities such as deceitful manipulation of one's own and other's reputation, and counter-strategies of closer observation. These possibilities seem also to be things that really happen in human communities.

The implications of Alexander's suggestion may become clearer if we think about it in concrete terms similar to those used by Robert Frank. Frank (1988:47-49) discusses the case of two individuals, Smith and Jones, who can pool their talents to establish an excellent restaurant. Smith is a talented cook but is awkward in dealing with customers and lacks good business judgment. Jones can't boil water, but he is good with customers and has good business judgment. The two form a good pair. Each has talent the other lacks. Together they can run a business that neither can run alone. But cheating could make the venture less profitable. Jones who will run the dining room and handle the cash register could skim from the register without Smith knowing. Smith who will run the kitchen could take kickbacks from food suppliers. Neither will be able to monitor the behavior of the other. If both cheat, the venture will not be profitable. If only one cheats, the venture will be profitable only for the cheater. Each party to this potential venture will be more willing to enter into a joint arrangement if he knows the other to be scrupulously honest. If both are scrupulously honest, the venture can be very profitable for both. But if either cheats, the other will not find the venture profitable. This is a clear example of a commitment problem in Frank's terms. In Alexander's terms, reputation is a crucial element. What if Smith and Jones have known each other all their lives? Neither has ever entered a joint business venture with the other, but both know third parties who have, and who vouch for the scrupulous honesty of the other. This element of community-wide reputation is then a resource each can use to open the door to a profitable business arrangement. In fact, any means by which one can convincingly demonstrate a commitment to honesty will be useful in persuading the other to enter the joint business venture.

What Frank refers to as commitments are the same things that Alexander refers to under the labels of reputation and self-image (Alexander 1987). He theorizes that we know that others will judge us and that we will come to have a reputation and that we must manage that reputation. (Our conscious thought process may not be framed in exactly these terms.) We deal with this situation by forming an image of the kind of person we wish to be and then strive to become that person. Our self-image is then an internal guide to behavior. If our self-image is that of an honest person, then we behave honestly even when we are not convinced that dishonest behavior will be detected. The underlying reason may be that, occasionally people would misjudge if they tried to be honest only when dishonesty were detectable. The best way to gain a reputation for scrupulous honesty is to be scrupulously honest. If such behavior imposes costs in the form of foregoing opportunities for personal gain through occasional cheating, the costs may be worth paying.

Frank (1988) drives home this view of self-image as a guide by discussing tipping on the road. We tip in restaurants, some would argue, so that we will get good service in the future when we return to the same restaurant. But if this is the case, why tip when traveling? Someone impressed with the importance of reputation might say we tip in strange, far away places to impress traveling companions. But what if we are traveling alone? Frank's answers that we tip while traveling alone in places we will never visit again because we reassure ourselves that we are the generous person that our self-image says we are. Alternately he says that by tipping we are buying self-respect.

Alexander's (1987) thinking runs parallel, but with one important exception. Alexander emphasizes that in the process of forming a self-image and letting it guide us we may to some extent indulge in self-deception. Alexander suggests that the man who returns wallets left in bus terminals (even though he could easily keep the money) may be deceiving himself. Once the amount of money is large enough and his pressing need great enough, he may stop deceiving himself and keep the money. I am sure that for some people in some circumstances, Alexander is right. On the other hand, some people who keep the money feel guilty about it for a long time and eventually will try to return it. Others may be unable to find the original owner of the money. After years of feeling guilty, they may make a special donation to charity to clear their conscience. After we discover we were deceiving ourselves about our honesty or generosity or whatever commitment we fell down on, our self-image may haunt us.

It is also relevant that despite the scrupulous honesty of many people, there are a few who make their living as confidence artists. These people are parasites on the majority, who rely on certain signs of commitment to honesty. Frank includes in his *Passions Within Reason* (1988) an interesting analysis of the relative advantages and disadvantages of inflexible honesty versus opportunistic honesty (being honest only when there is danger of being caught). His analysis suggests that both strategies may coexist under certain circumstances. Under certain conditions some people will be honest, others opportunistically honest. When this happens, there is a definite advantage to monitoring others to determine which they are.

Costly-to-fake signs of commitment

Consider another possibility explored by Frank (1988:99-102) and Cronk (1994): the "costly-to-fake principle." What if both Smith and Jones are members of a religious sect that demands strict honesty of its members and excommunicates any members who fail to meet this requirement. What if this religious sect also demands heavy contributions of money and observance of elaborate time-consuming rituals as a strict condition of its membership. Then each will have reason to trust the other because their membership in this sect is a "costly-to-fake" sign of honesty. Someone who was not really honest would be unlikely to go to the trouble of all the rituals, donations, and other strict observances just to persuade a business partner that he is honest. Costly-to-fake signs of commitment are very valuable to individuals with real commitment as a way of communicating their commitment in a believable way. They are also valuable to those who wish to assess the commitment of others.

Consider the role of fraternity hazings or Marine basic training. Both fraternities and the United States Marines demand strong commitments of loyalty, and in the case of the Marines, obedience. A condition of membership is an unpleasant experience that lasts for some time. This vastly diminishes the possibility that those lacking the proper commitment will become members of the organization. In the case of Smith and Jones, membership in a religious sect is a sign to all the community. In the case of a Marine recruit, his endurance of an ordeal is a condition for entry into the lower ranks of a hierarchic organization and a sign to his superiors. In one case (membership in a religious sect) the commitment is given to all who wish to witness it. In the other (Marine basic training), it is demanded by someone in a position of authority as a sign to the authority figure himself.

Another variant on the commitment theme was the basic training of U. S. Army draftees. Their basic training was less demanding, but nevertheless an unpleasant experience for most individuals who experienced it. Even though the alternative for draftees was worse (prison and a criminal record), basic training can still be seen as a way of communicating commitment. Here the main message initially comes from the Army command hierarchy. The message is, "You had better be committed to unquestioning obedience and possibly great personal sacrifice, and you had better show me that you are! If not, you will be subjected to even worse treatment than what you are getting now." The usual response is a credible sign of commitment. Alternately, Army basic training for draftees could be seen as a test to determine which of the unwilling recruits can stand up to a difficult situation. If seen this way, performing satisfactorily is still a sign to one's superiors that one can play the role satisfactorily.

A number of apparently maladaptive forms of exotic behavior may be examples of such signs of commitment to demanding standards imposed by particular societies (Irons, in press). Examples would include the subincision of young men among the Australian Aborigines; clitoridectomy and infibulation of women in the Sudanic region of Africa, and the former practice of binding women's feet in China. (Subincision consists of cutting the underside of a penis open and letting it heal with the urethra open; something like circumcision but more drastic. Clitoridectomy consists of removing the clitoris. Infibulation consists of scarifying the vaginal opening so that it heals shut with a tube inserted for drainage. (Clitoridectomy and infibulation are sometimes called female circumcision.) All of these are examples of costly signs of commitment imposed on individuals of low social status. In much of the Sudanic region of Africa, women have very low status. Among Australian Aborigines, young men occupy a very subordinate position to older men. Though harsher than the treatment of Army draftees, these ordeals may have a similar function of providing a costly sign of commitment.

Before their subordination to U.S. authority, the practice of counting coup among the Plains Indians provided another example of costly-to-imitate signs of commitment. Some of the more prestigious coup consisted of such things as turning around and charging the enemy directly when the body of one's war party was in retreat. In contrast to the above example, these signs were more voluntary in character. They represented commitments made by brave men rather than commitments demanded of all low status members of a social system. Nevertheless, they made sense in the same general framework of costly signs of commitment. They also made sense as ways of gaining status. There were many occasions on which Plains Indian men would recount for the other men of the tribe their coup, thus reminding others that they had done something of great value for the tribe and are therefore worthy recipients of favorable treatment by other members of the tribe.

Along with such costly-to-fake signs of commitment, a number of other forms of behavior can be interpreted as signs of commitment even if less costly and hence less reliable (Irons 1991). Familiar examples include: wearing a white shirt and necktie along with a well-shined pair of shoes, displaying a flag on memorial day, membership in a less demanding religious congregation than the one discussed above, giving to charities and displaying stickers on one's door attesting to the fact that one has given, and occasionally voicing agreement with general community standards of morality.

Punishment and moralistic strategies

Boyd and Richerson (1992) recently suggested another basis for self-sacrificing moral behavior by exploring the significance of punishments as ways of establishing patterns of reciprocity. They frame their discussion in terms of game theory and specifically appeal to the idea of evolutionarily stable strategies. Briefly, an evolutionary stable strategy is a strategy that cannot be improved on once the majority have adopted it. A very simple example is driving on one side of the road or another. Once the majority of individuals drive on the right, nothing can be gained by driving on the left. Once the majority drive on the left, nothing is to be gained by driving on the right. The advantageous thing to do is to imitate the majority. Tit for Tat discussed above comes close to being an evolutionarily stable strategy, although under certain circumstance it is not quite so. Such a strategy is called a robust strategy. A robust strategy is successful under a wide range of circumstances, but not under every conceivable circumstance.

In game theory, sometimes a stable or robust strategy emerges; sometimes two different strategies coexist; sometimes no stable pattern emerges. One can get a feeling for the nature of game theory by considering Frank's (1988) analysis of opportunistic honesty versus real honesty. His analysis shows that once the majority are genuinely honest, monitoring the honesty of other people becomes a waste of time; not monitoring becomes more advantageous than monitoring, and monitoring vanishes. Once monitoring vanishes, the advantages of opportunistic honesty go up since the chances of getting caught go down. Here, imitating the majority is not necessarily the most profitable strategy.

Boyd and Richerson (1992) explore the consequence of allowing players in a hypothetical game to punish other players if they make certain choices, that is to subtract points from the other players score immediately if they make the wrong choice. They found that something called "moralistic strategies" can easily become evolutionarily stable and can, in addition, establish the regular performance of costly acts in order to avoid punishment. A moralistic strategy consists of two parts, or two instructions about interacting with other individuals. The first part says that anyone who fails to perform some costly act should be punished. The second part says that any individual who fails to punish those who do not perform the act in question should also be punished. If the costly act is to reciprocate aid, then the player should punish those who do not reciprocate and moreover punish those who do not punish the non-reciprocators. Again the strategy invented here has an intuitive familiarity. We are all familiar with situations where *non*-punishment is itself punished. The label "moralistic" is well chosen to remind us of such situations.

Two familiar situations from recent history and from present day politics come to mind. During the McCarthy era in the United States, great effort was made to locate and punish communists (through black listing, a special form of ostracism). It was also part of the political ethos of that era to punish those who disapproved of the procedure of hunting for and punishing communists. Being "soft on communism" was a definite blot on a politician's reputation that could prevent reelection. The result was scrupulous avoidance of anything that could be interpreted as softness toward communism. The other familiar case is that of the attitudes of politicians in Arab countries toward Israel. They must punish Israel and also punish those who do not punish Israel. Being soft on Israel has occasionally been a ticket for assassination.

Moralistic strategies are logically an extension of Alexander's idea of indirect reciprocity mediated by reputation. Alexander (1987:85-86) includes in his definition of indirect reciprocity both helping those observed to help others and punishing those observed to hurt others. Boyd and Richerson add the ingenious (and intuitively familiar) instruction to punish those who fail to punish. In fact this is what human beings do at least some of the time. They police one another. They observe others and are nice to the nice and nasty to the nasty. They also reward and punish people according to how well they play the policing role itself (Irons in press). They do this especially when very sacred principles are believed to be involved, such as rooting out communism in the McCarthy era. The result can be heavy demands for conformity.

One aspect of this demand for conformity noted by Boyd and Richerson (1992) is that moralistic strategies can not only establish the practice of reciprocity, they can establish the regular practice of any costly act. On this account, such costly customs as subincision and female circumcision need no explanation other than that they are maintained by moralistic strategies. However, I would suggest an alternate view (Irons in press). Human beings are more imaginative and more flexible than the hypothetical maximizers who play game theorists' games. When faced with a costly behavior, they try to wriggle out of it, or at least modify it to decrease the cost. Because of this persistent tendency to renegotiate rules, a costly behavior that benefits no one but is maintained by a moralistic strategy is not likely to endure. The victims will try increment by increment to modify it and those who are obliged to punish will eventually cooperate because punishing is also costly. The punishers, who see punishing as a cost with no gain, will look for a way to modify the requirement that they punish without themselves being punished. As a result, the required costly behavior will gradually be modified so that it becomes less of a burden. Why then do subincision, female circumcision, and military basic training not disappear? The answer is that, while they cost some low-status individuals, they at the same time benefit certain high-status individuals. These high-status individuals are not interested in reducing the cost of punishing nonconformists; for them the costs are worth paying. Australian elders use subincision and the other harassing elements of the initiation of young men as a way to control young men. In a society where older polygynous men monopolize the marriageable women, control of young men by old men is crucial (from the point of view of old men). Similarly female circumcision is a way that men control their wives, and military basic training is a way in which the military hierarchy controls its lowest status members.

Another suggestion made by Boyd and Richerson (1992) is that individuals such as tribal chiefs, big men, and the rulers of archaic states are in effect parasitic punishers. They help to maintain the societies' overall pattern of cooperation by punishing non-cooperators and rewarding cooperators, but they do not themselves perform self-sacrificing acts of cooperation. The advantage of such a system to the parasites is obvious. The question is, why do the ordinary members of such societies accept the situation? The answer may be that the alternative of trying to abandon their membership in the group would impose a higher cost on them (Carneiro 1970). Whatever the reasons, the earliest human states seem to have been held together by rulers who played the role Boyd and Richerson (1992) have described as parasitic punisher. Coercion played a very large role in these societies and inequalities of access to status and resources were extreme. Conversely, recent historic trends are in the direction of greater equality. Elected rulers are less parasitic than hereditary ones (Betzig 1993).

Rules as ways of resolving conflicts of interest

Alexander (1987) suggests that moral rules serve as ways of resolving within-group conflicts of interest without doing too much damage to the interests of either party. With such a means of resolving conflicts of interest, some individuals would find group membership disadvantageous and would withdraw from the group. He further suggests that our intuitive sense of what is and what is not fair is an evolved capacity to identify rules that fail to do this and motivate attempts to change them. Rules can also clarify the expectation that people can act without harming one another (which side of the road to drive on is an example).

Moral sentiments are important but they often need explicit rules to clarify expectations and to assist in monitoring other individuals who may on occasion fail to be sufficiently motivated by moral sentiment alone. Frank's analyses of conditions favoring the coexistence of honesty and opportunism and Alexander's discussion of self-deception suggest that sentiments alone will not always create cooperative behavior. Thus most societies do not rely on sentiments and spontaneous rewards and punishments to maintain a pattern of cooperation. They back up sentiment with rules.

Explicit support of rules can also be a sign of commitment. Tipping on the road will engender self-respect. Telling one's associates that one should tip on the road, because it is unfair to waitresses and waiters not to, is a sign of generosity and adherence to a principle worth communicating. Once the majority states that one should tip on the road, saying that it is purely optional makes one look opportunistic. This is not a good signal to send associates in most social circles. In fact arguing that one need not tip on the road might do more harm to one's reputation than not tipping on the road. Once a certain form of behavior becomes the requirement of some rule, one often looks bad if one does not state agreement with the rule. The result is that the rule gets regularly stated and passed down over the generations.

Human beings not only have moral sentiments that can sometimes motivate self-sacrificing aid to others; they also find social rules very easy to understand and to deal with effectively. Recent research by Cosmides and Tooby (1987) and Tooby and Cosmides (1992) indicates that human beings are especially skilled at identifying individuals who break social rules. Considering the discussion above it is interesting that human beings should find it easy to learn to identify rule breakers.

One final point concerning rules needs to be made. I think that Alexander is only partly right when he suggests that rules are ways of resolving conflicts of interest. He is right, I think, in that this is the function of many rules, perhaps most. However, some rules are hard to interpret in this way. Take for example the rule against eating pork among Jews and Moslems. How can this be said to resolve conflicts of interest? Rules such as these do however make sense as signs of commitment. Both the Jewish and the Islamic faiths require a great deal in the way of ritual observance and dietary law, and these are signs of commitment to a particular community that are not easy for those lacking this commitment to imitate. They make sense as hard-to-fake signs of commitment.

Moral relativism

All human societies have social rules. In all societies, there is a belief that breaking these rules is wrong and following them is right. This is true although the extent of disapproval and approval involved may be very strong for some rules and very weak for others. Despite the universality of rules, however, the rules themselves vary a great deal among societies. In some cases, the exact rule is not as important as having a rule. Which side of the road the rules say one should drive on is unimportant, but clearly specifying one side is important. The side specified by each society is then a matter of historic accident.

There is, however, a host of more interesting reasons for variation among rules that societies have. The basic way of making a living in a society will certainly influence the society's rules. Hunting and gathering societies will have elaborate rules governing the division of the fruits of the hunt. Modern industrial societies have no need for such rules. Preliterate foragers on the other hand have no need for copyright laws. In many preliterate societies, such as the Yanomamo (Chagnon 1992), much of social life revolves around competition among men for wives. The Yanomamo allow polygyny and many men are polygynous. The result is not enough potential wives to satisfy every man's desire for at least one and maybe more wives. Much of the competition is played out through violence and threats of violence. About one-third of adult Yanomamo men eventually die a violent death with conflict over women or revenge being the underlying cause in most cases. The first marriages of women are arranged for them by their senior male kin while they are still children. The exchange of women in marriage is the strongest basis for political alliance among the Yanomamo and allies in their milieu of violence are a necessity. Given this, it is not surprising that their most basic rules have to do with who can marry whom and who can arrange the marriage. The rules state that people cannot marry within their own patriline (male line of descent) and that as a matter of strong preference they should marry cross-cousins (a cross-cousin is a cousin not in one's own patriline). These rules affect the practice of two patrilines exchanging women and remaining allied over several generations. Given the conflicts and alliances of Yanomamo society these rules make sense. However, in a modern industrial society like our own the considerations underlying marriage and the ways of arranging them are completely different and as a consequence the rules involved are also different.

The particular moral sentiments encouraged by different societies also vary greatly among societies. Among the Yanomamo the primary virtue for men is a commitment to defend kin in violent conflict. This willingness is often demonstrated by a number signs some of which may be hard to fake. A readiness to threaten violence when one's interests are threatened is one of these and it is often acted on in ritualized club fights in which the opponents take turns standing still while the other fighter bashes his head with a club as hard as he can. Men who are ready to challenge others to such club fights are genuine "tough guys" and the status is not easy to fake. The contrast with most of modern urban society is obvious. Our greatest virtues include a willingness to get a difficult job done no matter what (usually for an employer). We cultivate hard-to-imitate signs of an ability and willingness to do this. Frank (1988) suggests that the importance of a college degree lies not in the knowledge gained but rather in the fact that it is a hard-to-fake sign that a person will stick to the pursuit of a difficult goal over a number of years.

As noted above, human beings do not inherit an inflexible set of moral sentiments. Rather they inherit the capacity to develop a range of sentiments, and the circumstances they experience, especially those they experience while growing up, determine which sentiments they will develop. It is even more clear that human beings do not inherit belief in a particular set of rules. Rather, as they mature they develop a capacity to readily understand what rules are and how to use them to their own advantage. At the same time while growing up they learn the rules of their own society and develop a set of actual sentiments which as a rule integrate well with the rules of their society.

The result is that what is considered reprehensible in one society may be admired in another society. Individuals from different societies find it hard to agree on moral rules. This makes it hard to argue that there is such a thing as natural law, or natural rights. Since different societies arrive at very different rules and standards of morality, there is no way to argue that certain of these rules are natural and others are artificial. They are all natural in the sense that they harness the human potential to develop moral sentiments and to learn, follow, and manipulate rules. They are all artificial in the sense that specific rules have over time been invented by specific people, and that they reflect the experience of these particular people.

One can argue, as I would, that moral codes and sentiments that entail as little as possible in the way of differences of power and of coercion are preferable. However, this is simply a preference. I can argue that people can be very happy and lead very satisfying lives in such societies. However, very privileged members of societies characterized by vast differences in power and opportunity are almost certain to disagree and devise arguments for their positions that, for them, justify their position. McShea (1990) claims that human beings are enough alike that in a situation of calm passion, they can eventually agree on moral judgments. I would like to believe this, but do not.

Schweder, Mahapatra, and Miller (1990) document differences in moral judgment between residents of Bhubaneswar in Orissa, India and in Hyde Park, Chicago. The residents of Bhubaneswar think it is inherently wrong for widows to eat chicken or to wear brightly colored clothing (not just during a period of morning, but for the rest of their lives).

Residents of Hyde Park see no sense in these rules. Residents of Hyde Park agreed that, given the existing rules and sentiments, it might be better for widows to conform to the rules in Bhubaneswar given community pressure, but they also thought that Bhubaneswar would be a better place if they were to change their rule to conform to Hyde Park standards. Residents of Bhubaneswar were also willing to let residents of Hyde Park do as they pleased given their customs, but they felt that Hyde Park would be a better place if they adopted the Bhubaneswar rules regarding the behavior of widows. It will take more than reflection in a state of calm passion to bring Hyde Park and Bhubaneswar together. Perhaps a permanent mingling of and intermarriage of the two populations would bring them to agree on some hybrid form of morality, but this is not likely.

When one contemplates such horrors as genocide or slavery, it would be comforting to argue that these practices are somehow against nature and only possible under conditions of pathology. However, the above view about morality does not easily point in this direction. (I am open to any argument that can persuade me to the contrary.) Rather the above view points in the direction of relativism because it incorporates a belief in the flexibility of human moral sentiments and judgments and the openness of human beings to rules and practices set by tradition. It does not however argue that anything is possible. Human beings are capable of developing a range of moral sentiments depending on circumstances, but the range is probably not infinite. There is no society where the reward for hard work is starvation and where people exert great effort in order to achieve this reward. In a similar vein, Symons (1979) pointed out that there is no society in which people derive the highest pleasure from poking themselves in the eye with a stick. Many different human societies are possible, but not all are possible, or equally probable.

There is also another important way in which not everything is possible. There is an adaptive logic to the relationship between specific moral sentiments and the environments that evoke them. In environments where there is no law as we modern urban folks know it, people develop a commitment to take revenge for a wrong to themselves or a relative. It is in these environments that the commitment makes one safer. In environments where police, courts, prisons, and low crime rates make such a commitment unnecessary, it does not develop, or at least is not nearly as strong. The flexibility built into human nature is an adaptive flexibility. Within the range of conditions in which our ancestors evolved we tend to develop sentiments that are adaptive responses to the environments we experience.

Differences of power

As societies vary in their distribution of power, their moral rules vary. As noted, Alexander suggested that rules are ways for resolving conflicts of interest. In the case of Smith and Jones above (taken from Frank 1988), we can imagine that their business venture might begin with the drawing up of a contract – a set of rules governing their interaction in running their jointly owned restaurant. The rules would specify that the purchase of food and hiring of kitchen staff would be Jones' responsibility. Jones also would put together the menu, but he and Smith would meet to set prices. The rules might further specify that Jones would bring to the meeting an accurate estimate of the cost of each meal. Smith would hire the waiters, arrange for auditing and payment of taxes, etc. Assuming both men were indeed scrupulously honest and both were expected to put equal effort into the restaurant, the rules would probably not favor one partner at the expense of the other.

One test that has been suggested of the fairness of a society's rules comes from Rawls (1971). Rawls suggested that a set of fair rules would be ones that people would agree were fair if they could somehow study them before they were placed in the society and before they knew what position they would occupy in that society. A person performing Rawls' evaluation of the Smith-Jones contract before he knew whether he was to be incarnated as either Smith or Jones would probably agree that the arrangement was fair; he would accept it as just whether he became Smith or Jones.

Of course, this is a contract between two men, not a society. But, if the Smith-Jones restaurant should become a great success, grow into a national chain, and survive as a giant corporation for a hundred years, then it would be more like a society. New people hired by the chain would not negotiate a set of rules before accepting employment. They would think of the rules as something given; not something that they could renegotiate as they pleased. Still, if labor were scarce, and the chain had to compete for good employees with other chains, the rules governing employment might still pass the Rawls' test. If not, too many good employees might vote with their feet by leaving the firm.

However, what if jobs were scarce and unemployment widespread? Then the chain of Smith-Jones restaurants might decide to offer employment on tougher terms. Wages might be low and hours long. The power of bosses over those they supervise might be arbitrary. The bargaining power of the two parties (the employee and the Smith-Jones corporation) would be unequal and the conditions agreed to (the company rules) would be much more favorable to the corporation that to the employees. The company's rules might no longer pass the Rawls' test. The managers and owners of the company (the heirs of Smith and Jones) would have what Rawls' examiners would call an unfair advantage.

The rules of many societies are like the latter situation imagined for the Smith-Jones restaurant chain. The rules have been made up increment by increment over many generations, but not all members of the society have participated equally in this process. The rules of Yanomamo society appear to have been made up by men and are much more favorable to men that to women (Chagnon 1992; cf. also Alexander 1979). In a similar way, the rules of many Australian Aboriginal societies appear to have been made up by older men and appear to be designed to keep younger men under their control. That all men with luck eventually get to be old may seem to mitigate this unfairness in a way that the male chauvinism of Yanomamo society is not mitigated. However, I would guess that young Australian Aboriginal men grumble, and ethnographies make it clear they try to circumvent the rules. In highly stratified societies, the extent of deviation from Rawls-style fairness can be extreme, because one restricted class of people has made up the rules bit by bit over the generations. Often the moral sentiments that develop in these societies accept, to a large degree, the inequality that is built into the rules. The less privileged classes of such societies develop what Marxists would call false consciousness.

Is the question how to cooperate, or why cooperate at all?

Most of the discussion above concerning commitments (Frank 1988), indirect reciprocity (Alexander 1987), and moralistic strategies (Boyd and Richerson 1992) is concerned with strategies for establishing cooperation. That is, the discussion is concerned with means of preventing the separate and potentially competing interests of unrelated individuals from making cooperation unfruitful for some members of the group and thus leading to the break up of cooperative groups. This is the part of a theory of extensive reciprocity that has been hard for evolutionary biologist to explain without appeal to group selection.

There is however another question that needs to be answered. Why bother to cooperate at all? Why not simply live in small kin groups isolated from one another, as our ancestors probably did at some stage of evolution? This question is easier to answer. There are many things that groups of cooperating individuals can accomplish that a single individual cannot. Many fruitful forms of cooperation among unrelated on distantly related individuals can be found in the descriptions of the simpler societies that preserve more of the conditions of human evolution than modern urban societies. Group hunting can be more successful than individual hunting. Sharing among the families of a group can smooth out variations in the success of individuals in foraging for food. Sometimes valuable resources such as obsidian can be traded over great distances as a process that requires a degree of cooperation among trading partners.

However, Alexander (1987) suggests that there is one form of cooperation that has been especially important in the evolution of morality. Human groups compete with one another often in very violent ways, and in this type of competition the advantage to larger and better united groups was especially important. Thus, Alexander's view is that indirect reciprocity was the means of strengthening groups, and success in inter-group competition was the goal.

Conclusion

Behavioral ecologists and sociobiologists now have a coherent theory of the evolution of morality by individual selection. The advantages to morality are the ability to form larger and better-united groups for a wide range of purposes. Intergroup warfare may have been the most salient reason for needing larger cohesive groups (Alexander 1987). Such groups could only be formed if there was some way of making participation in the group advantageous for all members. It did not need to be equally advantageous for all members, but it needed to be preferable to abandoning the group (cf. Alexander 1974). This was especially important when the first non-kin alliances were formed in a social environment limited largely to kin cooperation.

This was accomplished through the evolution of moral sentiments that resolved the commitment problem of cooperating with non-kin (Frank 1988). Another side of the commitment coin was the habit of policing other members of one's community and rewarding the good and punishing the bad (Alexander 1987; Boyd and Richerson 1992). The business of displaying commitments and monitoring the commitments of others allowed a pattern of indirect reciprocity that resolved within-group conflicts of interest.

The result is that human beings display a unique form of sociality in which they are able to form very large, intricately cooperating groups that unite non-relatives. Another result is their acceptance of culturally inherited rules that help to shape their flexible moral sentiments one way or another, given a broad range of possibilities. Often a part of this process of becoming a member of a society held together by rules is the performance of costly behaviors that by themselves are maladaptive, but which may make sense as the price paid for membership in a successful group that confers important benefits.

As can be seen from the dates of the central ideas discussed here, this is a new theory. As yet there has been little in the way of theory evaluation specifically directed at this theory, but the theory is testable and probably will be evaluated through empirical work in the future.

References

Alcock, J.
  1993 *Animal Behavior: An Evolutionary Approach*, 5th Edition. Sunderland, MA: Sinauer Associates, Inc.

Alexander, R.D.
  1974 The Evolution of Social Behavior. *Annual Review of Ecology and Systematics* 5: 325-383.
  1979 *Darwinism and Human Affairs*. Seattle: University of Washington Press.
  1987 *The Biology of Moral Systems*. New York: Aldine De Gruyter.

Axelrod, R.
1984 *The Evolution of Cooperation.* New York: Basic Books.

Axelrod, R. and W.D. Hamilton
1981 The Evolution of Cooperation. *Science* 211: 1290-1396.

Betzig, L.
1993 World History: The 20-Minute Version. Paper presented at the Evolution and the Human Sciences Conference, London School of Economics, June 24-26, 1993.

Borgerhoff Mulder, M.
1991 Human Behavioral Ecology: Studies in Foraging and Reproduction. In *Behavioral Ecology,* 3rd Edition. J. R. Krebs and N. B. Davies, eds. London: Blackwell Scientific Publications.

Boyd, R. and P.J. Richerson
1985 *Culture and the Evolutionary Process.* Chicago: University of Chicago Press.
1991 Punishment Allows the Evolution of Cooperation (or Anything Else) in Sizable Groups. *Ethology and Sociobiology* 13: 171-196.

Carneiro, R.L.
1970 A Theory of the Origin of the State. *Science* 169: 733-738.

Chagnon, N.A.
1992 *Yanomamo,* 4th Edition. NY: Holt, Rinehart and Winston.

Cosmides, L. and J. Tooby
1987 From Evolution to Behavior: Evolutionary Psychology as the Missing Link? In *The Latest on the Best.* J. Dupre, ed. Pp. 77-306. Cambridge, MA: MIT Press.

Cronk, L.
1991 Human Behavioral Ecology. *Annual Reviews of Anthropology* 20: 41-75.
1994 Evolutionary Theories of Morality and the Manipulative Use of Signals. *Zygon* 29:81-101.

Darwin, C.
1858 *On the Origin of Species: By Means of Natural Selection or the Preservation of Favored Races.* London: John Murray.
1871 *The Descent of Man and Selection in Relation to Sex* (2 volumes). London: John Murray.
1965[1872] *The Expression of the Emotions in Man and Animals.* Chicago: University of Chicago Press.

Dawkins, R.
1989 *The Selfish Gene* (New Edition). Oxford: Oxford University Press.

Frank, R.H.
    1988 *Passion Within Reason: The Strategic Role of the Emotions.* New York: W. W. Norton and Company.

Gray, J.P.
    1985 *Primate Sociobiology.* New Haven, CT: HRAF Press.

Hamilton, W.D.
    1964 The Genetical Evolution of Social Behaviour (I and II). *Journal of Theoretical Biology* 7: 1-16,17-52.

Hume, D.
    1930[1751] *An Enquiry Concerning the Principles of Morals.* LaSalle, IL: Open Court Publishing Co.
    1978[1739] *A Treatise of Human Nature.* Oxford: Oxford University Press.

Irons, W.
    1991 How Did Morality Evolve? *Zygon* 26: 49-89.
    In press. The Significance of Evolutionary Biology for Research on Human Altruism. Loccumer Protokolle.

Lack, D.
    1954 *The Natural Regulation of Animal Numbers.* Oxford: Oxford University Press.

McShea, R.J.
    1990 *Morality and Human Nature.* Philadelphia: Temple University Press.

Rawls, J.
    1971 *A Theory of Justice.* Cambridge, MA: Harvard University Press.

Rice, O.
    1982 *The Hatfields and McCoys.* Lexington: University of Kentucky Press.

Richards, R.
    1986 *Darwin and the Emergence of Evolutionary Theories of Mind and Behavior.* Chicago: University of Chicago Press.

Richardson, D.C.
    1986 *Mountain Rising.* Oneida, KY: Oneida Mountain Press.

Ruse, M.
    1986 *Taking Darwin Seriously.* Boston: Blackwell.
    1990 Evolutionary Ethics and the Search for Predecessors: Kant, Hume, and All the Way Back to Aristotle? Loccumer Protokolle 78/89. Rehburg-Loccum: Evangelische Akademie Loccum.

Shweder, R.A.
    1990 Cultural Psychology –What Is It? In *Cultural Psychology: Essays on Comparative Human Development.* J. W. Stigler, R. A. Shweder, and G. Herdt, eds. Pp. 1-43.

Shweder, R.A., M. Mahapatra, and J.G. Miller
>   1990   Culture and Moral Development. In *Cultural Psychology: Essays on Comparative Human Development.* J. W. Stigler, R. A. Shweder, and G. Herdt, eds. Pp. 130-204.

Symons, D.
>   1979   *The Evolution of Human Sexuality.* Oxford: Oxford University Press.

Tooby, J. and L. Cosmides
>   1992   The Psychological Foundations of Culture. In *The Adapted Mind: Evolutionary Psychology and the Generation of Culture.* J. H. Barkow, L. Cosmides, and J. Tooby, eds. Oxford: Oxford University Press.

Trivers, R.L.
>   1971   The Evolution of Reciprocal Altruism. *Quarterly Review of Biology* 46: 35-57.

Wade, M.J.
>   1978   A Critical Review of Models of Group Selection. *Quarterly Review of Biology* 53: 101-114.

Williams, G.C.
>   1966   *Adaptation and Natural Selection.* Princeton: Princeton University Press.

Wilson, D.S.
>   1980   *The Natural Selection of Populations and Communities.* Menlo Park, CA: Benjamin/Cummings.

Wilson, E.O.
>   1978   *On Human Nature.* Cambridge, MA: Harvard University Press.

Wynne-Edwards, V.C.
>   1962   Animal Dispersion in Relation to Social Behaviour. Edinburgh: Oliver and Boyd.

Chapter 2   Evolutionary Psychology and the Search for Evolved Mental Mechanisms Underlying Complex Human Behavior

Linda Mealey

The goal of this chapter is to suggest that even such complex, uniquely human processes as moral decision-making have evolved through natural selection, and are thus not different in kind from basic animal instincts and primitive drives. I begin by a short description of the field of evolutionary psychology. Next, evidence is presented for the existence of modular structures in the brain that may control specific cognitive mechanisms that are related to moral behavior. Finally, I present a research design that would test whether specific tasks related to moral decision-making might be regulated by specific cognitive mechanisms.

The study of evolutionary psychology

A new sub-discipline has developed recently in the field of psychology called Darwinian, or evolutionary, psychology. As with sociobiology (the study of the biological and evolutionary bases of social behavior), Darwinian psychology draws its basic premises from the fields of evolutionary biology and ethology. Also like sociobiology, it attempts to investigate the biological origins and bases of human nature and human interactions without calling into play any non-materialistic elements (Cosmides and Tooby 1987 and Cosmides; Tooby and Barkow 1992).

Despite their overall similarities, most evolutionary psychologists would not identify themselves as sociobiologists, as there are differences in both the assumptions and the methods of the two groups (see, e.g., Symons 1987; 1989 and 1992; Tooby and Cosmides 1990a,b; and Cosmides, Tooby and Barkow 1992). First, whereas most sociobiologists begin their studies with the assumption that observed behavior is biologically adaptive (i.e., it optimizes reproductive fitness), evolutionary psychologists start with the assumption that observed behavior is the result of the action of psychological mechanisms that were selected because of their fitness-enhancing effects at some point during our evolutionary past, and therefore are not necessarily adaptive in our current environment. A second, related, area of disagreement is that most sociobiologists conceive of the human brain as an extremely complex general-purpose intellect which is designed to optimize behavior by tracking changes in the environment and modifying behavior accordingly. Thus, for sociobiologists, general intelligence, creativity, and the capacity to modify behavior through operant conditioning and social learning are considered to be extremely important attributes which evolved to ensure flexibility of behavior. Evolutionary psychologists, on the other hand, conceive of the human mind as an extensive set of independent modules (Fodor 1983), each of which was evolved in response to a particular challenge or selective pressure from our evolutionary environment. According to this perspective, each functional module of the psyche is attuned only to those specific features of the environment that it was designed to monitor, and, since each evolved independently, they are not necessarily in communication with one another. In this way, the modular psyche is thought to be much less flexible and adaptive than a general purpose problem-solving brain, and it is therefore expected to generate behaviors that may not be considered adaptive or intelligent in the current environment.

Cognitive psychologists have known for a long time that the human mind does not operate like a digital computer. We are not as consistent, we are not as "objective," we are not as "rational;" in some ways, we are not as smart as a pocket calculator. Yet there are some tasks, such as visual perception, motor coordination, and language learning, that no computer can even begin to master but that come easily to even the most profoundly retarded or brain-damaged human. Computers may be able to solve arithmetic problems to a million decimal places, but the human brain is wired so as to make it excel at things humans needed to do in order to survive and reproduce in a three-dimensional world full of objects, dangers, and most importantly, other humans. Evolutionary psychologists therefore, are attempting to understand the human mind by determining what kinds of problems evolving humans would have had to deal with, and then postulating, and testing for, psychological mechanisms which seem to be designed for solving those kinds of problems.

Because of their focus on fixed, domain-specific psychological mechanisms (as opposed to general-purpose learning mechanisms), evolutionary psychologists look for universals in behavior while sociobiologists look at individual differences. Evolutionary psychologists can also use the hypothetico-deductive method to make predictions about the nature of possible "adaptive modules" of the psyche, whereas sociobiologists are more constrained to post hoc explanation of already observed phenomena. Studies like the one reported herein are currently being designed to search for specialized cognitive mechanisms, with the hope that their discovery might explain some of the heretofore confusing limitations and inborn biases in human thinking. In this way, evolutionary psychologists hope to begin to understand some of the most complex, yet fundamental and universal human thought processes, emotions, and behaviors, including: language learning; selective attention, perception and memory; sexual emotions and interactions; processes of causal attribution, judgment, and risk-assessment; and, of particular interest to readers of this book, moral decision-making.

Evidence for specialized cognitive mechanisms

In order to address the evidence for the existence of specialized cognitive mechanisms in the human *psyche*, it will be helpful to first address another phenomenon which is at least analogous to, and possibly directly underlying, the idea of a modular psyche: the functional specialization of different parts of the *brain* itself. Since the structure of the psyche is in some sense dependent upon the structure of the brain that houses it, it might be that some functional mechanisms of the psyche map directly onto certain structural parts of the brain. Such a direct mapping is not necessary, but it is plausible (Shallice 1991), and even if it is not the case, the analogy between independent structural units and independent functional units is still a useful one.

That different parts of the brain exhibit functional specialization has been known for over a hundred years. Specialized structures and neural circuits have been discovered which regulate not only basic vegetative functions such as the maintenance of temperature homeostasis, but also more complex operations such as sleep and visual-motor coordination. The agreement between functional maps of the brain (as determined from studies of brain damage and electrical stimulation), cytoarchitectural maps (maps of different cell types), and projection maps (maps which literally trace neural pathways) is "stunning" (Kolb and Wishaw 1990). Gazzaniga (1989) reports "precise" overlaps between maps of brain structure and function. Together with evidence from comparative anatomy, this evidence for localization and specialization of function in the brain suggests an evolutionary pattern of the cumulative addition of new brain structures on top of old ones, rather than ongoing expansion, integration, or rewiring of pre-existing features (Kalat 1992; MacLean 1990). In other words, each new survival problem seems to have generated its own, new, self-contained problem-solving system.

Perhaps the best-studied examples of the functional specialization of different brain structures and areas are the fairly well-defined systems involved in the production and processing of language, memory and emotion. Yet, while it is widely acknowledged that the specialized structures underlying these complex processes have evolved through natural selection, it still remains an item of contention as to whether the behavioral and psychological correlates of activity in these areas have themselves, evolved in the same fashion. (See Pinker and Bloom 1990 and Panskepp 1982 for debates on the evolution of language and emotion respectively.) Perhaps the reticence to accept the same explanation for the existence of psychological processes as for the physical structures which underlie them suggests that our capacity for language, long-term memory, and complex emotion are, ultimately, of fundamental importance to the expression of cognitions and behaviors (such as moral decision-making), that we consider uniquely human. I will briefly examine three cognitive processes related to moral decision-making – emotion, logic, and memory – and review the evidence for their specialization in the brain.

Evidence for specialization of emotion

It is clear that emotions such as sympathy, anger, fear, guilt, and shame are related to human moral behavior (Link and Mealey 1992; Mealey 1995b). But when we analyze the nature of human emotions it is clear that some phylogenetically old structures underlie the emotional displays and expressions of both humans and other mammals. Those who specialize in the study of human emotion (e.g., Plutchik 1980; Izard 1977, 1991; and Ekman 1971) generally agree that there are some five to eight basic, or "primary," emotions which are hard-wired in the brain; are associated with certain behavioral and physiological responses (e.g., facial expressions and changes in autonomic functioning); are found cross-culturally and at an early age; and are reflexively produced in response to certain stimuli. MacLean (1992), Panskepp (1982), and Blanchard and Blanchard (1988) have each authored reviews concluding that these emotions arise from the activation of hard-wired neural circuits in the limbic system.

Griffiths (1990:183) points out that the phenomenological attributes of emotion argue for an adaptive, evolutionary explanation for the psychological structures of emotion as well as for the physical structures which underlie it. Emotions are generally involuntary (even "intrusive," he claims), and they do not seem as responsive to new information about the environment as do beliefs. Therefore, emotional responses to environmental stimuli are likely to be complex, organized, but "informationally-encapsulated" reflexes, which are "adaptive responses to events that have a particular ecological significance for the organism. That is, each emotion has its own eliciting stimuli, its own circuitry, and its own behavioral consequences. All these have been selected as a unitary functional psychological mechanism to deal rapidly with a particular environmental circumstance. These independent systems may be simultaneously stimulated (leading to "secondary" and "tertiary" emotions), but they do not interact or exchange information with one another or with other information-processing systems. Frijda (1988) expresses the same position. His "Law of Closure" states that "Emotions tend to be closed to judgments of relativity of impact and to the requirements of goals other than their own." This "closure, or control precedence," he states, ". . . may well be considered the essential feature of emotion . . . (The) notion of control precedence captures in some sense the involuntary nature of emotional impulse or apathy . . . (and) expresses what I think is the major, basic, theoretical fact about emotion its modularity" (pp. 354-355).

Mineka and Sutton (1992) emphasize the applied aspects of "control precedence" in their discussion of the cognitive biases that are often associated with strong emotions. Emotion seems unable to respond well to new or additional information from other cognitive systems. But it also seems to have a "pre-conscious" influence on other information processors. Anxiety, for example, results in an uncontrollable heightened attentiveness to threatening stimuli and potentially threatening aspects of neutral stimuli, while depression brings about a memory bias for mood-congruent (i.e., depressing) information (Mineka and Sutton 1992; Gotlib 1992). Other authors, too, suggest that cognition subserves emotion, rather than the other way around (Plutchik 1980:303; Kenrick and Hogan 1991:174).

Traditionally, the "social emotions," including love, guilt, shame, and remorse, have not been considered by most theorists to be primary emotions. As secondary or tertiary emotions derived from complex combinations and intensities of the primary emotions, their interpretation and expression were thought to be dependent upon learning and socialization. Those who have adopted the evolutionary approach, however, (such as Weisfeld 1980; Frank 1988; Nesse 1990; and Jankowiak 1992), suggest that the social emotions, also, have evolved as pan-human responses to certain environmental and social situations.

According to these models, the social emotions are biologically wired "commitment devices" (Frank 1988) which motivate adaptive social behavior. Which behaviors, and thus which emotions are adaptive when, varies with age, sex, status, and culture, so that while the emotions and their outward expressions are pre-wired, the particular circumstances and individuals which selectively elicit each emotion are learned. Each individual is biologically prepared to learn, based on reinforcement and punishment, which social emotions are appropriate for a variety of continuously changing social circumstances; once learned, the phenomenological and physiological experience of the emotion itself then further rewards, punishes, or otherwise motivates the individual toward or away from certain types of behaviors and social interactions. Frank (1988) and Caporeal, Dawes, Orbell and van de Kragt (1989) present data from a variety of studies which find that in social situations, emotional responses typically prevail over logic. These results, once again, suggest that the neural systems underlying emotions, even the complex social emotions, are independent, modular systems, informationally-encapsulated from other information-processors.

Evidence for specialization of logic

Moral decision-making relies on logic as well as on emotion. Is logic a domain-specific, evolved capacity? Intuitively, it would seem that if any cognitive capacity is general-purpose and not domain-specific, it would be the capacity to apply deductive logic. Indeed, formal logic is most often taught using abstract symbols which are intended to apply equally well across examples from varying content areas. Yet social scientists know that humans do not always behave "rationally," and economic models of choice and decision-making must take into account this irrational (or a-rational) nature of the human psyche. (See Abelson and Levi 1985 and Wang nd for reviews.)

Among the most widely studied of topics in this area is risk-taking behavior. Repeated studies show that when offered a variety of choices, most people prefer low risk options over high risk options, and a guaranteed outcome over a probabilistic outcome, even when the high risk or probabilistic option is statistically more likely to yield a high payoff; in other words, people are generally conservative and risk-aversive (Kahneman, Slovic and Tversky 1982). This approach to the world makes sense from an evolutionary perspective, in that throughout human history and pre-history before the appearance of intensive technology, big payoffs (like killing a mastodon instead of a deer) were unlikely to translate directly into reproductive fitness, whereas what might be considered a small cost today (like suffering a laceration), might have been deadly. Margolis (1988) takes an evolutionary perspective when he argues that risk-taking judgments are much like emotions in that they are quick, wired-in responses to important environmental stimuli, and are unlikely to be responsive to additional information from other assessment processes. Also like emotional responses, risk judgments lead to further biases in our subsequent thinking.

Recent studies of risk-taking and decision-making suggest that the heuristics we use to make such judgments are not only sometimes "irrational," but also frame-dependent and domain-specific. Tversky and Kahneman (1981), for example, demonstrated that simple changes in the wording of various risk options (emphasizing either loss or gain, but without changing the probability of various outcomes), leads to dramatic changes in the judgment or choice of subjects; this is an example of a framing effect. Cosmides (1989) and Cosmides and Tooby (1989) then demonstrated that decision-making in logic tasks is also heavily dependent upon the content of the examples (all else being equal); this is an example of do-main-specificity.

Most interestingly, Cosmides was able to show that subjects performed best on logical tasks when the task was imbedded in a context of social exchange; subjects were particularly good at using logic to determine when others were cheating on an agreement or breaking a social rule. Cosmides and Tooby (1992) subsequently demonstrated that familiarity with social rules and topics could not explain the results, nor could the social context per se. Across a variety of tests and conditions, subjects excelled at finding "law breakers" when those law breakers were other humans cheating in some social arrangement, but not when those law breakers were objects breaking natural or statistical laws; subjects were also unable to successfully apply the same logical rules when the task required finding altruists or cooperators. These results imply that the human psyche is designed not for a general ability to apply logic and intelligence equally to a variety of settings, but specifically for certain tasks, including the ability to ferret out cheaters from amongst a cooperating group.

Evidence for specialization of memory

When people operate within a moral social system, it is important to be able identify specific individuals and remember their past behavior (Mealey 1995b). The proposed research (discussed below) tests this ability. But just as there is no single general-purpose type of logic, there is no single general-purpose type of memory. Multiple memory systems have evolved, each of which is specialized to such a degree that the stimuli or problems that each system handles cannot be handled by any other system. Different memory systems may be both functionally incompatible and procedurally independent (Sherry and Schacter 1987; Tulving and Schacter 1990; Cooper and Schacter 1992).

Karl Lashley (and later, his student, Donald Hebb), conducted some of the earliest research exploring the possibility that memories are stored in specific parts of the brain. They hypothesized that, because memories are stored through conditioned associations, there must be specific places or neural circuits which somehow physically embody the mental connection between the associated stimuli or stimulus and response. Arguably, the simultaneous activation of two "reverberating circuits" (neural circuits which code for the perception of two different stimuli), could lead to the activation and strengthening of neural pathways which literally connect the two original circuits (Polster, Nadel and Schacter 1991).

Over the course of years of experiments in which he damaged portions of the cerebral cortex of trained rats, Lashley discovered that the amount of tissue he damaged was more important than the location of the damage. From this, he concluded that memories should not be thought of as physical, localized entities, but rather as a process (called "mass action"), in which the cortex works together as a whole, such that no one portion of the brain is more important than any other part.

Later reinterpretations of his work however, suggest that the original hypotheses were basically correct, but that hidden assumptions of the research methodology led him astray. One way in which Lashley's conclusions were problematic was that the brain functioning of rats is very different from that of humans, who have so much more "association cortex" (Camhi 1984). Also, Lashley investigated only cortical areas, not paying attention to the subcortical structures that we now know are so important (Camhi 1984; Kalat 1988). Lastly, the learning tasks which Lashley used may also have created a problem in that he used complex tasks such as maze learning, which relies on many different kinds of cues (such as vestibular, tactile, olfactory, and visual), each encoded differently and in different places. Thus, while Lashley's own experiments seemed to disprove his hypothesis that certain areas of the brain serve certain memory functions, more recent evidence leads us back to this original hypothesis (Carlson 1986; Polster, Nadel and Schacter 1991).

Some of the most current and compelling evidence for specialization of function in memory systems comes from the study of lesions and ablations. Lesions and ablations in specific areas of the brain, produced either intentionally or through natural causes, result in specific memory losses. For example, a man in Minnesota, after suffering a limited injury to the brain, emerged from the hospital otherwise normal except for an inability to remember the names of vegetables. Although he was able to recognize vegetables, even knowing how they are best eaten, he was unable to remember their names, even after prompting (Hart, Berndt and Caramazza 1985).

When a distinct lesion results in a specific memory loss, it can be assumed that the affected area plays some influential role in the genesis, storage, or recall of such memories. Extensive studies have concluded that memories for different types of tasks are stored differently and in different places (Carlson 1986; Desimone 1992). For example, various forms of visual memory (such as object and face recognition) are impaired by injury to the inferior temporal-occipital junction, whereas somatosensory memory (recognition of objects based on shape and feel) is damaged by injury to the superior bank of the Sylvian fissure in the posterior parietal lobe. Also, just as there are different places for memories of different sensory modalities, there are different places for long-term memories versus short-term memories, even within a modality. The ability to learn a long-term visual discrimination task, but not the ability to recognize objects that were just seen, is impaired by destruction of the temporal stem. Farah (1992) summarizes the literature on the agnosias (deficits in object recognition) and concludes that there are multiple, independent, and domain-specific processing units which underlie both the perception and the recognition of various types of stimuli.

We also have discovered that there is a different long-term memory for storage of facts (declarative memory) than for retention of skills (procedural memory). The well-known, textbook case which demonstrates this distinction is that of H.M., a severe epileptic prone to violent seizures. In an attempt to lessen his seizures, surgeons performed a bilateral ablation of H.M.'s hippocampus, amygdala and parts of the surrounding cortex. While the procedure had its intended effect of decreasing the severity and frequency of seizures, there was also an unforeseen consequence: H.M.'s memory for remote past events remained intact (i.e., he had no retrograde amnesia), but memory for recent events was grossly impaired (i.e., he had almost complete anterograde amnesia). What became particularly interesting about this case and subsequent cases like it, was the finding that H.M. could store few new "facts" (declarative memory) but could improve on certain skilled tasks (procedural memory) *despite no conscious memory of any previous exposure to the tasks* (Carlson 1986; Kalat 1992). These (and other) cases provide strong evidence for the existence of very different systems of memory which function in different capacities and which are not necessarily accessible to one another, i.e., they too, are informationally-encapsulated (Shallice 1988; 1991). More subtle testing reveals the existence of such separate memory systems in normal (intact) individuals as well (Tulving and Schacter 1990; Cooper and Schacter 1992).

Research on other animals suggests that we may find even more specialized memory systems when we use the evolutionary approach and look for systems which are designed to solve a particular ecological problem. Memory for song learning in birds is a good example, as this system has restrictions both on what can be learned and when the learning can take place (Sherry and Schacter 1987). Most songbirds will not learn the phrases of other even closely related species, even when the song phrases are presented using the same procedures that lead to the acquisition of the conspecific song phrases; it is clear that some songs are preferentially admitted to memory while others are excluded. Additionally, in most birds song learning is restricted to a particular time period during development, and the timing of these critical periods is directly related to changes in the brain (Alvarez-Buylla, Kirn and Nottebohm 1990). Zebra finches and white crowned sparrows, for example, learn their songs during a single critical period early in development, while canaries can learn new songs every year, but only during restricted seasons when hormonal activity initiates neuronal proliferation in the brain's song centers.

Imprinting is another type of memorization that has clear restrictions on what is learned and when learning takes place. Imprinting is the memorization of significant environmental or social stimuli such as one's nest site, parent's features, or, for migratory species, landmarks and stellar constellations. The well-known example of salmon homing is an example of imprinting upon an olfactory stimulus. In all these cases, restrictions of what features of the environment are admitted into memory and when the learning can occur make these memory systems functionally incompatible with other systems, further suggesting that evolutionarily important tasks are likely to be solved by distinct, independent modules.

In humans, face recognition is such a task, and clearly the memory system which has evolved to solve this task is one that utilizes a different system than other types of memory (Davies 1978). Individuals suffering from prosopagnosia have an inability to visually recognize familiar faces although they can still identify people using other sensory channels, such as by sound of voice. That prosopagnosia is a memory deficit rather than a visual deficit is made clear by the fact that such patients can accurately describe, in minute detail, photos of faces, or even faces of their conversation partner, yet they cannot associate the face with a name or any other personal attribute stored in their otherwise intact memory. Prosopagnosia is a result of damage to the inferior temporal-occipital lobe junction, and thus is spatially, as well as functionally, distinct from other memory systems. In fact, studies using monkeys have documented the existence of particular cells in this area which seem to fire only in response to the presence of a monkey or human face in the visual field (Perrett, Rolls and Caan 1982 cited in Camhi 1984). Thus, face recognition is likely the result of a specialized evolutionary module designed to deal with a specific ecological problem.

A test for a heretofore unknown psychological mechanism for moral decision-making

I postulate that there exist specialized cognitive mechanisms which selectively attend to the moral behavior of others. These mechanisms serve to code and retrieve information pertaining to individuals of high status, and individuals who, based on previous behavior, may pose a future threat.

Rationale

As it becomes apparent that our emotions, our ability to utilize logic, and even our memory processes are specially designed features whose properties seem to be the result of evolution, it is not surprising that arguments over human nature have turned to the one remaining realm of cognition that is sometimes thought to separate us from the rest of the animal kingdom: morality. Yet it is perhaps that very realm which evolutionary psychologists would posit as the most likely of all to exhibit attributes which are clearly the result of evolutionary jerry-rigging. After all, the breakthrough which first established sociobiology as a predictive science, and not just another form of ethology or natural history, was its ability to explain and predict, with striking statistical accuracy, the relative distribution and dispensation of altruistic versus selfish acts across a wide variety of species and situations.

The idea that human moral behavior, like that of other species, should be something shaped by natural selection, stems from the belief that one of the most important, if not *the* most important, feature of early *Homo*'s environment was the behavior of nearby conspecifics (Humphrey 1976, 1983; Tooby and Cosmides 1990a). In our pre-technological world, much more so than today, cooperation or deception on the behalf of trusted others was likely to be a matter of life and death. It would seem imperative to have some kind of mechanism or heuristic suggesting whom to trust and whom to watch, whom to help and whom to deny.

That such heuristics do exist is in no doubt, as suggested by the results of multitudinous sociobiological and game theoretic studies. In particular, the variables of kinship, status, and reciprocity are pre-eminent. For some theoretical discussions see e.g., Hamilton (1964a,b, 1975) on kinship, Weisfeld (1980) on status, and Trivers (1971), Axelrod and Hamilton (1981), Axelrod (1984), and Axelrod and Dion (1988) on reciprocity. For examples of empirical studies on kinship see Wang (1992 and nd) and Barber (1992 and 1994). For empirical studies on status see Mazur (1973), Ginsburg and Miller (1981), and Savin-Williams, Small and Zeldin (1981). See Essock-Vitale and McGuire (1980,1985) for empirical studies on reciprocity.

For any of these situational variables to be important determinants of behavior, there must exist some sort of cognitive mechanisms which respond to them. That is, for kinship to be an important factor in the elicitation of cooperation, trust, or altruism, there must exist one or more kin recognition mechanisms. Likewise, there must exist one or more status recognizing mechanisms. And, to base behavior on the likelihood of future reciprocity, there must be mechanisms for individual recognition and the ability to recall an individual's past behavior. A variety of such mechanisms have been discovered in other species (e.g., Colgan 1983, Gouzoules and Gouzoules 1987, Fletcher and Michener 1987, Dewsbury 1989 and Hepper 1991). It is the goal of the study proposed below to search for such a morality-related mechanism in humans.

General evidence

Research in a wide variety of fields (primatology, ethology, linguistic anthropology, personality, and social psychology) has suggested that social status and trustworthiness are key personal attributes. In each discipline, factor analyses find that status (dominance) and trustworthiness (friendliness) emerge either as the two primary dimensions of interaction, or at least as two of a small number of primary dimensions.

Studies of primate behavior clearly delineate the roles of social status and friendship as secondary only to the role of kinship relations in determining social interactions (see e.g., Chance 1988 and Dunbar 1984). Non-human primates spend an inordinate amount of time and energy monitoring each others' behavior, and most of their communication revolves around issues of status, friendship, and trust. Non-human primates instinctively utilize (and recognize) specialized vocal expressions, facial expressions, body postures, and movements as indicators of dominance, submission, threat, or appeasement (e.g., Plutchik 1980; Walters and Seyfarth 1987; Zeller 1987; Argyle 1988). Studies of human ethology and kinesics find similar patterns in the use and interpretation of these expressions, postures, and movements across varied cultures and age groups (e.g., Andrew 1963; Ekman 1975; Morris 1977; Camras 1980; Ohala 1983; Keating and Bai 1986; Leffler, Gillespie and Conaty 1982; Hinde 1987; Eibl-Eibesfeld 1989; and Provine and Yong 1991). These findings suggest that the messages such signals communicate were important aspects of our social environment early in our evolutionary history.

Concern regarding "social reputation" seems to be a human cultural universal. Kenrick and Hogan (1991) suggest that when people think about other people, two questions come to mind: "Is this person dominant or submissive?" and, "Is this person an agreeable person with whom to associate?" Evidence from linguistics, kinesics, and social psychology studies support this notion: dominance and trustworthiness emerge repeatedly and cross-culturally, as primary dimensions of the terms used to describe others (Hogan 1982). Lorr and McNair (1965), for example, reported a set of correlated dimensions of interpersonal interaction which could be ordered in circular fashion; the primary (north-south) dimension of the circle was dominance-submission, with the lesser (east-west) dimensions being affection-detachment and nurturance-mistrust. Similarly, Romano (1974) concludes that the two major dimensions of communication expressed through body language are power (dominance) and liking/disliking. White (1980) performed independent factor analyses of personality descriptor terms of three different spoken languages: the A'ara language of Santa Isabel, Solomon Islands; the Oriya languages of the state of Orissa in India; and English. He found similar conceptual themes underlying the meanings and uses of the descriptors in all three languages; he labeled them "dominance/submission" and "solidarity/conflict." These same dimensions (albeit often given different names), also emerge as factors on personality tests and when people are asked to describe their own personality and emotions (Plutchik 1980; Hogan 1982; Wiggins and Broughton 1985; Gehm and Scherer 1988).

These findings from primatology, ethology, linguistics, and personality and social psychology support our belief that the variables of dominance/submission and trustworthiness/ untrustworthiness may have been of particular importance to early humans, and that we, therefore, may have developed innate subconscious or preconscious ways of assessing and responding to them. Thus, an evolutionary need to recognize and remember faces of cheaters and individuals of high status may have led to the development of a specialized memory system that preferentially codes these attributes automatically.

Specific evidence

Direct evidence for status-detection mechanisms or threat-detection mechanisms in humans is not abundant, but such modules have been identified in other animals through both ethological and neurological techniques. Tinbergen's classic "hawk/goose" study (1948 cited in 1951:69) exemplifies the ethological approach: he found that a silhouette which resembled a flying hawk (a threat) when moved in one direction, would elicit an immediate fear response in ducks and geese, whereas the same silhouette was ignored when it was moved in the opposite direction to resemble a flying goose (which was non-threatening). The neurological approach has been applied more recently. For example, Kendrick and Baldwin (1987) identified specific cells in the sheep brain which would fire selectively in response to a) the face of a conspecific, b) high status individuals (faces of conspecifics with large horns) and c) threat stimuli (faces of dogs or humans).

Although it would be unethical to do this type of neurological study on humans, ethological studies can be done. One such study recently yielded evidence that humans preconsciously selectively attend to threatening stimuli- specifically, angry faces. Hansen and Hansen (1988) found that angry faces in happy crowds were found and processed more efficiently than happy faces in angry crowds. It has also been demonstrated that infants can distinguish between angry, sad, or fearful faces, and that they selectively and instinctively avert their gaze away from photos of angry faces (Schwartz, Izard and Ansul 1985). These findings suggest that there is a threat-detection feature built into face-processing, and that detection of such a stimulus has a particular and instinctive affective meaning. These data are compatible with our own hypothesis that people also have such a device built into the memory process, and that they should, therefore, be more efficient and more selective in remembering faces of individuals who had previously been perceived as a threat, than in remembering those who were not so perceived.

The studies by Hansen and Hansen and by Schwartz, Izard and Ansul both point to innate specialization in the processing of faces. These studies complement substantial earlier research which found a variety of independent heuristics and biases in the processes of face encoding, face recognition, and face recall. As mentioned before, face recognition itself has been documented to involve a different type of memory than other types of recognition memory. This memory has been extensively studied and found to be influenced by many variables including: the sex, attractiveness and arousal level of the subject, as well as the age, sex, attractiveness, and race of the target face (Goldstein 1977; Shepherd 1981).

A review by Davies (1978) found that when subjects rate faces on global factors (such as intelligence or attractiveness) or when a descriptive statement is presented along with the face, the subjects recall the faces better later. Winograd (1976 and 1978) and Patterson and Baddeley (1977) reported that memory is poorer for faces judged solely with respect to physical features than faces judged based on perceived traits. More recently, Tanaka and Farah (1993) demonstrated that the initial coding of faces is also based less on specific features than on holistic appearance. Together, these studies suggest that one's subjective perception of a face is of major importance in determining whether and how the face is later recalled.

Rodin (1987) put the study of face recognition into an evolutionary/ecological perspective by finding that faces were preferentially recalled when they were perceived as likely to be of later significance. I expect that one's subjective perceptions of the status and trustworthiness (or lack thereof) of a face are likely to be critical elements of their total perception. This hypothesis is bolstered by data from Bower and Karlin (1974), who showed that recognition of faces was substantially better for subjects who were asked to report their assessment of the face's likableness or honesty than those simply asked to report the face's sex, and that subjects who were asked to assess the face's honesty did the best of all.

Given the evolutionary rationale for the existence of a specialized module to re-member identifying features of individuals who may pose a future threat, and the empirical evidence that face recognition is based on holistic attributes rather than specific identifying characteristics, I designed an ethological study to specifically look for a memory which keyed in on the faces of individuals who were portrayed as possible future threats.

Study design and predictions

The study is based on the hypothesis that humans have evolved multiple threat-detection mechanisms (Davey 1995 and Mealey 1995a). I predict that when sub-jects are shown neutral faces with accompanying descriptions that vary on levels of trustworthiness and status, they will tend to better recall faces that were associated with low trustworthiness and those associated with high status. Specifically, I predict that there will be statistically significant effects of both status and trustwor-thiness, and that there will be an interaction effect as well, such that high status, low trustworthiness faces will be recalled at a rate significantly greater than that predicted by the additive effect of the two variables.

Approximately 100 subjects will be told that they will be participating in a study of the reliability of attractiveness ratings, and that they will be asked to judge some photos twice, a week apart. They will then be presented 36 photos and asked to rate the attractiveness of each depicted individual. Each photo will have a (fictional) descriptive sentence typed below. (For example: "J.H. is a vender at baseball games who, after finding a wallet containing $250, located the owner us-ing the driver's license.") The descriptions, similar in length and wording, will differ on the dimensions of trustworthiness and status (the description above being one for high trustworthiness and low status). Each subject will view six of each of six photo/description types in a 2x3x2 design. High versus low status photo/descriptions is a two-level, within-subject variable; high, neutral, or low trustworthiness photo/descriptions is a three-level, within-subject variable; and sex of subject is a two-level, between-subjects variable included because females tend to be better than males at face recognition tasks (McKelvie 1978, Nesse, Silverman and Bortz 1990). Stimuli will be presented in a counterbalanced fashion so that each photo gets each type of description, in order to control for the quality of the photos, facial uniqueness, and other variables which could affect subject's judgments of, and later recognition of, the photos.

When subjects return for their second session a week later, they will view 72 photos, one-half of which will be new, and one-half of which they will have viewed before. None of the photos will be presented with descriptions the second time. Subjects will be asked to again rate all photos on attractiveness, but additionally, to identify which of the photos they recognize from the previous session. The dependent variables are thus: attractiveness ratings at time one when descriptions are available, attractiveness ratings at time two when only the subjects' memory of the descriptions is available, and whether a repeated photo was recognized or not.

We expect, first of all, that people will rate high status individuals as more attractive than low status individuals (even though all the photos have already been preselected for their averageness). We also expect people to rate trustworthy individuals as more attractive than untrustworthy individuals. Both predictions fit the evolutionary perspective, but could equally be explained from other perspectives. Thus, the key prediction of this study in terms of testing the evolutionary model is the prediction that subjects will recall faces of "cheaters," especially high status "cheaters," better than they will recall the faces of trustworthy and/or low status individuals. These results would give evidence that a separate memory system exists which is specialized for the selective storage and recognition of potentially threatening individuals – a system which was predicted based on our knowledge of the kinds of social problems people faced throughout our evolutionary history.

Implications and suggestions for future research

The wealth of literature on strategies that people use to detect deception, as well as the technologies that have been developed in order to further enhance that ability, is are indicators of the great value we place on such ability. (See Zuckerman, DePaulo and Rosenthal 1981, Mitchell and Thompson 1986, and esp. Ekman 1992.) Many of the social problems facing us today (such as deception) are similar to those that faced our pre-technological ancestors. Thus, it would not be at all surprising to find that nature had already evolved a set of psychological mechanisms to perform tasks for which we now have developed complex technological and social structures. We have set up huge, elaborate social structures and rules to aid us in social judgments, risk assessment, and detection and punishment of cheating. I predict that future studies will discover that underlying our (nominally) objective, rational rule systems are some not-so-rational, but evolutionarily adaptive, preconscious and subconscious psychological mechanisms that contribute to the design and exercise of those systems. Patterns and biases in the attribution process, in making judgments about believability and trustworthiness, and in doling out rewards and punishments to others, are all moral cognitions or behaviors that are likely to be explained by evolved psychological mechanisms. (See a recent review and plea for further work in Hans, 1992, as well as the following commentary by Saks 1992, and Vidmar 1992). Furthermore, some of the major moral and social problems of our time, including racism, sexism, and ethnocentrism, are also likely to stem from the operation of underlying cognitive biases and mechanisms that were selected during our evolutionary history (Reynolds, Falger and Vine 1987).

To the extent that we want to change or mold the moral behavior of our children or ourselves, it is imperative that we understand the proximate mechanisms and stimuli involved in the formation of moral judgments (Link and Mealey 1992, Mealey 1995b). Obtaining such understanding does not necessarily require taking an evolutionary approach, but such an approach could certainly facilitate the speed with which we discover such mechanisms and the stimuli that trigger them. Then, to the extent that we do have a general problem-solving ability, we might choose to design and redesign our social structures in ways that best fit, or, alternatively, circumvent, the pre-wired biases of our preconscious.

References

Abelson, R.P. and A. Levi
  1985 Decision Making and Decision Theory. In *Handbook of Social Psychology,* 3rd edition. G. Lindzey and E. Aronson eds. New York: Knopf.

Alvarez-Buylla, A., J.R. Kirn, and F. Nottebohm
  1990 Birth of Projection Neurons in Adult Avian Brain May be Related to Perceptual or Motor Learning. *Science* 249: 1444-1446.

Andrew, R.J.
  1963 Evolution of Facial Expression. *Science 142*: 1034-1041.

Argyle, M.
  1988 *Bodily Communication.* London: Methuen and Co. Ltd.

Axelrod, R.
1984   *The Evolution of Cooperation.* New York: Basic Books.

Axelrod, R. and D. Dion
1988   More on the Evolution of Cooperation. *Science* 242: 1385-1390.

Axelrod, R. And W.D. Hamilton
1981   The Evolution of Cooperation. *Science* 211: 1290-1396.

Barber, N.
1992   Are Interpersonal Attitudes, Such as Machiavellianism and Altruism,
        Modified by Relatedness of their Targets? Presented at the Fourth Annual
        Meeting of the Human Behavior and Evolution Society, Albuquerque, NM.
1994   Machiavellianism and Altruism: Effect of Relatedness of Target Person
        on Machiavellian and Helping Attitudes. *Psychological Reports* 75: 403-
        422.

Blanchard, D.C. and R.J Blanchard
1988   Ethoexperimental Approaches to the Biology of Emotion. *Annual Re-
        view of Psychology* 39: 43-68.

Bower, G.H. and Karlin, M.B.
1974   Depth of Processing Pictures of Faces and Recognition Memory. *Jour-
        nal of Experimental Psychology* 103(4): 751-757.

Camhi, J.M.
1984   *Neuroethology.* Sunderland, MA: Sinauer Associates Inc.

Camras, L.
1980   Social Dominance and Human Motivation. In *Dominance Relations: An
        Ethological View of Human Conflict and Social Interaction.* D.R. Omark,
        F.F. Strayer and D.G. Freedman, eds. New York: Garland Press.

Caporeal, L.R., R.M. Dawes, J.M. Orbell, and A.J.C. van de Kragt
1989   Selfishness Examined: Cooperation in the Absence of Egoistic Incen-
        tives. *Behavioral and Brain Sciences* 12: 683-739.

Carlson, N.R.
1986   *Physiology of Behavior,* 3rd edition. Boston, MA: Allyn and Bacon,
        Inc.

Chance, M.R.A.
1988   *Social Fabrics of the Mind.* East Sussex, UK: Lawrence Erlbaum.

Colgan, P.
1983   *Comparative Social Recognition.* New York: Wiley-Interscience.

Cooper, L.A. and D.L. Schacter
1992   Dissociations Between Structural and Episodic Representations of Vis-
        ual Objects. *Current Directions in Psychological Science* 1(5): 141-149.

Cosmides, L.
    1989   The Logic of Social Exchange: Has Natural Selection Shaped How
          Humans Reason? Studies with the Wason Selection Task. *Cognition* 31:
          187-276.

Cosmides, L. and J. Tooby
    1987   From Evolution to Behavior: Evolutionary Psychology as the Missing
          Link. In *The Latest on the Best: Essays on Evolution and Optimality*. J.
          Dupre, ed. Cambridge, MA: MIT Press.
    1989   Evolutionary Psychology and the Generation of Culture, Part II: Case
          Study: A Computational Theory. *Ethology and Sociobiology* 10: 29-30.
    1992   Cognitive Adaptations for Social Exchange. In *The Adapted Mind:*
          Evolutionary Psychology and the Generation of Culture. J.H. Barkow, L.
          Cosmides and J. Tooby, eds. New York: Oxford University Press.

Cosmides, L., J. Tooby, and J. Barkow
    1992   Introduction: Evolutionary Psychology and Conceptual Integration. In
          The Adapted Mind: Evolutionary Psychology and the Generation of Cul-
          ture. J.H. Barkow, L. Cosmides and J. Tooby, eds. New York: Oxford
          University Press.

Davey, G.
    1995   Preparedness and Phobias: Specific Evolved Associations or a General-
          ized Expectancy Bias? *Behavioral and Brain Sciences* 18(2).

Davies, G.M.
    1978   Face Recognition: Issues and Theories. In *Practical Aspects of Mem-*
          ory. M.M. Gruneberg, P.E. Morris and R.N. Sykes, eds. New York: Aca-
          demic Press.

Desimone, R.
    1992   The Physiology of Memory: Recordings of Things Past. *Science* 258:
          245-246.

Dewsbury, D.A.
    1989   Comparative Psychology, Ethology, and Animal Behavior. *Annual Re-*
          view of Psychology 40: 581-602.

Dunbar, R.I.M.
    1984   *Reproductive Decisions: An Economic Analysis of Gelada Baboon*
          Social Strategies. Princeton University Press.

Eibl-Eibesfeld, I.
    1989   *Human Ethology*. New York: Aldine de Gruyter.

Ekman, P.
    1971   Universals and Cultural Differences in Facial Expressions of Emotion.
          In *Nebraska Symposium on Motivation*. J. Cole, ed. University of Ne-
          braska Press.
    1975   Face Muscles Talk Every Language. *Psychology Today* 9(4): 35-39.

1992 *Telling Lies: Clues to Deceit in the Market Place, Politics, and Marriage*, 2nd edition. New York: Norton Pub.

Essock-Vitale, S.M. and M.T. McGuire
1980 Predictions Derived from the Theories of Kin Selection and Reciprocation Assessed by Anthropological Data. *Ethology and Sociobiology* 1: 233-243.
1985 Women's Lives Viewed from an Evolutionary Perspective. 2. Patterns of Helping. *Ethology and Sociobiology* 6: 155-173.

Farah, M.J.
1992 Is an Object an Object an Object? Cognitive and Neuropsychological Investigations of Domain Specificity in Visual Object Recognition. *Current Directions in Psychological Science* 1(5): 164-169.

Fletcher, D.J.C. and C.D. Michener.
1987 *Kin Recognition in Animals*. Wiley-Interscience, New York.

Fodor, J.A.
1981 *The Modularity of the Mind*. Cambridge, MA: MIT Press.

Frank, R.H.
1988 *Passions Within Reason: The Strategic Role of the Emotions*. New York: W. W. Norton and Co.

Frijda, N.H.
1988 The Laws of Emotion. *American Psychologist* 43: 349-358.

Gazzaniga, M.S.
1989 Organization of the Human Brain. *Science* 245: 947-952.

Gehm, T.L. and K.R. Scherer
1988 Factors Determining the Dimensions of Subjective Emotional Space. In *Facets of Emotion: Recent Research*. K.R. Scherer, ed. Hillsdale, New York: Lawrence Erlbaum.

Ginsburg, H.J. and S.M. Miller
1981 Altruism in Children: A Naturalistic Study of Reciprocation and an Examination of the Relationship Between Social Dominance and Aid-Giving Behavior. *Ethology and Sociobiology* 2: 75-83.

Goldstein, A.G.
1977 Experimental Evidence for Face Recognition. In *Psychology in the Legal Process*. B.D. Sales, ed. Spectrum Publications, Old Tappan, NJ.

Gotlib, I.H.
1992 Interpersonal and Cognitive Aspects of Depression. *Current Directions in Psychological Science* 1(5): 149-154.

Gouzoules, S. and H.G. Gouzoules
1987 Kinship. In *Primate Societies*. Eds. B.S. Smuts, D.L. Cheney, R.M. Seyfarth, R.W. Wrangham and T.T. Struhsaker. University of Chicago.

Griffiths, P.E.
  1990 Modularity, and the Psychoevolutionary Theory of Emotion. *Biology and Philosophy 5*: 175-196.

Hamilton, W.D.
  1964a The Genetical Evolution of Social Behavior. I. *J. Theoretical Biology* 7: 1-16.
  1964b The Genetical Evolution of Social Behavior. II. *J. Theoretical Biology* 7: 17-52.
  1975 Innate Social Aptitudes of Man: An Approach from Evolutionary Genetics. In *Biosocial Anthropology*. R. Fox, ed. London: Malaby Press.

Hans, V.P.
  1992 Obedience, Justice and the Law: PS Reviews Recent Contributions to a Field Ripe for New Research Efforts by Psychological Scientists. *Psychological Science 3(4)*: 218-221.

Hansen, C.H. and R.D Hansen
  1988 Finding the Face in the Crowd: An Anger Superiority Effect. *Journal of Personality and Social Psychology* 54: 917-924. Harper and Row.

Hart, J., R.S. Berndt and A. Caramazza
  1985 Category-Specific Naming Deficit Following Cerebral Infarction. *Nature 316*: 439-440.

Hepper, P.G.
  1991 *Kin Recognition*. New York: Cambridge University.

Hinde, R.A.
  1987 *Individuals, Relationships, and Culture: Links Between Ethology and the Social Sciences*. Cambridge University.

Hogan, R.
  1982 A Socioanalytic Theory of Personality. In *Nebraska Symposium on Motivation*. G.B. Melton, ed. University of Nebraska Press.

Humphrey, N.K.
  1976 The Social Function of Intellect. In *Growing Points in Ethology*. Eds. P.P.G. Bateson and R.A. Hinde. Cambridge University Press.
  1983 *Consciousness regained*. Oxford University Press.

Izard, C.E.
  1977 *Human emotions*. Plenum Press.
  1991 *The Psychology of Emotions*. Plenum Press.

Jankowiak, W.R.
  1992 *Love, Lust and Found in Anthropology*. Presented at the Fourth Annual Meeting of the Human Behavior and Evolution Society, Albuquerque, NM.

Kahneman, D., Slovic, P. and Tversky, A.
  1982 Judgment Under Uncertainty: Heuristics and Biases. New York: Cambridge University Press.

Kalat, J.W.
1988 *Biological psychology,* 3rd edition. Belmont, CA: Wadsworth Pub.
1992 *Biological psychology,* 4th edition. Belmont, CA: Wadsworth Pub.

Keating, C.F. and D.L. Bai
1986 Children's Attributions of Social Dominance from Facial Cues. *Child Development* 57: 1269-1276.

Kendrick, K.M. and B.A Baldwin
1987 Cells in Temporal Cortex of Conscious Sheep Can Respond Preferentially to the Sight of Faces. *Science* 236: 448-450.

Kenrick, D. and R. Hogan
1991 Cognitive Psychology. In *The Sociobiological Imagination.* Mary Maxwell, ed. SUNY Press.

Kolb, B. and I.Q. Wishaw
1990 *Fundamentals of Human Neuropsychology,* 3rd edition. San Francisco, CA: W.H. Freeman and Co.

Leffler, A., D.L Gillespie and J.C. Conaty
1982 The Effects of Status Differentiation on Nonverbal Behavior. *Social Psychology Quarterly* 45(3): 153-161.

Link, R. and L. Mealey
1992 *The Sociobiology of Sociopathy: An Integrated Evolutionary Model.* Presented at the Conference on the Biology of Morality, Bethel College, St. Paul, MN and the Fourth Annual Meeting of the Human Behavior and Evolution Society, Albuquerque, NM.

Lorr, M. and D.M. McNair
1965 Expansion of the Interpersonal Behavior Circle. *Journal of Personality and Social Psychology* 2(6): 823-830.

MacLean, P.D.
1990 *The Triune Brain in Evolution: Role in Paleocerebral Function.* New York: Plenum Press.

Margolis, H.
1988 *Patterns, Thinking, and Cognition.* University of Chicago Press, Chicago.

Mazur, A.
1973 A Cross-Species Comparison of Status in Small Established Groups. *American Sociological Review 38(5):* 513-530.

McKelvie, S.J.
1978 Sex Differences in Facial Memory. In M.M. Gruneberg, P.E. Morris and R.N. Sykes (Eds.). *Practical Aspects of Memory.* New York: Academic Press.

58

Mealey, L.
    1995a Enhanced Processing of Threatening Stimuli: The Case of Face Recognition. *Behavioral and Brain Sciences* 18(2).
    1995b The Sociobiology of Sociopathy: An Integrated Evolutionary Model. *Behavioral and Brain Sciences* 18(3).

Mineka, S. and S.K. Sutton
    1992 Cognitive Biases and the Emotional Disorders. *Psychological Science* 3: 65-69.

Mitchell, R.W. and N.S. Thompson
    1986 *Deception: Perspectives on Human and Nonhuman Deceit.* SUNY Press.

Morris, D.
    1977 *Manwatching: A Field Guide to Human Behavior.* New York: Harry Abrams Inc.

Nesse, R.M., A. Silverman, and A. Bortz
    1990 Sex Differences in Ability to Recognize Family Resemblance. *Ethology and Sociobiology* 11: 11-21.

Ohala, J.J.
    1983 Cross-Language Use of Pitch: An Ethological View. *Phonetica* 40: 1-18.

Panskepp, J.
    1982 Toward a General Psychobiological Theory of Emotions. *Behavioral and Brain Sciences* 5: 407-467.

Patterson, K.E. and A.D. Baddeley
    1977 When Face Recognition Fails. Journal of Experimental Psychology: Human Learning and Memory 3(4): 406-417.

Pinker, S. and P. Bloom
    1990 Natural Language and Natural Selection. *Behavioral and Brain Sciences* 13: 707-784.

Plutchick, R.
    1980 *Emotion: A Psychoevolutionary Synthesis.*

Polster, M.R., L. Nadel and D.L. Schacter
    1991 Cognitive Neuroscience Analyses of Memory: A Historical Perspective. *Journal of Cognitive Neuroscience* 3(2): 95-116.

Provine, R.R. and Y.L. Yong
    1991 Laughter: A Stereotyped Human Vocalization. *Ethology* 89: 115-124.

Reynolds, V., S.E. Falger and I. Vine
    1987 *The Sociobiology of Ethnocentrism: Evolutionary Dimensions of Xenophobia, Discrimination, Racism and Nationalism.* Athens, GA: University of Georgia Press.

Rodin, M.J.
1987   Who is Memorable to Whom? *Social Cognition* 5(2): 144-165.

Romano, A.
1974   *Kinesics: Understanding Body Language*. Media kit. Produced by
W.A. Wandling and M.L Knapp, Center for Advanced Study of Human
Communication, Los Angeles.

Saks, M.J.
1992   Obedience Versus Disobedience to Legitimate Versus Illegitimate
Authorities Issuing Good Versus Evil Directives. *Psychological Science*
3(4): 221-223

Savin-Williams, R.C., S.A. Small and R.S. Zeldin
1981   Dominance and Altruism Among Adolescent Males: A Comparison of
Ethological and Psychological Methods. *Ethology and Sociobiology* 2:
167-176.

Schwartz, G.M., C.E. Izard and S.E. Ansul
1985   The 5-Month-Old's Ability to Discriminate Facial Expressions of Emotion. *Infant Behavior and Development* 8: 65-77.

Shallice, T.
1988   *From Neuropsychology to Mental Structure*. Cambridge University
Press.
1991   Précis of "From Neuropsychology to Mental Structure." *Behavioral
and Brain Sciences* 14: 429-469.

Shepherd, J.
1981   Social Factors in Face Recognition. In *Perceiving and Remembering
Faces*. Eds. G. Davies, H. Ellis and J. Shepherd. New York: Academic
Press.

Sherry, D.F. and D.L Schacter
1987   The Evolution of Multiple Memory Systems. *Psychological Review*
94(4): 439-454.

Symons, D.
1987   If We're all Darwinians, What's the Fuss About? In *Sociobiology and
Psychology: Ideas, Issues, and Applications*. Eds. C.B. Crawford, M.F.
Smith and D.L. Krebs. Hillsdale, NJ: Lawrence Erlbaum.
1989   A Critique of Darwinian Anthropology. *Ethology and Sociobiology* 10:
131-134.
1992   On the Use and Misuse of Darwinism in the Study of Human Behavior.
In *The Adapted Mind: Evolutionary Psychology and the Generation of
Culture*. Eds. J.H. Barkow, L. Cosmides and J. Tooby. New York: Oxford
University Press,.

60

Tanaka, J.W. and M.J. Farah
  1993   Parts and Wholes in Face Recognition. *Quarterly Journal of Experimental Psychology* 46A(2): 225-245

Tinbergen, N.
  1951   *The Study of Instinct.* Oxford: Oxford University.

Tooby, J. and L. Cosmides
  1990a The Past Explains the Present: Emotional Adaptations and the Structure of Ancestral Environments. *Ethology and Sociobiology* 11: 375-424.
  1990b On the Universality of Human Nature and the Uniqueness of the Individual: The Role of Genetics and Adaptation. *Journal of Personality* 58: 17-67.

Trivers, R.L.
  1971   The Evolution of Reciprocal Altruism. *Quarterly Review of Biology* 46: 35-57.

Tulving, E. and D.L. Schacter
  1990   Priming and Human Memory Systems. *Science* 247: 301-306.

Tversky, A. and D. Kahneman
  1981   The Framing of Decisions and the Psychology of Choice. *Science* 211: 453-458.

Vidmar, N.
  1992   Procedural Justice and Alternative Dispute Resolution. *Psychological Science* 3(4): 224-228.

Walters, J.R. and R.M. Seyfarth
  1987   Conflict and Cooperation. In *Primate Societies.* B.S. Smuts, D.L. Cheney, R.M. Seyfarth, R.W. Wrangham and T.T. Struhsaker, eds. University of Chicago.

Wang, X.-T.
  1992   *An Evolutionary Analysis of the Framing Effect in Decision Making.* Presented at the Fourth Annual Meeting of the Human Behavior and Evolution Society, Albuquerque, NM.
  (nd)   Multivariate Framing Effects on Human Choice Behavior: A Search for Rationality Behind "Irrational" Decision Making Biases. (unpublished ms).

Weisfeld, G.E.
  1980   Social Dominance and Human Motivation. In *Dominance Relations: An Ethological View of Human Conflict and Social Interaction.* D.R. Omark, F.F. Strayer and D.G. Freedman, eds. New York, Garland Press,

White, G.M.
  1980   Conceptual Universals in Interpersonal Language. *American Anthropologist* 82: 759-781.

Wiggins, J.S. and Broughton, R.
  1985 The Interpersonal Circle: A Structural Model for the Integration of Personality Research. In *Perspectives in Personality* (Vol. 1). R. Hogan and W. Jones, eds. JAI Press Inc. Greenwich, CT.

Winograd, E.
  1976 Recognition Memory for Faces Following Nine Different Judgments. *Bulletin of the Psychonomic Society 8(6)*: 419-421.
  1978 Encoding Operations Which Facilitate Memory for Faces Across the Life Span. In *Practical Aspects of Memory*. M.M. Gruneberg, P.E. Morris and R.N. Sykes, eds. New York: Academic Press.

Zeller, A.
  1987 Communication by Sight and Smell. In *Primate Societies*. B.S. Smuts, D.L. Cheney, R.M. Seyfarth, R.W. Wrangham and T.T. Struhsaker, eds. University of Chicago.

Zuckerman, M., B. DePaulo and R. Rosenthal
  1981 Verbal and Nonverbal Communication of Deception. In *Advances in Experimental Social Psychology*. L. Berkowitz, ed. New York: Academic Press.

Chapter 3   The Selection of Moral Behavior by its Consequences

Carole J. Young

At the heart of the sociobiological debate is the issue of moral behavior –
specifically, if humans and other animals act to survive and reproduce their genes
in their offspring, how and why do such behaviors as altruism and self-denial appear? In recent years the arguments generated in this debate have taken diverse
forms, and it is not within the scope of this chapter to summarize them all. Two
approaches, however, have qualities that I believe make them particularly compatible, and their concatenation may yield a possible explanation for at least some
altruistic and cooperative aspects of moral behavior. The viewpoint of the sociobiologist will be mainly that of R. D. Alexander (1987), and the radical behaviorist
viewpoint will be that of B. F. Skinner (1987).

Genetic selection as a basis for morality

Alexander (1987) argues that moral systems have been selected because they are
reproductively successful for individuals who experience conflicts and confluences
of interest among themselves. Each individual's interest is in preserving and passing along to the next generation his or her genetic materials. The gene is the unit
of survival in this endeavor, not the person, and so the successful gene is the one
that enhances the reproduction of its carrier, and to a lesser degree, the reproduction of other individuals who may carry copies of the same gene. The probability
that two individuals carry the same gene, summed over all the genes in their re-
spective genotypes, expresses the extent of the interests the two individuals share.
On average, common interest will be greatest between relatives, and the self-
sacrificing behavior for relatives that a huge variety of species exhibits could be
attributed to this common interest. Except for identical twins, however, there will

always be genetic conflict of interest between individuals. Alexander argues that moral systems have arisen to keep the common and conflicting interests in dynamic balance.

Moral systems are peculiarly human because of a level of cognitive development that allows prediction and manipulation of a highly social future involving primarily other humans. These systems are based on indirect reciprocity, wherein some forms of self-sacrificial behavior are performed for the benefit of others in the presence of interested spectators with whom the benefactor may one day interact. The self-sacrificial or "altruistic" element of behavior is a difficult problem for evolutionary theory, as is the indiscriminate nature of some altruistic behaviors in humans. Alexander attempts to explain how even indiscriminate altruism could be selected because it is reproductively successful.

Alexander begins by pointing out that plasticity of behavior has evolved in animals generally because conditions in the world vary predictably among predictable alternatives. An animal that is able to match its behavior to the current conditions under which it finds itself will enjoy a marked survival and reproductive advantage. In humans this plasticity has evolved to a greater degree than in any other known animals because, for much of our history as a species, our main hostile force has been other people. Thus was the stage set for the selection of increasingly complex thought processes and social systems, specifically, the ability to learn by imitation and verbal instruction as well as direct experience. Boyd and Richerson (1985) have done extensive research attempting to demonstrate through mathematical modeling how and why such a complex cultural system has evolved in humans. They conclude that in a variable environment, when the costs of trial and error are high, the ability to acquire information by imitation and instruction would be selected even more strongly than the ability to learn by direct experience.

Alexander believes that the earliest forms of moral behavior were probably helping behaviors performed under a system of direct reciprocity. Our ability to remember those we have helped (or not helped) and those who have helped us in return (or not helped us), would create a reproductive advantage that would favor retaining such abilities and behaviors in the gene pool. A system of mutual helping could result in each individual receiving from others more reproductive benefit than s/he gives away. In a system like this a few cheaters could probably survive and reproduce, but they are unlikely to become plentiful. Such a situation makes direct reciprocity an evolutionarily stable strategy (Maynard-Smith 1976).

It must be noted that where the biologist sees the possibility of genetic selection of certain helping behaviors, the behavioral scientist emphasizes social learning as the mechanism of preservation of such behaviors. From a developmental point of view, infants are born into this world with a general capacity to learn any kind of behavior, and the social environment takes over from there, cultivating cooperative and/or competitive behaviors that suit that culture (Mussen and Eisenberg-Berg 1977). The "rules" determining what animals find reinforcing and punishing are selected by genetic evolution, but once they've been instilled into the gene carriers, the learning occurs relatively independently. Most any variations of cultural and personal practices could be selected by reinforcement and punishment, within certain broad constraints, of course (Pulliam and Dunford 1980). Some researchers argue that development of moral behavior may be helped along by innate tendencies that children possess, for example, responsiveness or empathy toward others (Blum 1987). Others, however, see the "natural" state of human children as one of egocentric selfishness that the culture must counter by inculcating a set of anti-hedonistic rules into its members (Campbell 1978).

Another approach to reciprocal altruism, developed by Trivers (1971) and further tested by Axelrod (1984) claims that reciprocal altruism can arise spontaneously, without foresight, in a population of "selfishly" behaving individuals, and once established can be impregnable to a defecting or cheating strategy. It can arise if a small cluster of individuals (possibly related but not necessarily) begin cooperating with each other, and have a large enough probability of interaction with each other to make the benefits of cooperating over the long run outweigh those of defecting (Axelrod 1984). The cooperating individuals may be able to recognize each other, but don't need to if they are able to stay in constant contact or meet in designated locations. Reciprocal cooperation can remain stable as long as the probability of future reciprocity is large enough, but can deteriorate if it appears to any party that the relationship may be nearing an end.

These two approaches to reciprocity are not totally incompatible with each other. A genetic basis for altruism could underlie the developmental model, and the various cultural forms of altruistic behavior could be manifestations of it (Wispé 1978). Trivers (1971) definitely sees reciprocity as a class of behaviors favored by natural selection.

Although genetic selection of altruistic behavior remains only a theoretical possibility, Alexander (1987) continues building his argument upon this foundation. He proposes that a system of indirect reciprocity among humans sprang from mutual cooperation. Because humans are so adept at vicarious learning, individuals who notice exchanges between others will quickly learn whom to help: those who are likely to return the favor. Indiscriminate helping of others could work to one's individual advantage. By being known and remembered as a helper of others, one becomes the recipient of help offered by others expecting to be paid back by your generosity. The long term benefits of acquiring an honest or helpful reputation, under the right conditions, can outweigh the short term benefits of cheating (Link and Mealey 1992). Frank (1988) has proposed that this situation can lead to certain emotions or passions, such as fairness, to be valued above one's own immediate gain.

Alexander emphasizes that a system of indirect reciprocity requires adequate memory abilities, consistent behavior from individuals over time, application of precedents to new situations, and widespread teaching of ideas of right and wrong. Regarding the first of these, humans undoubtedly have the general memory capabilities for such a system to function. Cognitive research has been illuminating some fascinating possibilities regarding how the memory of humans or monkeys operates on knowledge of other's social behavior. An extensive study of vervet monkeys, coupled with studies of baboons and chimpanzees, has led Cheney and Seyfarth to conclude that "primates seem to be able to remember past interactions and to adjust their cooperative acts, depending on who has behaved altruistically toward them in the past" (1990:291). The researchers go on to emphasize that this ability in nonhuman primates appears to be quite domain-specific, in that certain cooperative actions may be exchanged regularly, but objects rarely are. Also, knowledge that is acquired in one domain, for example, social relations, is infrequently generalized to other domains, such as foraging. In humans, some evidence for domain specificity has been accumulating, leading to presentations such as Gardner's *Frames of Mind* (1983) and Fodor's *The Modularity of Mind* (1983), but the consensus still seems to be that humans' knowledge is more accessible to them and applicable from one domain to another (Cheney and Seyfarth 1990). This does not eliminate the possibility, however, that within domains certain cognitive mechanisms have been selected to deal with particular adaptive demands, and that although these mechanisms may operate on general content to which they are applied, they are best suited, or "tuned" to dealing with particular types of information. Cosmides (1989) has summarized years of research showing how human reasoning abilities may have been shaped by natural selection to deal with information regarding social exchange. Research is also underway (Mealey, Daood, and Krage 1992) to explore the possibility that humans are cognitively biased to remember the faces of people who are described as having high status (powerful) or those described as being untrustworthy (likely to collect a benefit without paying back).

Second, indirect reciprocity also requires consistent behavior over time. This trait has been a point of contention between psychologists for quite some time (see Ross and Nisbett 1991, for a review). People's behavior is much more influenced by situational factors than most of us realize. This doesn't really pose a serious problem for Alexander's claims, however. Humans are not only very good at remembering people's behavior but also the situations in which it occurs. Certain sets of circumstances, as well as certain people, hold status as "good investment risks." Alexander's basic proposal is not compromised.

Alexander's third prerequisite, ability to apply precedents to new situations, is a skill at which humans far outdistance other species, but here also there are limitations. For example, when solving a series of problems that are similar in structure and in appearance, humans quickly grasp the rule or strategy leading to the solution, and will apply it consistently even when it may not be the most efficient available (Luchins 1942). However, when superficial aspects of problems are substantially dissimilar, people have difficulty applying successful strategies from one problem to another. Cosmides (1989) notes that dissimilarities of content in reasoning problems can readily produce this disjunction. However, as a prerequisite for the type of moral system Alexander is proposing, our ability to apply precedents to new situations is more than adequate. If this ability were studied within the context of social interactions (as one of those domain-specific skills described earlier), it may well prove to be remarkable.

Fourth, humans certainly have elaborate networks of verbal and social learning whereby we spread stories of heroes, saints, and good Samaritans. These people are celebrated as objects of respect and emulation because they are benefactors of others, sometimes to the detriment of themselves. Above all, we teach our young ones that having the appearance of a generous helper of others, not interested in one's own personal gain, is of paramount importance. The operative word is "appearance." Helping behavior always exacts its costs from the benefactor and so it could not be selected if it regularly exacted more in costs than it gave in benefits.

Each individual is motivated to give the impression of spending with no expectation of return, but to actually spend less in helping others than what is received. As Link and Mealey (1992) have described, this situation results in a dynamic balance between the selection of better strategies for cheating and better detection of cheaters.

This, Alexander argues, is why self-awareness and consciousness have been selected in humans. We must see ourselves as others see us in order to successfully manipulate their view of us. Apparently, this ability is exclusive to humans among the primates. Monkeys and apes occasionally act as if they knew what others were thinking, but so far none of these instances fails to be explained by behavioral learning principles (Cheney and Seyfarth 1990). Human consciousness, Alexander believes, is the mechanism that allows us to override the immediate costs of helping for the future potential rewards, and to calculate the likelihood and magnitude of those rewards. Although we are conscious for purposes of making these complex judgments, we are unconscious of our true motives, so we can persuade others. Our presentation of ourselves as self-sacrificing is not only deceptive toward others, it is also self-deceptive. If we all truly believe we are acting in others' interests rather than our own, and thereby persuade others to invest in us, we reap a reproductive reward.

Furthermore, the nature of our intergroup competition makes cooperation and altruism more profitable at some times than at others. Consciousness, Alexander claims, has been selected because it provides us the ability to switch from cooperation to advantage-taking as the situation warrants.

Behavioral selection as a basis for morality

The strict behaviorist, such as B. F. Skinner, would probably concur with most of this account, except for the characterization of human behavior as anticipatory. Evolutionary biologists have been attempting for years to persuade the rest of us to view evolution as a selection process operating at the level of individual genes. Evolution does not look ahead as if to design the ultimate surviving animal; it merely retains through reproduction those randomly occurring variations that are the most viable. In light of this, it is surprising that Alexander would burden his theory with a consciousness that looks ahead in anticipation of future rewards, when the behavior that is being observed can be explained without it, by viewing behavior as the product of previous environmental conditions.

Skinner argues (1987) that most human and animal behavior other than that which is reflexive is selected from a repertoire of widely ranging behavioral variations. Just as biological reproduction retains some genetic variations in the gene pool and lets others disappear, so reinforcement, or strengthening by consequences, retains some behavioral variations in the animal's repertoire and eliminates others. If you follow Skinner's reasoning to its culmination, animals, including humans, are not behaving a certain way now because they anticipate it will bring rewards in the future; they are behaving a certain way now because that behavior has been rein- forced (or selected) by past conditions. Humans may think and say that they "expect" a certain event to take place as a result of some action, but it's not the future event nor even the cognitive state that produces the behavior, but rather the past contingencies.

To think about human behavior in this way demands a drastic reshaping of as- sumptions for most people, and even many behavioral psychologists would not agree with it (see Bandura 1974, for example). But it suggests how a system of indiscriminate altruism might have arisen without consciousness playing a causal role.

How does behavioral selection fit into a sociobiological approach to moral behav- ior? Animals have been selected who are capable of generating variations in be- havior, and whose behavioral repertoire is susceptible to reshuffling by their environment in certain ways beneficial to survival and reproduction. Much more is known about the second stage of this process than the first, due to decades of re- search on the effects of reinforcement on behavior. It hasn't always been thought of as a selection process (that is a fairly recent development) but the observations collected over the years are compatible with the idea of selection. Recently, Ep- stein (1991) has focused on the capability to generate variations in behavior. "Generativity" is viewed as a combinatorial process acting upon already existing behaviors. Using the principles of reinforcement, extinction, automatic chaining, and resurgence, and assuming that these principles operate continuously and con- currently on the probabilities of all possible behaviors occurring in a certain situa- tion, a mathematical models can be devised that emulates human and animal behavior in that situation. The next logical step, which is already underway in be- havioral laboratories, is to extend the model to describe generation of multiple repertoires of behavior and how they compete and interact with each other.

This level of selection is "nested" under the level of genetic selection, as Plotkin and Odling-Smee (1981) have presented in their multiple-level model of evolution. Certain types of situations generate variable but restricted repertoires from which the environment selects, and it is simply untrue that any behavior whatsoever could be conditioned by constant reinforcement. Several decades of research have been spent elucidating the relationship between the innate behavioral repertoire and the influence of learning upon it (see Bolles and Beecher 1988, for a collection of papers). Pulliam and Dunford (1980) have devised an equation modeling the learning process that captures both the innate tendency for a particular behavior to occur and the cumulative effects of experience with the environment. Models like this are the wave of the future.

Thinking about behavior as a generation and selection process helps to fill in the evolutionary gap between animals working only for their own benefit and beginning to work for the benefit of others. The action of helping another individual doesn't have to somehow be "produced" by a gene to get its start. The mechanisms that generate variability in behavior could easily extend behaviors one might do for one's self or one's offspring to nearby others. If nearby others exhibit similar variability of behavior, a system of mutual helping and reinforcement could readily spring up (e.g., you groom me; I'll groom you). A necessary assumption, and probably a reasonable one, is that receiving help from another will be reinforcing. Such a system would have an even stronger foothold, at least initially, if it operates among related individuals, because the benefits of mutual helping will increase reproductive fitness.

The proliferation of helping behaviors among a small group of mutual cooperators would be influenced by several other principles of learning. The process of stimulus discrimination is one whereby animals learn to respond differently in the presence of different cues (Schwartz and Robbins 1995). The higher rate of reinforcement available from certain individuals in an animal's environment would select helping behavior in the presence of that individual. This describes a system of direct reciprocity such as one might find among monkeys, for example (Cheney and Seyfarth 1990). Furthermore, it is now widely recognized among behaviorists that signals for reinforcement elicit approach as well as various other behaviors depending on the nature of the cue (Holland 1977) and the nature of the reinforcement (Jenkins and Moore 1973). Again we see that helping or cooperative behavior probably results from the combination of an innate behavioral repertoire and the application of selection pressure by reinforcement.

Harlow's (1959) summary of how learning sets develop during extended discrimination training reminds us of the dynamic balance that is ongoing between selection by reinforcement (tending to narrow an animal's range of displayed behavior) and generativity (tending to increase variability of behavior). An animal that has been consistently responding to the correct stimulus in a choice discrimination problem (the one that's reinforced) may spontaneously shift to the other stimulus. Harlow attributed this to an animal's tendency to explore; it could as easily be a manifestation of Epstein's (1991) generativity. When an animal shifts like this, and if no reinforcement is forthcoming, it immediately returns to the reinforced stimulus, as would an animal who spontaneously proffers an act of generosity to another and receives no reinforcement. The price the animal pays for such a "testing of the waters" is smaller than the benefits gained by the continuous generation of new combinations of behavior. And it is only by such spontaneous emission of behavior that reinforcement, when it is forthcoming, can select, preserve, or strengthen that behavior.

Stimulus generalization is the tendency for animals to respond to similar stimuli in the same manner, and could probably also be included in Epstein's list of generativity mechanisms. Generalization allows an animal to form a concept of a "reciprocating individual" and to respond helpfully to all who appear to fall into that class. The variety and complexity of concepts animals are capable of abstracting is amazing (Mazur 1990).

Generalization also occurs among responses or behaviors that are in the same class. Behaviorists have puzzled for decades about how reinforcement actually affects behavior, given that even a simple behavioral response is never performed exactly the same way twice. An animal performing a simple response to earn reinforcement is not learning a precise set of movement patterns, but rather "an entire class of interchangeable movements" (Mazur 1990:115).

Imitation is one of the best examples of how a class of behaviors can increase in frequency because certain imitative behaviors have been reinforced in the past. Generalized imitation, that is, the performance of imitative responses that are never directly reinforced, has been amply demonstrated in humans (e.g., Weisberg, Stout, and Hendler 1986). The effects of reinforcement generalize to members of the same response class, and what may appear to be "novel" behaviors can occur because they are variations of previously reinforced responses. Imitation in humans is also influenced by whether the model is reinforced or punished for the exhibited behavior. This is explained from a strictly behaviorist position by appealing to the similarity of what is observed happening to the model and what has happened to the observer in previous experiences with imitation and its consequences (Mazur 1990).

Given the operation of these behavioral principles, it is reasonable to propose that a class of helping behavior could be reinforced and could spread among a group through generalization and reinforced imitation. The behaviors in the class would be built from the elements of the animal's already established repertoire. And although they may be initially established by direct reciprocity, they become indiscriminate (offered to other individuals, who may or may not ever reciprocate) because of the reinforcement that comes to those who are recognized for such generosity. I believe such a system could arise due to the operation of the principles just described without anticipatory consciousness and self-awareness playing a causal role.

This is not to argue that humans do not anticipate or form expectations about future events or that we do not consciously reflect upon our own best courses of action or upon possible actions and attitudes of our conspecifics. But these abilities may be only a byproduct of our highly developed language skills that describe our learned ways of behaving (Skinner 1974). These abilities need not be prerequisite, and they may not confer any reproductive advantage. Conscious reflection, anticipation, and self-awareness are not needed as "overrides of the . . . immediate costs and benefits" (Skinner 1987:10). It has been demonstrated that even a pigeon can learn to bypass immediate reinforcement to some extent. If a pigeon is placed in a Skinner box and given a choice of two responses that it can make, one that brings a small reward very quickly and the other that brings a larger reward after a longer time, the pigeon can and will learn to work for the larger delayed reward. The crucial factors are the differences in the size of reward and the length of delay (Rachlin and Green 1972). This behavior is not "hardwired" or genetically encoded; it is learned. The pigeons who perform this way have extensive experience in discrimination tasks, and have always been trained under the most consistent conditions. When we watch children developing, we realize that part of the discipline that children learn is how to delay gratification – how to put off their reinforcers and do the unpleasant tasks right away. How well this is learned depends upon the consistency with which children are reinforced (Millar and Navarick 1984).

Consciousness is not necessary for the complex analysis of costs and benefits of certain behaviors, and it seems unlikely that such analyses are performed. Reinforcement can produce behavior in animals that makes it seem as though they are calculating costs and benefits when, in fact, simple principles are being followed. For example, a variety of animals (and humans in some situations), when given a choice of responses with different rates of reinforcement available for each, will display a phenomenon called matching. They will distribute their behavior to the responses in approximately the same ratio as reinforcement is available (see Mazur 1990, for a summary). It appears the animals have cleverly figured out how to get the most reinforcement for their effort (referred to as optimization or maximizing). But when an experimental set-up forces the animal to abandon matching in order to optimize reinforcement, animals do not act to optimize the amount of reinforcement earned; they simply match (Baum 1981; Mazur 1981). At present, it appears most likely that matching behavior is produced either by a molar strategy called "melioration" (Vaughn 1985) or a molecular strategy of momentary maximization (Hinson and Staddon 1983; Silberberg, Warren-Boulton, and Asano 1988). There is some evidence that matching occurs while animals are foraging in their natural environments, suggesting that it may confer a survival and reproductive advantage (Houston 1986).

It is also questionable whether consciousness has been selected in humans because it makes us better deceivers of others, as Alexander has proposed. So many animals in this world are successful deceivers of others, even of their own kind, that it seems humans could have evolved this ability without consciousness. As Cheney and Seyfarth (1990) have pointed out in their discussion of deception among monkeys and baboons, "even the most compelling observations are only consistent with higher-order intentionality and cannot be used to confirm it" (p. 216).

So, why are we conscious? The radical behaviorist would say consciousness is a byproduct of our highly developed language skills, and current physiological research would bear out the claim. Research on split-brain patients has demonstrated that the "silent" modules of our brains are busy carrying out functions with little or no input from our "consciousness." What the speaking or conscious parts of our brain appear to do is construct a plausible story line to explain the behaviors produced by the silent players (Gazzaniga 1992).

Cooperative levels of selection

To summarize, natural selection produces creatures who respond to certain reinforcing stimuli, and the reinforcement can then begin to select behavior according to its own rules, nested of course within the genetic level of evolution. Skinner claimed, "Because a species that quickly acquires behavior appropriate to a given environment has less need for an innate repertoire, operant conditioning could not only supplement the natural selection of behavior but also replace it" (1987:52). If he meant, as radical behaviorists originally claimed, that any animal can be taught any behavior within its physical capabilities using any reinforcer that has been shown to be effective for that animal (Watson 1930), he was mistaken. There have been many examples of how even the correct and consistent application of reinforcement has failed to produce the desired behavioral change. The Brelands (1961), in their article "The misbehavior of organisms," coined the term "instinctive drift" to refer to the situations where a particular combination of stimuli, behavior, and reinforcer (usually food) produced an innate behavior that interfered with the behavior being taught. This innate behavior, present in the animal's repertoire because of natural selection, directly prevents the animal from performing the response required for reinforcement, and could (if the trainer would be so mean) result in the animal starving to death.

These examples and many others (see Bolles and Beecher 1988) serve to illustrate, as Schwartz (1986) has argued, that the unquestionable success of operant conditioning in the laboratory is not sufficient to support the claim that learning can override instinctual behavior. When reinforcement is applied to a behavior occurring in its natural environment, subject to all the influences operating there, the result is far from predictable. However, maybe Skinner meant that some behaviors that are counter-reproductive could be acquired and maintained by reinforcement in a sizable enough group of people to make it appear that natural selection is being thwarted. Skinner explained that this could happen because reinforcement has both a strengthening effect and a pleasing effect. Its strengthening effect is its ability to reproduce a behavior or to retain it in the repertoire. Its pleasing effect is how it makes the animal feel: enjoyment, or something synonymous (Pulliam and Dunford 1980). The enjoyment of reinforcers probably evolved later than their effectiveness, for to be pleased or attracted by a reinforcing stimulus would enhance its effectiveness and bestow a benefit on those endowed with such reactions. The problem arises because the pleasing effects of reinforcers can themselves begin to mold behavior, and can do so in counter-reproductive ways. We all are capable of acting in ways that we know are bad for us, because we like the way it makes us feel or the reinforcers it brings us. The question is, could such behavior be widespread and persistent? And even if it could, and an entire species succeeded in reinforcing itself into extinction, would that mean that operant conditioning had overridden natural selection, or vice versa?

Building on the foundation of natural selection, the behaviorist can construct explanations for some aspects of moral behavior that are composed of established principles of learning. This approach temporarily sets aside the issues of human consciousness, foresight, and attribution of motives to others, and concentrates upon the continuity and observability of animal and human behavior.

References

Alexander, R.D.
   1987   *The Biology of Moral Systems.* Hawthorne, NY: Aldine de Gruyter.

Axelrod, R.
   1984   *The Evolution of Cooperation.* New York: Basic Books.

Bandura, A.
   1974   Behavior Theory and Models of Man. *American Psychologist* 29: 859-869.

Baum, W.M.
   1981   Optimization and the Matching Law as Accounts of Instrumental Behavior. *Journal of the Experimental Analysis of Behavior* 36: 387-403.

Blum, L.
   1987   Particularity and Responsiveness. In *The Emergence of Morality in Young Children.* J. Kagan and S. Lamb, eds. Chicago: University of Chicago Press.

Bolles, R.C. and M.D. Beecher, eds.
   1988   *Evolution and Learning.* Hillsdale, NJ: Lawrence Erlbaum Associates.

Boyd, R. and P.J. Richerson
   1985   *Culture and the Evolutionary Process.* Chicago: University of Chicago Press.

Breland, K. and M. Breland
    1961   The Misbehavior of Organisms. *American Psychologist* 16: 681-684.

Campbell, D.T.
    1978   On the Genetics of Altruism and the Counterhedonic Components in Human Culture. In *Altruism, Sympathy, and Helping: Psychological and Sociological Principles*. L. Wispé, ed. New York: Academic Press, Pp. 39-57.

Cheney, D.L. and R.M. Seyfarth
    1990   *How Monkeys See the World: Inside the Mind of Another Species*. Chicago: University of Chicago Press.

Cosmides, L.
    1989   The Logic of Social Exchange: Has Natural Selection Shaped How Humans Reason? Studies With the Wason Selection Task. *Cognition* 31: 187-276.

Epstein, R.
    1991   Skinner, Creativity, and the Problem of •pontaneous Behavior. *Psychological Science* 2: 362-370.

Fodor, J.
    1983   *The Modularity of Mind*. Cambridge, MA: M.I.T. Press.

Frank, R.H.
    1983   *Frames of Mind: The Theory of Multiple Intelligences*. New York: Basic Books.
    1988   *Passions Within Reason: The Strategic Role of the Emotions*. New York: W. W. Norton and Co.

Gazzaniga, M.S.
    1992   *Nature's Mind: The Biological Roots of Thinking, Emotions, Sexuality, Language, and Intelligence*. New York: Basic Books.

Harlow, H.R.
    1959   Learning Set and Error Factor Theory. In *Psychology: A Study of a Science* (Vol. 2). S. Koch, ed. New York: McGraw-Hill.

Hinson, J.M. and J.E.R. Staddon
    1983   Hill-Climbing by Pigeons. *Journal of the Experimental Analysis of Behavior* 39: 25-47.

Holland, P.C.
    1977   Conditioned Stimulus as a Determinant of the Form for the Pavlovian Conditioned Response. *Journal of Experimental Psychology: Animal Behavior Processes* 3: 77-104.

Houston, A.
    1986   The Matching Law Applies to Wagtails' Foraging in the Wild. *Journal of the Experimental Analysis of Behavior* 45: 15-18.

Jenkins, H.M. and B.R. Moore
  1973 The Form oOf the Autoshaped Response with Food or Water Reinforc-
        ers. *Journal of the Experimental Analysis of Behavior* 20: 163-181.

Link, R. and L. Mealey
  1992 *The Sociobiology of Sociopathy: An Integrated Evolutionary Model.*
        Paper presented at the conference, The Biology of Morality: An Interdis-
        ciplinary Dialogue. Bethel College. St. Paul, Minnesota. March, 1992.

Luchins, A.S.
  1942 Mechanization in Problem Solving. *Psychological Monographs* 54
        (Whole No. 248).

Maynard Smith, J.
  1976 Evolution and the Theory of Games. *American Scientist* 64: 41-45.

Mazur, J.E.
  1981 Optimization Theory Fails to Predict Performance of Pigeons in a Two-
        Response Situation. *Science* 214: 823-825.
  1990 *Learning and Behavior.* Englewood Cliffs, NJ: Prentice Hall.

Mealey, L., C. Daood, and M. Krage
  1992 Selective Memory for Faces of Cheaters and Individuals of High Status.
        Paper Presented at the Conference, *The Biology of Morality: An Interdis-
        ciplinary Dialogue.* Bethel College. St. Paul, Minnesota.

Millar, A. and D.J. Navarick
  1984 Self-Control and Choice in Humans: Effects of Video Game Playing as
        a Positive Reinforcer. *Learning and Motivation* 15: 203-218.

Mussen, P. and N. Eisenberg-Berg
  1977 *Roots of Caring, Sharing, and Helping: The Development Of Prosocial
        Behavior in Children.* San Francisco: W. H. Freeman and Co.

Plotkin, H.C. and F.J. Odling-Smee
  1981 A Multiple-Level Model of Evolution and its Implications for Sociobi-
        ology. *The Behavioral and Brain Sciences* 4: 225-268.

Pulliam, H.R. and C. Dunford
  1980 *Programmed to Learn: An Essay on the Evolution of Culture.* New
        York: Columbia University Press.

Rachlin, H. and L. Green
  1972 Commitment, Choice and Self-Control. *Journal of the Experimental
        Analysis of Behavior* 17: 15-22.

Ross, L. and R.E. Nisbett
  1991 *The Person and the Situation.* New York: McGraw-Hill.

Schwartz, B.
  1986 *The Battle for Human Nature: Science, Morality, and Modern Life.*
        New York: W. W. Norton.

Schwartz, B. and S.J. Robbins
   1995   *Psychology of Learning and Behavior*, 4thj edition. New York: W. W. Norton.

Silberberg, A.F., R. Warren-Boulton, and T. Asano
   1988   Maximizing Present Value: A Model to Explain Why Moderate Response Rates Obtain on Variable Interval Schedules. *Journal of the Experimental Analysis of Behavior* 49: 331-338.

Skinner, B.F.
   1974   *About Behaviorism*. New York: Alfred A. Knopf, Inc.
   1987   *Upon Further Reflection*. Englewood Cliffs, NJ: Prentice-Hall.

Trivers, R.L.
   1971   The Evolution of Reciprocal Altruism. *The Quarterly Review of Biology* 46: 35-57.

Vaughn, W.
   1985   Choice: A local analysis. *Journal of the Experimental Analysis of Behavior* 43: 383-405.

Watson, J.B.
   1930   *Behaviorism*. Chicago: The University of Chicago Press.

Weisberg, P., R. Stout, and M. Hendler
   1986   Training and Generalization of a "Yes-No" Discrimination With a Developmentally Delayed Child. *Child and Family Behavior Analysis* 8: 49-64.

Wispé, L.
   1978   Toward an Integration. In L. Wispé, ed. *Altruism, Sympathy, and Helping: Psychological and Sociological Principles*. New York: Academic Press.

Chapter 4 Taste, Natural Law, and Biology: Connections and Separations Between Ethics and Biology

Garrett E. Paul

The disciplines of biology and ethics have largely gone their separate ways in the world (although they may, in some respects, claim a common founder: Aristotle). This separation has recently been criticized, however, and there have been renewed attempts to find connections between them, partly in response to the sociobiology debate. Attempts to bridge the gap may be made from the side of biology or from the side of ethics. This paper takes the second approach, looking at the contours and causes of the division, and considering some approaches in western moral philosophy and theology that might offer clues about how to go about re-making these connections. These approaches include the various natural law traditions, process philosophy and theology, and the doctrine of creation in Christianity. The paper closes with a brief consideration of how re-establishing these connections might affect the sociobiology debate.

The separation of science and ethics

Can we use what is (biology and evolution) to inform us about what ought to be (ethics and morality)? An old dictum in Western moral philosophy holds that *de gustibus non distputandum est*: matters of taste are not subject to dispute. In the West during the century now almost past, this dictum has been expanded to include ethics and morality as well. Ethics, for most Western thought (in theory if not in practice), has become a matter of taste. This reduction of ethics to taste has been identified as emotivism: "the doctrine that all evaluative judgments and more specifically all moral judgments are nothing but expressions of preference, . . . attitude or feeling" (Macintyre 1981:11). For emotivism, the sentence "This is good" means "I approve of this; do so as well" (Stevenson 1944, cited in Macintyre 1981:12). Emotivism makes the sharpest possible distinction between fact and value, assigning fact to the realm of objective reality, and value entirely to the realm of individual preference and feeling. Hence, according to this view, fact and value have nothing to do with each other; science (fact) is believed to have nothing in common with ethics (value or morals).

This separation between fact and value corresponds to the social situation of modern selves, who live sharply divided lives, impaled on the spit between external facts and internal emotions. This division reflects, and is reflected in, the division between the two chief personas of contemporary society, the manager and the therapist. The manager is a utilitarian individualist, the therapist an expressive individualist (Bellah et al. 1985:32-35). The manager and the therapist are often the same person, but this person lives two lives that have little or nothing in common. Knowledge becomes separate from feeling, so that one's emotions and preferences are construed as independent of anything that one knows. (For the social and historical causes of this division, see Macintyre 1981:35-59; Bellah et al. 1985:275-286.)

Several more dichotomies correspond to this division between fact and value, science and preference, manager and therapist. Nature has been separated from history. Naturalistic (i.e., scientific) modes of explanation, which rely on regularity, observability, predictability, and universality, have become divorced from historical modes of explanation, which rely on unrepeatability, internal motivation, unpredictability, and uniqueness (Dilthey 1989; Troeltsch 1914). All molecules of water behave the same under the same conditions, but Charles V and Martin Luther will never behave the same again under the same conditions, because there is, by definition, only one Charles V and one Martin Luther, not to mention only one Germany and only one Holy Roman Empire and only one sixteenth century, etc.

Moreover, science tends towards monistic explanations, looking for single causes and principles, always seeking the simplest explanation and resisting exceptions: natural selection and random variation are regarded as explaining the origin of all species, with no exceptions. There was even an influential and controversial "Monist Society" in Germany in the late 19th and early 20th centuries, which was dedicated to aggressive advancement of this view. It was led by the biologist Ernst Haeckel, whose writings enjoyed phenomenal popularity (Haeckel 1900). Meanwhile, developing in the completely opposite direction, modern emotivist ethics has tended more and more towards pluralism, recognizing an enormous variety of ultimately inexplicable and incommensurable preferences.

Science tends towards determinism, since it permits nothing to be exempted from the nexus of cause and effect. But emotivist ethics has, on the contrary, moved towards voluntarism, emphasizing human will and choice. Voluntarism views the world as something to be changed according to one's desires and preferences; the will exists outside the nexus of cause and effect and intervenes in that nexus to cause desired change. Thus, for the emotivist (and perhaps for most modern peoples), the world becomes the raw material upon which one seeks to impose one's will.

Finally, while the above developments were largely independent of developments in theology and religion (both 20th century science and emotivist ethics have largely ignored or deprecated religious faith)[1] there is a parallel dichotomy or tension in Christian theology. This is the dichotomy of creation and redemption. The doctrine of creation emphasizes the givenness of nature and culture, both of which are created by the First Person of the Trinity (God the Creator). The doctrine of redemption emphasizes the fallenness of the world and society, and their liberation through redemption by the Second Person of the Trinity (Christ). Christian theology has repeatedly sought to keep these two elements in a creative tension. Moral theologies that overemphasize creation (like most traditional Lutheran theology) tend to emphasize exclusively the givenness and unchangeability of the orders of creation, on which Christ has little impact. Moral theologies that overemphasize redemption (like most sectarian and liberation theologies) tend to emphasize exclusively the corruption of the present order, which Christ will replace. Gnostic versions of Christianity go so far as to eliminate the First Person of the Trinity and the doctrine of creation altogether, leaving a purely spiritual Jesus who imparts an other-worldly wisdom. Christianity, then, embodies dichotomies similar to those found in western moral philosophy and science – which should not be that surprising, since all three have had significant impact on one another (Gilkey 1959).

We have, then, several dichotomies: fact/value; nature/history; monism/pluralism; determinism/ voluntarism; creation/redemption. But let us return now to our initial question: whether matters of "taste" are subject to dispute. We shall investigate it further by means of an analogy.

---

[1]While religion did not play an immediate role in the above developments, it does seem that the growth of the sectarian movement in Christianity during the 16th and 17th centuries, with its rejection of the established social order of church and state, contributed (unintentionally) to the growing emphasis on choice, individualism, and voluntarism in the 18th and 19th centuries.

The analogy: is taste not subject to dispute?

Ethics and morality, as we have seen, are widely held to be a matter of taste, and therefore indisputable. This development contradicts the scientific portrait of reality upon which western society's ubiquitous technology relies — the very technology that has, ironically, made emotivism possible. From the – of science, taste is a biological reality, and so too is eating behavior, subject to biological description. Let us examine this question in greater detail by taking up a closer examination of the question of taste in the more literal and restricted sense of the taste of food. Can the taste of food be a subject for dispute?

Now it may seem self-evident that the taste of various foods is an utterly subjective and personal matter. I may like sauerkraut and bratwurst and detest grits and red-eye gravy, while you may like grits and red-eye gravy and detest sauerkraut and bratwurst, but our mutual friend may detest all of these and eat tofu. Another friend may eat potato casseroles. Or, we may think all of these foods taste good. And we cannot say anything more about what they and you and I eat, except that we have different tastes. Or can we?

In fact, there are several ways in which we can say more. First, perceived taste can be measured and reported. This may not tell you whether you should like the taste of something, but it can predict whether you are more or less likely to like the taste of something. Second, tastes are influenced by social and historical background, and these patterns can be studied and measured, making additional predictions possible. Third, even though food exists for us as taste, it also exists as chemicals and nutrition. These can be empirically investigated. The chemical makeup of sauerkraut and grits does not vary according to individual taste. The nutritional implications of bratwurst and red-eye gravy vary according to individual human bodies, but not according to taste. If you have high cholesterol, bratwurst is bad for you regardless of whether it tastes good to you or not. When it comes to nutrition, food involves questions of what is good for the body: which foods promote or inhibit heart disease and cancer, which foods can or cannot be eaten safely by diabetics or alcoholics, etc. And questions of the good of the body inevitably involve biology.

The dilemma is particularly vivid in the potentially fatal contradiction of the anorexic woman whose body is starving and yet who thinks (feels? emotes?) that she is growing thinner and hence more attractive. This concrete dichotomy between the preference of the person and the biology of her body has grave implications.

Hence there is much more to food than taste. Food entails a host of relatively objective phenomena that cannot be reduced to personal taste. In particular, one cannot ignore the nutritional and disease implications of various foods if one wishes to enhance one's life and health. Hence matters of taste are subject to dispute – even when we consider taste in its most literal sense, as the taste of food. It is noteworthy that this point can be seen most clearly when we have recourse to the social and natural sciences.

There are two objections of which we must take note at this point: One could simply refuse to be concerned about one's health and lifespan, and then claim that nutrition is irrelevant to her/his individual choice of food. In that case it would seem that choice can still be reduced to taste. Or, one could deny the relevance of biological information to one's own body, as many anorexics do. Both objections are logical and self-consistent, particularly if life is not an absolute good. Yet they go against common sense and actual human practice, and seem to be highly problematic, if not implausible, views.

Natural Law theory as an attempt to make the connections; a brief history of natural law

If the identification of ethics with taste seems implausible even in the most literal sense, in what ways can we seek to expand our understanding of ethics beyond mere taste? How can the divorce between value and fact, between internal and external, be overcome?

One way to approach this question is to look at some of the ways in which connections were made before the divorce became effective. This is not the only possible approach, and it carries within it the peculiar temptation to think that the past can be restored. Yet this approach can assist us as we attempt to rethink for today the problems caused by this separation in the past.

One recurring attempt to connect value and fact in the history of western moral philosophy has been the tradition of natural law. Natural law theory has a long, rich, and complex tradition, reaching back to Aristotle and the Stoics. It is, for that reason, quite difficult to define. For our purposes we can describe it as the conviction that there is present, in nature, an order from which we can discern something of how human beings ought to live. This order is thought to be universal, unvarying, and not limited to any one culture or society; judgments based on it are objective and in no way arbitrary. The different schools of natural law vary greatly, however.

Aristotle (who predated the formal development of natural law theory) believed that what is good for human beings is not simply a matter of opinion, but can be discerned from a careful study of human behavior. For example, careful observation of human confidence and fear could lead to the conclusion that the best way to express confidence and fear is as courage, and not as cowardliness or recklessness (Aristotle 1962:1115a-1116a). Human happiness for Aristotle was not simply a matter of opinion; conclusions about happiness and the good life for humans could be drawn from the observation of external circumstances.

Natural law in the narrower sense is largely a product of Stoicism. Stoic philosophy perceived the world as ruled by a law that was rational and universal, not limited to the crumbling *polis* of ancient civilization, nor to any single state, region, race or color. This understanding was subsequently appropriated in Christianity, which identified natural law with the divine will and reason of the God of Israel, the creator of the world (Troeltsch 1991a:329-331).

Thomas Aquinas formulated an imposing synthesis of natural law in the 13th century. Aquinas combined Aristotle with Augustine, and observed a world where all life gave evidence of purpose and teleology, where all things are directed toward God as their end (Aquinas 1948:429-438). From a careful reading of those ends, according to Aquinas, one can determine what is true and good, and what is right for every living being.

Today, however, natural law has fallen on very hard times. It has been criticized for a variety of reasons. Some of the most potent objections have grown out of modern science. Nature, it is objected, is not static, but changing. Nature is not unvarying and universal, but manifests difference and change from time to time and from place to place. Furthermore, nature does not act according to ends and goals. Since Darwin, biologists have ceased to speak in terms of intention and order, and now speak in terms of adaptation. Science does not see in nature any *telos*, or goal of its development. Variation is, as Darwin held, random, betraying neither purpose nor intention nor goal. On these terms it is held that Aristotle and Aquinas were poor guides for scientific inquiry.

Other objections have come from various movements dedicated to social change. Natural law theory has been seen as a conservative force and an impediment to change because of its claims to invariability and objectivity, and because of its conviction that there is something good about the present "natural" order. Thus did Marxists object to attempts to justify human inequality by appeals to nature, and feminists (until recently, at least) rejected any attempt to read woman's destiny from woman's body: "Anatomy is not destiny!" It should be no surprise then, that some of the most vigorous objections to sociobiology come from Marxists and feminists (Bancroft 1985:25-27).

Finally, the sheer variety and difference in various natural law theories have been taken as evidence against the whole project of discovering any authoritative natural law. If natural law is universal and unvarying, then surely those committed to discovering it should have achieved some measure of agreement by now.

There have been other intellectual forces at work in dismantling the natural law synthesis, notably reformed and sectarian Protestantism's insistence on revealed law. Also, there have been a host of social forces stemming from the industrial revolution and the changes it produced in human relationships. But for now it is sufficient to note that we have returned to the place where started our reflections: the separation between fact and value, between biology and ethics.

We are left, then, with what Kant would call an antinomy, or what lesser mortals call a contradiction. It seems that we cannot find any connections between value and fact, and yet it also seems that we cannot separate them into two distinct and mutually exclusive realms. Neither natural law nor emotivism appears coherent. It is of little comfort to note that Kant's own resolution of this antinomy has not enjoyed unquestioned acceptance (Kant 1929:A444-A456).

Attempting to re-make the connections: Where does this leave us?

Whenever we find ourselves confronted with mutually contradictory and incoherent answers, I tend to think that we are asking the wrong question. Wrong answers are often the result of wrong questions. Unfortunately, the right questions are not yet clearly discernible. But there are various threads that might, upon further examination, prove to be helpful in weaving renewed connections between biology and ethics. Most of this will take the form of reconceptualizing the dichotomies summarized at the beginning of this paper.

First, a concept of nature as dynamic rather than static and unchanging could open the way to a renewed dialogue between biology and ethics. This emerges from the observation that nature as we know it, although it evinces signs of regularity, is far from unchanging. Indeed, nature has a history. Similarly, all history takes place in nature. Consistent application of these insights could enable a reconceptualization of the nature/history dichotomy. This is an insight often associated with the process philosophy of Alfred North Whitehead (1978).

Second, the dichotomy between determinism and voluntarism in ethics could be challenged by substituting a responsibility or action/response model for the cause/effect model in moral action. This would entail a rejection of determinism, because moral action (indeed, all human actions) would be viewed as response to a situation, not a mechanical reflex; and it would entail a rejection of voluntarism, because the will would seek not to impose itself on the world, but to respond to it (Niebuhr 1963:47-68). This view has been called "soft determinism," that the number of choices that any moral agent has are significantly limited by a large degree of determinacy in every situation. It stops short, however, of the "hard determinism" that would eliminate all indeterminacy and choice (Gustafson 1975:7-14).

Third, the fact/value dichotomy could be overcome by understanding that value emerges in response to fact. Value emerges from fact and then helps to create new fact, from which new value emerges, and so on. To give an example: the value called democracy did not simply happen in the brains of John Locke, Thomas Jefferson, et al. Instead, a variety of facts – the development of the printing press, the growth of literacy, the emergence of capitalism, the physical distance of the American colonies from Great Britain, the weakening power of the French nobility – helped to create the value of modern democracy. But, in turn, democracy itself became a fact that helped to create new facts – the Declaration of Independence, the French Revolution, the U.S. constitution, the Montgomery bus boycott – which themselves helped still other values to emerge. Value and fact co-inhere within one another.

Fourth, renewed interest in the body and the body's connectedness with nature, particularly in feminist thought (Griscom 1985), helps to undermine the body/mind and nature/history dichotomies as well as the fact/value dichotomy. This development suggests still another possibility for re-establishing a connection between morality and biology, the science most closely connected with the human body.

Fifth, in the area of Christian moral theology, it would be helpful to place renewed emphasis on the doctrine of creation, and on the dynamic relationship between creation and redemption. Creation should be viewed not as a once-for-all, finished event, but as a continuing event in which we are called to be co-creators (Gilkey 1980:90-93). Similarly, the redemption of a fallen world (including nature and history) needs to be kept in close tension with the goodness of a created world. This, finally, implies the need for a dynamic relation between the First and Second Persons of the Trinity, and, in turn, the need for a dynamic, not static concept of God. This may have implications for the monism/pluralism dichotomy as well; the unity and plurality of the creation need to be held in the same creative tension as the unity and plurality of the Godhead. Views tending in this direction can be found in movements as diverse as process theology, ecological theology, and Trinitarian theology.

Sixth, and finally, attention needs to be paid to the social location of biology and biologists, something that critics of sociobiology in particular have been quick to point out. While this is sometimes done with the goal of discrediting science (Harding 1992), it need not be so. Such observations should remind us, however, that science too has a history and a context.

Conclusion: What does this mean for the sociobiology debate?

I have sought to call attention to the contradictions and incoherencies caused by the separation of biology and ethics, a separation manifested in the dichotomies listed at the beginning of this paper, and have tried to suggest ways in which some connections could be reestablished. I did not mean to suggest that these contrasts can be altogether eliminated in some sort of fuzzy "holism." Instead, I hold to the image of connections: making connections between realms that have been separated, restoring communication and tension where now there is simply a vacuum. This could open a way for a renewed dialogue between ethics and biology. What might such a dialogue mean for the sociobiology debate?

First, we need to overcome the monism/pluralism and determinism/voluntarism dichotomies. Wilson firmly plants himself on the monist side of the first dichotomy when he identifies his work as scientific materialism and contrasts it with traditional religion (Wilson 1978:190-193). Yet he implicitly recognizes the necessity of moral choice among plural alternatives in responding to our genetic trajectories (Wilson 1978:198-199, 208). Hence his explanations still allow for a plurality of moral choices that are shaped, but not dictated by, genetics. While "genes are necessary conditions for the possibility of developing human community, even Wilson would not argue that they are sufficient" (Gustafson 1979:45). But if they are not sufficient, then a monist, monocausal explanation of human behavior will not suffice. Wilson contradicts his own monism. However, we should welcome sociobiology's insistence on the genetic components (not determinants) of human behavior as a needed if overstated corrective to the excesses of emotivism and pluralism that abound in ethics today.

Similarly, the determinist slant of sociobiology could be corrected by appeal to the responsibility model identified above. It is not that we are somehow "free" of our genetic inheritance, nor that we are completely "controlled" by it; rather, we respond to it. Scientific knowledge of that inheritance, as it becomes increasingly available, is an important part of formulating that response. But it is not, as Wilson thinks, all-sufficient for reaching that response.

A model for how connections between ethics and sociobiology might be profitably established has been recently developed for ethics and psychology. Eschewing the determinist Freudian language of human "drives" and "instincts," we may speak instead of human "tendencies" and "needs" (Browning 1983:68-71, 89-95; 1987:161-163; 1991:102-105; Midgely 1978; Singer 1981). The language of "drives" and "instincts" strongly suggests that human beings have no significant control over their behavior, but are simply acting out a genetic program. However, to speak of human "tendencies" and "needs" suggests that, while we cannot ignore our genetic inheritance, we still have freedom in how we respond to it. To take an obvious example, we all have sexual and reproductive needs and tendencies. Yet there are a variety of ways to meet these needs and tendencies (including, in some cases, celibacy)! Moreover, human beings (including sociobiologists) customarily identify some ways of meeting these needs as better than others, and some as unacceptable.[2]

Following this broad insight, we can speak of values that emerge from our genetic inheritance and our human tendencies and needs; and we may also speak of conflicts between various values (for instance, between self-preservation and altruism,

---

[2] Even if we disagree (as we do) about which ways of meeting these needs are or are not acceptable, it is more important to observe that humankind universally does strive to distinguish the acceptable from the unacceptable.

or between sexual needs and respect for sexual integrity). We may, following William James, recognize saintly religious behavior as "adapted to the highest society conceivable, whether that society ever be concretely possible or not" (James 1961:296).

Despite Wilson's poor prognosis for theology (Wilson 1978:192), this approach also suggests the possibility for a theology enriched and informed – not controlled – by sociobiological insights into the origin and adaptive function of religion. Again following James, the adaptive function of religion can even be seen as an argument for its truth (James 1961:398), even if theology must continue to attribute that function to something beyond human biology. This is particularly true for those theologies that pay careful attention to the empirical existence of religion and view themselves as the intellectual self-interpretation of a religious community (Troeltsch 1991b:1-62).

If we follow this path, we can purge the insights of sociobiology of their scientific triumphalism. Sociobiology could then show greater promise for re-conceptualizing the language of ethics, enhancing our understanding of moral behavior, and providing a needed alternative to the indeterminacy and voluntarism of twentieth century moral philosophy and theology.

References

Aristotle
  1962 *Nichomachean Ethics*. Trans. by Martin Ostwald. New York: Macmillan.

Aquinas, T.
  1948 [1260] Summa Contra Gentiles. In *Introduction to St. Thomas Aquinas*. Anton C. Pegis, ed. New York: Modern Library.

Bancroft, N.
  1985 [1980] Women in the Cutback Economy. In *Women's Consciousness, Women's Conscience*. B. Hilkert Andolsen, C. Gudorf, and M. Pellauer, eds. Minneapolis: Winston Press. Pp. 19-31.

Bellah, R.N., R. Madsen, W.M. Sullivan, A. Seidler, and S.M. Tipton
  1985 *Habits of the Heart*. Berkeley: University of California Press.

Browning, D.
  1983 *Religious Ethics and Pastoral Care*. Philadelphia: Fortress Press.

90

1987   *Religious Thought and the Modern Psychologies*. Philadelphia: Fortress Press.

1991   *A Fundamental Practical Theology*. Minneapolis: Fortress Press.

Dilthey, W.

1989 [1883]   *Introduction to the Human Sciences*. Ed. and trans. by Rudolf A. Makkreel and Frithjof Rodi. Princeton: Princeton University Press.

Gilkey, L.

1959   *Maker of Heaven and Earth: A study of the Christian Doctrine of Creation*. Garden City, N.J.: Doubleday and Co.

1980   *Message and Existence*. New York: Seabury.

Griscom, J.L.

1985   *On Healing the Nature/History Split in Feminist Thought*. In *Women's Consciousness, Women's Conscience*, Barbara Hilkert Andolsen, Christine Gudorf, and Mary Pellauer, eds. Minneapolis: Winston Press.

Gustafson, J.M. Pp. 85-98.

1975   *Can Ethics be Christian?* Chicago: University of Chicago Press.

1979   Sociobiology: A Secular Theology. In *The Hastings Center Report* 9: 44-45.

Haeckel, E.

1900 [1899] *The Riddle of the Universe at the Close of the Nineteenth Century*. Trans. by J. McCabe. London: Harper and Brothers.

Harding, S.

1992   Why Physics is a Bad Model for Physics. In *The End of Science? Attack and Defense*. Richard Q. Elvee, ed. Lanham, Maryland: University Press of America.

James, W.

1961 [1902]   *The Varieties of Religious Experience*. New York: Collier Books.

Kant, I.

1929 [1787]   *Critique of Pure Reason*. Trans. by N. K. Smith. New York: Macmillan.

Macintyre, A.

1981   *After Virtue*. Notre Dame: University of Notre Dame Press.

Midgely, M.

1978   *Beast and Man: The Roots of Human Nature*. Ithaca, N.Y.: Cornell University Press.

Niebuhr, H.R.

1963   *The Responsible Self*. New York: Harper and Row.

Singer, P.
  1981 *The Expanding Circle: Ethics and Sociobiology.* New York: Farrar, Straus, and Giroux.

Stevenson, C.L.
  1944 *Ethics and Language.* New Haven: Yale University Press.

Troeltsch, E.
  1914 Historiography. In *Encyclopaedia of Religion and Ethics.* J. Hastings, ed
  1991a [1911] Stoic-Christian Natural Law and Modern Secular Natural Law. In *Religion in History.* Ed. and trans. by J.L. Adams. Minneapolis: Fortress Press. Pp. 321-324.
  1991b [1925] *The Christian Faith.* Trans. by G. E. Paul. Minneapolis: Fortress Press.

Whitehead, A.N.
  1978 [1929] *Process and Reality.* Corrected edition. D. R. Griffin and D. W. Sherburne, eds. New York: The Free Press.

Wilson, E.O.
  1978 *On Human Nature.* Cambridge: Harvard University Press.

Chapter 5   Inadequacies of Sociobiological Explanations Of Altruism

Gregg Johnson

The debate over the extent, origin, causes and implications of altruism in social animals, including humans, has intrigued scholars from many disciplines. The progress of the dialogue has often been obstructed by the morass of terms, many of which carry different meanings in different disciplines. Some would argue that all seemingly charitable behavior indeed has a selfish motive and thus true altruism does not exist. Others would call "altruism" any behavior that benefits others, even if there is clearly a selfish motive involved. The dialogue should continue, however, since it seems apparent that altruistic behavior has contributed significantly to the global success of our species. We need a clear understanding of the mechanisms and factors controlling altruism if we wish to develop strategies to prevent wars, civil strife, domestic abuse, racial and social injustice and moral degeneracy at many levels.

Sociobiologists argue that lessons from other social animals may hold clues to the commonalties and trends in social evolution. Darwin summarizes the human condition: ". . . to do good unto others as you would that they should do unto you is the foundation stone of morality" (Darwin 1871). This doing of good to others (called the "Golden Rule" in the Bible and "altruism" by academics), must remain a primary focus of human intellectual pursuit if we are to survive and thrive as a species. We must continue the search for the meaning, origin, effects and functions of altruism in order to preserve and nurture our social life. For it is from this position of strength that we can lay hold of other social ills and address them corporately.

In Webster's Dictionary, altruism is defined as "the principle of living for the good of others." Many authors would insist that true altruism means relinquishing personal resources to another with no potential for short term or long term return.

They observe that most purported examples of such altruistic behavior mask an underlying selfish motive though often unbeknownst to the initiator. Under such a definition, true altruism is demonstrably rare when screened through a sieve for potential long term gain. Tipping of waitresses, giving blood, or donation to charities raises one's stock as an altruist, and one's status as a worthy partner, friend, or confidante. The revelation of potentially selfish advantage leaves relatively few true acts of altruism, and those that appear unselfish can be excused as rare, maladaptive behavior that will not thrive.

Most biologists prefer a more clearly bounded definition of altruism. For example, Robert Trivers says that altruism is any act that confers a benefit on someone at a cost to the other in terms of resources or reproductive potential. Trivers leaves open the possibility of calling charitable acts altruism even though there is clear evidence of selfish gain in return (Trivers 1985). It is the intent of this paper to argue for the existence of a significant extended altruism, found only in the human species, an altruism that cannot have arisen or been maintained in the population by conventional evolutionary processes of natural selection. First, I will review several types of altruism discussed in the ethology literature Second, I will outline several developments in the evolution of altruism identified by sociobiologists. Third, I will present evidence that human extended altruism deviates from these trends. Finally, I will suggest problems with the strict biological explanations for altruism.

Types of altruism among social animals

Trivers identifies three basic types of altruism. *Kinship altruism* is caregiving or self-sacrificial acts applied only to relatively closely-related kin groups in which the altruism will benefit the survival of those genetically like the altruist. The intensity of this altruistic investment between two individuals directly correlates with the degree of relatedness. Maternal relationships with offspring produce the strongest interactions and can be referred to as maternal instinct. Paternal relationships are usually less intensely altruistic. The reason for this is that monogamy is relatively rare. Promiscuity and polygamy, the more common mating strategies of social animals, favors aggressive promiscuous males who have the small investment of sperm and often little parenting responsibilities, while females have relatively few offspring, bear far more of the gestating and parenting burden and therefore tend to be much more selective about mates. Consequently, females also tend to have much stronger altruistic interactions with offspring (Symmons 1979). More distantly-related individuals elicit even less altruistic behaviors in rather direct proportion to their genetic similarity.

Among seasonally monogamous songbirds such as the mountain bluebird, if a mated pair looses its mate, it may attract a new mate. If the new mate is male it will not help in the nest cleaning, grooming, and feeding of an existing clutch. If the new mate is a female, they have rarely been observed to adopt the existing clutch. Extremes of maternal altruism exist such as in the cricket, *Anurogryllus muticus*, which allows herself to be eaten by the offspring to give them a good nutritious start in life (Hardin 1977). Trivers argues that the net gain to a benevolent genotype from any altruistic behavior must exceed the reproductive result without such benevolent effort. If by being altruistic more of the altruists offspring and genes populate subsequent generations than would have been likely had the altruist channeled all energy into his own individual reproductive efforts, altruistic genes will increase. Examples of maternal instinct and kinship altruism abound among social animals including humans. We find immediate and extended families helping one another among most peoples. Among tribal people however, the limits of such extended kin groups rarely exceed 150 before aggressive tendencies cause the splitting of the group (Wilson 1980).

Reciprocal altruism is Trivers' second type of altruism. This is an extension of kinship altruism beyond the immediate kin group to members of a tribal group. Often groups are matrilocally arranged, such that females stay with their birth group while males leave and join unrelated groups often through tests of aggressive prowess. Reciprocal altruism flourishes where groups remain together in rather stable interactions even though unrelated and where a significant altruistic investment will be rewarded in time. Generally reciprocal altruism involves rather small investments by a large number of individuals in a group. Richard Alexander (1987), subdivides this category into direct and indirect, immediate and delayed payoff. The potential exists that ones small investment at a time of personal resource plenty will be compensated with a large return in a time of need. The alarm calling of prairie dogs perched at burrow entrances, warn foraging cadre members that there is approaching danger. The alarm call system is vital to forager and group survival yet produce minimal cost for the call initiator. (King 1959). Many birds of prey, and rodents practice the same alarm system. In some cases alarm calls are recognized across species. The caller usually places himself in more danger by drawing attention to his position, yet the risk may be worth it if it saves several kin or the gene for such behavior thrives because even though unrelated, affinity groups with such alarms survive better than those without. Human conventions such as giving a person phone change, helping a stranded motorist to a service station, sharing food from ones excesses, sending gifts, or giving of donations to charities may all be forms of such reciprocal altruism which place groups with such behavior at an advantage.

Cooperative altruism, Trivers' third type, involves several individuals aiding each other in a given time-space framework. The return on altruistic investment is more immediate with several individuals gaining more from collaboration than they could working individually. Mature male baboons may form alliances to maintain control of a troop which individuals separately may loose to younger stronger males. They thus come to one another's aid, surround and protect a member when mating, or gang up on subordinate members to coerce conformity to the group. (Strum 1987) Members of a chimpanzee troop may band together to help each other tree and capture young vervet monkeys or baboons. Several female African wild dogs may help each other nurse and care for collective pup litters. (Wilson 1975) Wolf packs and Lion prides would fare poorly without cooperative hunting within the group. Black backed gulls will pair and jointly defend their territory (Lorenz 1963).

The process of cooperative altruism is most pronounced among the primates. The grooming behavior common to most primates serves both a cleaning process and social bonding function. Individuals injured in areas that they can not reach are routinely ministered to by group members through cleaning, licking, and grooming the wound. Chimpanzees in adjacent cages will share food when one is given more than the other. Several chimps will work together to pull on a rope to get a box of food for one hungry chimp, even when two out of the three have been previously adequately fed (Hornstein 1976). Examples of this type of cooperation is abundant among human groups. Barter and monetary systems make complex specialization and cooperation extensive. "You scratch my back and I'll scratch yours" is a principle of human social behavior that can be found extensively. Farmers help each other complete the planting and harvests. Groups will band together to build a church, park, or other community project. Carpenters work in teams of three because they are more efficient than each working alone.

Richard Alexander (1987) suggests that a fourth type of altruism exists in a much lower frequency. Unreciprocated, non-kin or indiscriminate altruism, he suggests, arises periodically as an aberration or mutant extreme of the other forms of altruism. This form I will refer to as *extended altruism*. Extended altruism is the truly unselfish act for which it is difficult to devise any genetic return that would allow such behavior to be selected for. Alexander argues that such behavior is maladaptive, routinely selected against, and remains in low frequency in the human population.

This form of extended altruism embodied in the "Golden Rule" certainly appears rare to nonexistent among other social animals. I would argue, however, that it exists among humans at a much higher frequency than Alexander allows. It certainly appears more widespread than one would expect of a completely maladaptive gene. Military heroism evidenced by soldiers falling on live hand grenades to protect their comrades were the cause for granting over 200 medals of honor to Americans during World War II. There are numerous examples of civilian efforts to rescue survivors from dangerous conditions including earthquakes, floods, and auto accidents. One man hanging onto a piece of the fuselage from flight 207 that crashed in the Delaware river continued to catch a rope ladder from the rescue helicopter and pass it to his comrades in the water with him. He eventually slipped below the water and drowned. One can site the many who adopt or care for foster children. There are anonymous donors to impersonal charities. Fifty percent of Americans are active during some point in their life in volunteer activities such as the Peace Corps, Vista, Red Cross, or the Salvation Army. Seventy percent of people contribute to charities even though many are no longer tax deductible (Hunt 1990). The investments of time and energy are far more than can be attributed to reciprocal or cooperative altruism. It is unlikely they will receive similar pay back for their efforts. The efforts of Mother Teresa and missionaries like her, some of whom have lost their lives in efforts to minister to totally unrelated cultural groups. All of these are examples of extended altruism. It is this capacity in humans, I would submit, that has elevated our species above all others in terms of human success and social complexity

Sociobiologists suggest that we might find insight into our own social behavior by identifying common themes and trends in the social behavior of non human species and charting their evolutionary pilgrimage. Wynne-Edwards (1969) has identified several trends in the evolution of altruism. These principles have arisen from a wide range of studies on various social mammals. Human extended altruism violates these principles at several points and raises the possibility that extended altruism is not a part of the normal evolutionary process and must then have different origins.

Developments in the evolution of altruism

Kinship-based altruism appears to be found throughout the social animals whether primitive or advanced, simple or complex, and appears to be one of the earliest forms of altruism. In its most rudimentary form it is simple maternal care. Males are much less involved in this behavior across species. Social groups are often matrilocally organized. Paternal altruism is seen (e.g., defense against attack), but to a significantly lesser degree than maternal altruism. Thus, kinship altruism is mainly demonstrated by the mother. Caregiving, care soliciting, shared nurturing and nursing of young are much more intense among lionesses than among the male lions (Wilson 1975). This caregiving and soliciting is expressed in ritual food sharing, grooming, play, corporate protection and care of the injured or young, and involves extended kin groups such as those seen among baboon and chimp troops. Many ungulate mothers will take on great odds to protect their young, such as moose fending off a wolf pack or wildebeest confronting hyenas. Many ground nesting birds will feign an injured wing and lead potential predators away from the nest at their own personal risk.

Like other mammals, human females tend to display a stronger altruistic bond with offspring than do males. Hormonal changes facilitate this bond; at the time of birth, a burst of Oxytocin stimulates milk production and awakens strong bonding instincts (Durden-Smith and Desimone 1983). In general, however, human altruism seems to be much more evenly distributed between the sexes and does not seem to have its roots in maternal instinct. Volunteerism, philanthropy, and other evidences of extended altruism seem much less gender-specific.

A second development in the evolution of altruism is that reciprocal and cooperative altruism is more prevalent when the social group is smaller and more cohesive. Small groups invading new territory have high levels of allegiance and affinity and are very dependent upon one another to cope with hostile environments. They engage in a high degree of altruism, insuring the health and stability of the group. Meercats post sentries to sound alarm while others forage, dig new dens, or tend to the defenseless young. Alarm calling, food sharing, grooming and protecting are common reciprocal acts found in many social animals. This type of altruism begins to degenerate and disappear when animal groups become large and approach the carrying capacity of the habitat. Under these stressful conditions, survival dictates that every individual fend for herself. There is a high degree of social fluidity with much migration, social mixing, and crowding. The chance of one's altruistic acts being noticed, catalogued, and reciprocated are much reduced. Chimpanzee troops reach a critical number where tensions overwhelm altruistic tendencies and the group splits (Goodall 1980). In baboon troops, alliances and reciprocal care-giving disintegrate when the troop gets larger than 150 individuals (Sturm 1987). Thus, reciprocal and cooperative altruism have evolved to be most intense in small groups.

However, human extended altruism seems as vibrant in large groups as in small. There are many stories of unselfish sharing and extended altruism during the great depression and during other times of human need. Stories abound of families hiding and caring for wounded enemy soldiers. Many of the Industrialized nations (both Socialist and Capitalist) have institutionalized altruistic behavior. Examples include the provision of foreign aid to underdeveloped countries and the U.S. Marshal Plan to rebuild post-World War II Europe. Some may argue that selfish motives lie behind such programs. Yet they seem to have arisen from genuine extended altruistic concerns and have become more numerous as human social complexity has increased.

A third development in the evolution of altruistic behavior is that animal groups under stress who have chronic elevated levels of adrenaline tend to have less altruistic behavior and engage in more self-serving and even abnormal behavior than do unstressed groups. Rats that are crowded or foot shocked become hyperaggressive, abandon caregiving, ritualized social interactions, normal grooming, and even maternal behavior, and engage in bouts of abnormal and destructive behavior (Flannelly, et. al. 1984).

Clarence R. Carpenter (1964) set up a Rhesus monkey colony in Puerto Rico. Under normal conditions, the monkeys display a rich variety of altruistic behavior in grooming, feeding, and "aunting" (care of the young by non-mothers). However, during the voyage from India the monkeys were in unfamiliar and cramped spaces. The stress of this period and the early settlement of the colony produced hostile behavior, devoid of any displays of altruism. Eight of the ten mothers killed their offspring. Much fighting, hoarding of food, and other aggressive displays dominated social interaction.

We can also note that human congeniality diminishes under stress. During wars and periods of social unrest, humans are capable of just as heinous behaviors as the rhesus monkeys . Thus in both animals and humans one can find the potential for hostile and destructive behavior under stressful circumstances. On the other hand, human extended altruism seems to persevere under stressed environments where typical mammalian altruism wanes. Communities ravaged by tornado, flood, hurricane, or earthquake find unusual camaraderie and altruism. War stories of protection and heroism abound. During the Great Depression, people cared for neighbors who were out of work and without food. Of course, crisis precipitates looting and aggressive acts, but it also produces true altruistic behavior. This contrasts with the behavior of animal groups in similar situations.

A fourth development in animal social behavior is that the more dominant an individual is, the more she tends to be selfish and less inclined to cooperative and reciprocal altruistic acts. Trivers observes that dominant individuals who command most of the resources do not gain significantly from cooperative or reciprocal help. In groups from chimpanzees to lions, researchers document despot behavior among the dominant males, with caregiving and care soliciting behavior much more common among lower ranking animals (Trivers 1971).

One can find examples of this type of behavior among human male groups which possess a hierarchical structure. It may express itself in subtle corporate ladders or more rigid and hostile rank ordering such as in the military, or in street gangs. In most such cases, high rank carries power, privilege and resources. Those in such positions tend not to exercise the same level of altruistic concern as do their subordinates. It may be that there is a relationship between elevated levels of testosterone, dominance, and the reduction of altruistic behavior. Human extended altruism, however, *does* appear among the wealthy and powerful as well as among the oppressed, as witnessed by the philanthropy of many corporate leaders. Though data suggest that the wealthy give a smaller percentage of their income to church or charity, a significant number of foundations, charities, and schools are funded largely by wealthy philanthropists. It seems, then, that there are ample examples of altruism by dominant individuals, and that dominant individuals frequently display extended altruism.

A fifth development is that reciprocal and cooperative altruism will be strongest among those with the strongest reproductive potentials and will decline as reproductive potentials wane. Thus, middle aged animals will have the strongest drive toward altruistic endeavors and group bonding. In many animals, the cohesion of the social group is maintained primarily among the reproductively active members. Older animals are excluded from the group. Therefore, altruism may be controlled, not only by genes, but by epigenetic factors such as hormones which have shifting influence on those genes over the life cycle. Reproductively active groups of lions, African wild dogs, as well as many social carnivores synchronize their conception and birthing such that litters may be cared for collectively. Shared caregiving duties free some mothers to hunt or to provide for others' young in the event a mother is killed. Post-reproductive males and females of such groups are often driven off or at least are less involved in such altruistic behavior. Among humans, baby-sitting cooperatives and neighborhood childcare programs may reflect a similar altruism based on reproductive needs. However, extended altruism among humans seems much more complex and inclusive. For example, adoption of foreign babies does not seem to be an example of simple reciprocal altruism. Also, human altruism extends well beyond the reproductive years. Individuals who are well past reproductive age may in fact make more contributions than the young to volunteer causes and charities that benefit society as a whole, rather than benefiting a small, genetically-similar group.

A sixth evolutionary development in altruism manifests itself as social groups become larger than a few extended kin (such as baboon and macaque troops which may exceed 100 members). In these cases, the reciprocal benefits of random altruistic acts may be minimal or lost entirely. Types of altruism and their display become troop-specific and part of a learned "culture," with particular benefits, depending on the particular habitats where the troop resides. This culture springs from genetic underpinnings and follows its own evolutionary path. An adult male baboon will often oversee the play of juveniles to intervene in squabbles and to instruct in appropriate levels of aggressive play (Washburn and Devore 1961). Separate cultural patterns are present in different baboon troops and may also lead to their adaptive success. Another example of group-specific altruism occurs when young chimpanzee females learn parenting skills by practicing on the infants of relatives. This "aunting" practice which teaches caregiving skills is a unique expression of altruism among some groups, but may manifest itself differently among other groups.

Human extended altruism seems more than just cultural variant, however, since it seems to occur in all cultures. One can find evidence of extended altruism among primitive tribes such as the !Kung of South Africa. The !Kung are very solicitous and empathetic. For example, a hunter who has killed a large game animal will enlist others to help carry, cut and distribute the kill so as not to take sole credit for his achievement and thereby cause jealous feelings among his tribesmen (Hunt 1990). To a lesser degree, such empathy and extended altruism permeates industrialized societies.

Sociobiologists attempt to explain extended altruism as having underlying selfish motivations. Richard Alexander argues that humans have evolved a substantial capacity for indoctrination and self deception in order to accommodate religious mandates for extended altruism. Such religious conformity allows for more universally accepted social rules and consequently more widespread and stable social interactions and structures. Missionary martyrs or the work of Mother Teresa could be explained as maladaptive extremes of altruism. These acts are interpreted as overzealous acts arising from the human capacity for self-deception, and are based on the tendency to accept indoctrination. Yet we still have spontaneous, unconditional altruistic acts such as soldiers jumping on hand grenades to save their foxhole mates, people risking their lives to rescue unrelated children from a burning house, or civilians harboring Jews during World War II under threat of their own life. The frequency and intensity of these heroic acts overwhelms Wilson and Alexander's claims that indoctrination and self deception account for feats of extreme altruism. There seems to be an innate capacity buried deep within human nature that facilitates this kind of reflexive, heroic response. This capacity to spontaneously act out the "Golden Rule" is found nowhere else among social animals.

Several problems exist when attempting to derive a biological origin for this type of extended altruism. If extended altruism exists, it could not have arisen from a "selfish gene." This kind of unselfish altruism seems too pervasive to be explained away as aberrant and maladaptive, and efforts to explain it as a complex form of reciprocal or cooperative altruism seem to contradict the evolutionary developments seen in other species as presented above, where reciprocity and cooperation diminish to nothing as the population becomes large, fluid, or transient.

Among non-human animals it is possible to find kinship altruism where a parent will sacrifice his life for offspring, but the practice of reciprocal altruism is much more measured and cautious, and is "calculated" on the basis of a return on the investment. Even if one argues that all acts of altruism must be selfish, the human examples given above go far beyond the rather superficial and low energy investment behavior observed in reciprocal altruism. These examples exist in large populations where relatively few reciprocal benefits could be expected. The chance that someone might return a good deed is small; thus one would expect the frequency of reciprocal altruistic acts to likewise be reduced. However, human acts clearly involve non-kin and have no particular cooperative advantage to the initiator. On this basis it seems we must seek other explanations for the existence and complexity of altruism in humans.

Humans have developed many distinctives. These include the use of fire, production and use of tools, burying of their dead, the use of language, the existence of a self image, reasoning, forethought, the development of complex social systems, the development of the idea of the supernatural, and the frequency of extended altruism. However, many of these characteristics have been documented in other primates in rudimentary forms and appear to be different from humans "more by degree than kind" as Darwin had originally suggested. Jane Goodall, Diane Fossey, Harry Harlow and other primate specialists have found that these animals have complex social structures, can acquire language, can make and use tools and can demonstrate self awareness, reasoning, forethought and planning. Most characteristics that appeared earlier to be distinctives of human behavior are now recognized as amplifications of characteristics that are found in other mammalian species.

There remains, however, one distinctive that apparently does not exist in any other species: the facility to "love one's neighbor as one's self" (extended altruism). It is tempting to suggest that this capacity, more than any other, makes humans distinct from all the rest of the animal kingdom and that it is this characteristic that has led to our species' success. Extended altruism allowed humans to preserve genetic diversity and to adaptively radiate into new global niches. An additional explanation for human success could be that *culture* was the adaptive mechanism that allowed humans to occupy diverse niches. This ethic of extended altruism, embedded in the human spirit, embellished and transmitted in human culture, provided a powerful adaptive advantage for the human species, yet could not have arisen by normal selfishly-based natural selective processes.

One cannot build an evolutionary scenario that accounts for the emergence of extended altruism. Thus, those that are bound to explanations which demand selfish roots for behavior must argue that extended altruism is a mutant, maladaptive anomaly. However, one cannot automatically assume that because a trait is broadly adaptive, it must therefore be genetic in origin. A behavior pattern passed on through a *cultural* heritage can be adaptive as well. Extended altruism seems to be pan-human and pan-cultural. However, it cannot be accounted for by socio-biological explanations, because, by definition, it is not genetically adaptive for the individual.

The long range consequences of evolutionary processes are fairly well spelled out in the fossil record. The natural history of a species over time is to become specialized, genetically homogenous, and thus more vulnerable to extinction as the environment changes. Organisms near the center of the phylogenetic tree tend to be more primitive and more generalized. Organisms on the periphery of the phylogenetic tree can be viewed as more specialized and derived. They tend to have less genetic diversity. They occupy a narrower geographic area and are less able to adapt to novel environments. The fossil record is full of examples of species such as saber tooth tigers, woolly mammoths and dinosaurs that were specialized and succumbed to changing environments. The average life-span for such specialized species is about 20 million years.

Nevo (1978) charted the genetic diversity and heterozygosity of major groups of species on the periphery of the phylogenetic tree. As his data show, these species become more genetically homogeneous over time. However, humans deviate significantly from this trend. Although they are on the periphery of the phylogenetic tree, they have a vast diversity of alleles for all of the genes tested. The human species retains the genetic diversity more characteristic of long lived, generalized species. Thus humans have the ability to become highly efficient and adaptive in specialized niches, and yet to accommodate to totally new niches. How is this diversity maintained?

I would suggest that this diversity is due in large part to the human capacity to provide extended altruism to unrelated people. This means that individuals possessing genetic traits that are maladaptive in the present environment will be the beneficiaries of this extended altruism. This altruism may have diffused the strong selection pressures which have been the theme of evolution in other species, both at the individual and at the group level. This extended altruistic behavior may have been one of the most important adaptations for giving our species its wide adaptive success.

Extended altruism may be maladaptive for individuals, but because it exists, it provides a preadaptation for novel environments by preserving the necessary genetic diversity. Sociobiological theory cannot completely and adequately explain human extended altruism. Extended altruism is pan-cultural, and, while prejudicing the survival or reproduction of the individual, seems to aid general and long-term adaptation of the species as a whole.

References

Alexander, R..
   1987   *The Biology of Moral Systems.* New York: Aldine de Gruyter.

Blum, L.A.
   1980   *Friendship, Altruism, and Morality.* Boston: Rutledge and Kegan Paul Publishing.

Caplan, A.L.
   1978   *The Sociobiology Debate.* New York: Harper and Row.

Carpenter, C.R.
   1964   *Naturalistic Behavior of Nonhuman Primates.* Penn. State University Press.

Daly, M., and M. Wilson
   1978   *Sex Evolution and Behavior.* North Scituate, MA: Duxbury press.

Darwin, C.
   1871   *The Descent of Man and Selection in Relation to Sex.* New York: Appleton.

DeWaal, F.
   1989   *Peacemaking among Primates.* Cambridge: Harvard University Press.

Flannelly, K.J., and R.J. Blanchard
   1984   *Biological Perspectives on Aggression.* New York: Alan R. Liss Inc.

Hardin, G.
   1977   *The Limits of Altruism.* Bloomington, IN: Indiana University Press.

Hartl, D.L.
  1981 *A Primer of Population Genetics.* Sunderland, MA: Sinauer Associates
        Press.

Hornstein, A.H.
  1976 *Cruelty and Kindness.* Englewood Cliffs, NJ: Prentice Hall.

Hunt, M.
  1990 *The Compassionate Beast.* New York: William Morrow and Company.

King, J.
  1959 Social Behavior in Prairie Dogs. In *Readings from Scientific American:
        Animal Behavior.* T. Eisner and E.O. Wilson, eds. San Francisco: W.H.
        Freeman.

Lorenz, K.
  1963 *On Aggression.* New York: Harvest Books.

Mansbridge, J.J.
  1990 *Beyond Self Interest.* Chicago: University of Chicago Press.

Strum, S.C.
  1987 *Almost Human.* New York: W.W. Norton.

Symons, D.
  1979 *The Evolution of Human Sexuality.* New York: Oxford University
        Press.

Trivers, R.
  1971 Evolution of Reciprocal Altruism. *Quarterly Review of Biology* Vol.
        46:35-57.
  1985 *Social Evolution.* Menlo Park, CA: Benjamin Cummings Press.

Washburn, S.L and I. DeVore
  1961 Social Life of Baboons. In *Readings from Scientific American, Animal
        Behavior.* T. Eisner and E.O. Wilson, eds. San Francisco: W.H. Freeman.

Wilson, E.O.
  1978 *On Human Nature.* Cambridge: Harvard University Press.
  1980 *Sociobiology: The New Synthesis.* Cambridge: Harvard Univeristy
        Press.

Wynne-Edwards, V.C.
  1963 Intergroup Selection in the Evolution of Social Systems. *Nature* 200:
        623-626.

Chapter 6   Sociobiological Explanations of Altruistic Ethics: Necessary, Sufficient, or Irrelevant?

Jeffrey P. Schloss

"Man is neither angel nor brute, and the unfortunate thing is that he who would act the angel acts the brute."

Pascal, *Pensee* 358

Introduction

"From whence comes love, where does it have its origin and its source; where is the place, its stronghold, from which it proceeds?"

Kierkegaard, *Works of Love*

General Issues

A comprehensively naturalistic world-view demands an empirically based explanation for the origin of biological diversity (Dewey 1910; Himmelfarb 1968; Ruse 1979a). In the same way, an inclusive biological account of human nature and social behavior demands an evolutionary explanation of morality, and in particular, ostensibly sacrificial or non-reciprocal cooperative behavior – "unselfish goodness."

Darwin himself acknowledged that the existence of a characteristic in any species, "formed for the exclusive good of another, would annihilate my theory, for such could not have been produced through natural selection" (Darwin 1859). No structural traits threatened to pose this dilemma, but sacrificial behaviors and the instincts that motivated them, did. Darwin eventually speculated on the origin of social instincts, human conscience (which in its mediation of conflict between instincts, causes us to "differ profoundly from the lower animals;" 1871:89), and on the greater social cooperation or higher moral standard of "civilized" humans versus "savages." But his accounts were not concretely based on or even completely reconcilable with, his own evolutionary mechanism of natural selection.

He was aware of the quandary, acknowledging it appeared impossible that the number of those "with social and moral qualities . . . or the standard of their excellence, could be increased through natural selection, that is, by the survival of the fittest" (1871:163). As a way out, he flirted with Lamarkianism (". . . after long practice virtuous tendencies may be inherited"), and group selection (". . . increase . . . in the standard of morality will certainly give an immense advantage to one tribe over another"). Nevertheless, he was wont to conclude about the ultimate origin of social instincts, and the deeper affections upon which they are based, that though it might seem "hopeless to speculate," nevertheless, "we may infer that they have been to a large extent gained through natural selection" (1871:80). By *infer*, he of course meant *be confident* (Rachels 1990). The empirical debt of maintaining such confidence in natural selection as the explanatory currency of the realm, he was deferring to future trustees of his theory.

Indeed, more recently E. O. Wilson has returned to the issue by describing biological altruism – the sacrificing of an organism's reproductive success for that of another – as "the central theoretical problem" in comprehensively explaining social behavior in the light of natural selection (Wilson 1975:3). The challenge is powerful and self-evident: how could the genetic underlayment promoting a behavior that resulted in a reduction of individual fitness, be successfully transmitted and maintained by natural selection within populations?

And more than just a scientific theory is challenged. It is also a challenge to a human need to make sense of what can appear as "the antithesis of the naturalistic fallacy: what is, in the biological world, normally ought not" (Williams 1988:383). This involves more than the culture shock of replacing natural theology (which "discovered in Nature evidence of God's existence and confirmations of his moral demands") with evolutionary naturalism (which finds "only confirmation of his absence.") (Kaye 1986:2). For what kind of world is it that would appear to confirm the absence of a good designer? Profoundly gripping (post-Paleyan) perceptions of the nasty workings of nature usher in a scientific and existential quandary: how can goodness itself can have any "natural" place in "a world which depends so entirely and so systematically on cruelty" (Ruse 1988:414), governed by a "cosmic process" that is morally abhorrent (Huxley 1894)? On this Darwinian encumbrance, we are still making payments: "For followers of Darwin, the familiar theological 'problem of evil' was turned inside out: evil could henceforth be assumed, and the existential paradox which demanded explanation became, in fact, *the problem of goodness* "(italics in original; Oates 1988:444). Kierkegaard's contemplation becomes modernity's lamentation: "From whence comes love?"

Sociobiological Explanation

Before continuing, it is necessary to describe and delimit the range of theoretical approaches to be considered. Although virtually all contemporary behavioral scientists acknowledge the significance of evolutionary theory, there is extraordinary and well-noted variation in the extent to which it is used as an interpretive framework for behavioral observations, even amongst those attempting an empirical approach (Tobach 1978; Ghiselin 1973; Wilson 1977; Breuer 1982; Kaye 1986; Fox 1989; Greenwood 1989; Degler 1991). This results, in part, from the crumbling of a "precarious truce" in which "social scientists agreed not to deny the reality of human evolution, so long as nobody attempted to make any intellectual use of it" (Midgley 1982:xi). But even evolutionary explanations themselves exhibit nothing close to consensus on the relationship between natural selection and human cultural evolution (Alexander 1979, 1987; Symons 1979; Cavalli-Sforza and Feldman 1981; Hrdy 1981; Lumsden and Wilson 1981; Boyd and Richerson 1985). Although sociobiological and evolutionary approaches are occasionally lumped together and even referred to interchangeably (Ruse 1986a,b), for the purposes of this treatment I will use three attributes to distinguish expressly sociobiological explanations from the larger domain of general evolutionary and evolutionarily consistent approaches −three stable, tripodal legs on which it is claimed the theory "rests comfortably" (Barash 1982:62).

First, sociobiology's foundational (or default) explanatory framework is *biological*. That is to say, the origin and maintenance of major, universal behavior patterns in human beings, as in other animals, are believed to be explainable by evolutionary influences on the genotypic characteristics of populations. This is because the functional nature of human behavior is not conceived of as uncoupled from ultimate biological causation: genes influence behavior. That is not to suggest a rigid or even an environmentally mediated genetic determinism. Given a specified set of environmental conditions, complex social behaviors can *not* be reliably "elicited with the predictability of a reflex," as Lorenz (1966) hyperbolically asserted before the sociobiological attempt to integrate ethology with population genetics. But definitive characteristics of human social behavior are believed to be made sense of by evolutionary theory. Sociobiology is therefore the search for "the biological basis of all social behavior" (Wilson 1975:3). Second, sociobiology represents an emphatically neo-Darwinian subset of general evolutionary theory, because of the central role given to natural selection over and against group selection or non-selective mechanisms of genetic change. Third, "strong" sociobiology, which seems to be the form most readily or at least most prolifically applied to the analysis of human ethical systems, asserts that behavior not only maintains fitness, but is "designed by natural selection to maximize fitness" (Daly and Wilson 1983:22; Barash 1977; Irons 1991; Alexander 1979).

These three distinctives support the conviction that the major thrust of all human behavior, including morality, is not explainable "except as an inherited predisposition to maximize the number of offspring" (Wilson 1978:41). The ultimate function of human behavior, then, is viewed as optimizing reproductive success. One is tempted to paraphrase Dobzhansky by observing, "nothing in sociology (or philosophy for that matter . . .) makes sense except in the light of evolution" (Dobzhansky 1973). In fact, Wilson himself asserts as much (1975:3).

If behavioral repertoires are viewed as biocultural adaptations not necessarily caused, but at least facilitated by genes (themselves the products of evolution), and if evolution is directed by a natural selection that optimizes reproductive success; then biological altruism (the sacrificing of one's own reproductive success for that of another) could not exist as a stable trait in natural populations. More precisely, it could not have a genetic basis that is maintained by natural selection at the level of single individuals or loci. Behaviors involving risk or *apparent* sacrifice can nevertheless be explained if their ultimate impact is to actually increase rather than decrease fecundity or direct reproductive success (individual fitness), or the proportionate representation of an individual's genome in the next generation via reproduction of itself or others of like genotype ("inclusive" fitness). Kin selection (making or risking a sacrifice for a genetically related individual) can accomplish this (Hamilton 1964). Reciprocal altruism (risking sacrifice for a member of a social unit from which the likelihood of compensatory return more than offsets the probability of reproductive disadvantage) can also accomplish this (Trivers 1971).

According to sociobiology, then, our biological nature does not dictate particular behaviors, but it does both constrain and enable the domain of possible behaviors. Genetically disinterested "love" is without biological basis. Kinship- or stratification- delimited cooperation, however, is likely to be genetically favored within natural populations of social organisms with relatively low fecundity. The popularized ethological stereotype of humans as aggressive hunter apes (Ardrey 1966; Lorenz 1966; Morris 1967; Tiger and Fox 1971), is supplanted by that of humankind as gregariously social, evidencing behavioral cooperation that is innate but strictly limited by the *de facto* bounds of genetic (although not necessarily conscious) self interest. Can radically selfless altruism exist in such a world?

Sacrificial love

"The assumption of pure egoism may not be enough to explain all human actions. If so, will we not discover this sooner by presuming that it is?"
Garrett Hardin (1977:3)

". . . one must believe in love; otherwise one will never become aware that it exists"
Soren Kierkegaard (1847:32)

There are three distinct axes of disagreement, representing three different types of questions, in the sociobiological analysis of human sacrificial behavior. The first question is one of definition: when we speak of unselfish behavior, are we speaking of genetic consequences or personal motivations? The second is an ostensibly empirical question: does genuine sacrifice exist as an evident characteristic of human beings, or does it not exist? The third is theoretical: to whatever extent sacrifice exists, is it explainable by "strong" sociobiological theory? The cells of this 2^3 explanatory matrix are filled with speculative theoretical variants.

Analytical focus on genes or motives?

The first question is in principle the easiest to resolve. If we are conducting an evolutionary analysis, the only meaningful measure of sacrifice, the only meaningful measure, period, is fitness. The dilemma of altruism in sociobiology is ultimately about the impacts of behavior on the transmission of genes: differential reproductive success. As simple as that is, it is tremendously theoretically significant. But it is hardly universally interesting.

The issue compels such wide attention, though, because it hasn't stopped there, for a variety of reasons. First, although evolutionary theory focuses on reproductive outcomes, moral theory entails some notion of the significance of intention. Any evolutionary explanation of ethics will therefore have to take account of intentions.

Second, humans are conscious beings that do act, or appear to act, from affective motive and/or rational intention. This fact doesn't go away just because we focus our attention at a genetic level of analysis. And because any psychological state is itself genetically mediated, even if fitness *is* the primary variable being evolutionarily maximized, intentions may be related to the function in two different ways. It may be that particular motives or intentions (either selfish or unselfish, either cognitive or affective) are necessary to generate particular fitness-enhancing behaviors, as Darwin claimed of sociality (1871). Or it may be that such behaviors require no specific conscious causes, but that they necessarily result in certain psychological states. In either case, sociobiological theory ends up discussing motive.

Even when the theory itself does not demand it, motives just seem to slip into the conversation. Sometimes it is an intentionally speculative foray to "see where it takes us" (Barash 1977). Or sometimes it is possibly an unintentional lapse, resulting in the blurring of concepts, as when Williams describes ". . . natural selection as a process for maximizing selfishness" (1988:399). The teleological connotations of suggesting that natural selection is *for* anything, plus describing what it maximizes in terms not of mere reproduction, but of selfishness, make for provocative, if not ambiguous, reading indeed.

However, the loss of rhetorical rigor mentioned above is not always unintentional. When our subjective experience of nature enters in, descriptive precision may be traded for declarative power. For while the process and products of natural selection entail quantitative results without qualitative purposes, we often experience the living world in value-laden terms of function. Unlike being struck by lightning, being struck by a rattlesnake involves becoming a casualty of "what are clearly weapons, precisely designed and used to produce a victim"(Williams 1989:385). And many are forced to see only self-interest in a world symphonically exploding with biological armaments that kill, maim, enslave, torture, deceive, and manipulate (Huxley 1894; Dawkins 1976; Williams 1988). Barash attempts to convey this view of the world by proclaiming: "Evolutionary biology is quite clear that 'What's in it for me?' is an ancient refrain for all life" (1977:167).

This "ancient refrain," is therefore filled with insinuation of selfish motive, and function "clearly as a rhetorical tool . . . virtual parables of Darwinism that are used not merely factually but representatively: they are intended to present the inner truth of nature" (Oates 1988). It is certainly legitimate and important to make empirically consistent assertions about the nature of nature. That has helped us recover from the glaucomic optimism of Paleyism. But we must recognize the difference between using facts of nature to document a hypothesis and using images from nature to illustrate a world view. For example, when Williams describes snake fangs as weapons, his imagery indeed reflects the design features of biological structure; but when he makes an analogy between group selection and "systematic genocide," his anthropomorphism goes far beyond and even contraverts what is known of intergroup competition – since extinctions are chancy and purposeless, a better metaphor might be his own "lightning strike" (Williams 1989:196). Evolutionary biology, or some interpretations of it, are definitely "quite clear" about the ruthless selfishness of all life. Whether life itself, including our observations of human life, are equally clear is exactly what is at issue.

Finally, the idea of selfish intention is occasionally and completely inappropriately invoked in an attempt to make sense of or even debunk a helping behavior that appears to detract from the performer's reproductive success. E. O. Wilson suggests that the sacrifices of Mother Theresa and other religious altruists are motivated by the promise of heaven and supremacist attitudes toward non-believing "outgroups" (Wilson 1978). This may or may not be accurate, but it does nothing to address the issue of fitness.

In sum, the sociobiological controversy over altruism involves a question: is it biologically possible to develop and sustain behaviors that result in the reproductive detriment of the individual? It has nothing to do with *intentions,* and applies to non-sentient creatures as well as to human beings. However, because motives cannot be ignored when considering humans, substantial care must be exercised to rigorously clarify terms of discussion (Wilson 1992).

Does love exist?

The question of whether genuine sacrifice does or does not exist as a human characteristic was introduced as *ostensibly* empirical. It turns out, however, that this question is not easily answered for several reasons. First, it is methodologically quite difficult to assess sacrifice. If it is construed psychologically, there are obvious phenomenological hurdles to evaluating the motives of others, and existential problems with appraising our own motives. And in both cases, *a priori* views of human nature wield great interpretive influence. As Kierkegaard reminds us, love believed finds all things proof; love doubted finds all proofs wanting. Thus, "There is nothing, no 'in such a way,' of which it can be said that it unconditionally proves the presence of love or that it unconditionally proves there is no love" (Kierkegaard 1962:30).

On the other hand, if sacrifice is understood in genetic terms, as it ought to be in an evolutionary context, it ends up being extremely difficult to determine the fitness effects of specific human behaviors. First, we must meaningfully categorize individuals according to behavioral phenotype. This entails epistemological problems with developing categories that relate to what genotype informs and the environment "sees" – discerning, as it were, "the correct typology of description, the natural suture lines along which the phenotype of the individual is to be divided" (Lewontin, et al. 1984:247). It is also made observationally difficult by the extraordinary temporal, cultural, and developmental plasticity of human behavior.

Next, we must accurately determine inclusive fitness rather than mere fecundity or differential mortality for individuals. (And it is at the level of individual organisms rather than specific loci that fitness must be examined, because we don't know specific behavioral genes).

Last, if we should be able to identify "behavior types" and determine fitness differentials between them, we must demonstrate such differences are *due* to a particular behavior. This is the rub, for while we can infer causation, we cannot demonstrate causal agency without experimental manipulation, or vast amounts of rigorously controlled comparative data. It difficult enough to determine whether a relatively straight forward behavioral phenotype such as dietary cholesterol merely correlates with, let alone causes, simple *mortality*, let alone fitness.

Even if we succeed in doing all the above, for a behavior ultimately to qualify as biologically altruistic, any fitness reduction must be due to the agency of the *benefactor* and not to the competitive wiles of an exploiting *beneficiary*. This again poses methodological difficulties, in addition to raising meta-level interpretive problems with making judgments about the teleonomic "function" of behavioral characteristics. Darwin chose his words well when acknowledging his theory would find any trait problematic that "was formed for the exclusive good of another . . ." For if the good of another results from exploiting a trait originally formed "for" its possessor's own good, the observation is arguably less problematic.

Thus not only is the weight of theory against the existence of genetic altruism, but the conditions of proof are against establishing its presence even it does exist. This makes the controversy fairly intractable, especially since the *burden* of proof in any question of this kind is always on the affirmative: it is only the existent, never the absent, that can be empirically confirmed.

Finally, should we actually demonstrate that a uniquely human behavior (such as voluntary, lifelong poverty or celibacy) increases the fitness of others at the expense of the actor (we have not), we then must ask whether such behavior can be said to be a representative characteristic of humans, rather than an uncharacteristic, even pathological deviance (Ruse 1986b). At a friend's urging some time back, I tried a swig of his imported cigar. Yet I have no reservations about describing myself as an inveterate non-smoker – especially after the experience. So it may be with occasional occurrences of what might pass for human altruism. We are still left with the judgment of whether or not to describe ourselves as "inveterate non-altruists."

Given the above difficulties, evolutionary thinkers evidence considerable disagreement over whether human behavior is genuinely altruistic, although individual analyses often fail to acknowledge that uncertainty (Campbell 1975a,b; Alper 1978; Cavalli-Sforza and Feldman 1981; Breuer 1982; Boyd and Richersen 1985; Richards 1986a,b,c; Burhoe 1988; Wenegrat 1990; vs. Ghiselin 1974; Dawkins 1976, 1982; Barash 1977, 1982; Alexander 1979, 1987; Trivers 1985; Ruse 1986a,b; Williams 1988; Irons 1991). In the midst of the ongoing controversy however, we can say that clearly altruism does not exist in such obvious forms and such magnified proportions as to extinguish debate. If most of us are indeed heavy smokers, much of it must be going on behind the shed!

What, then, is not hidden from view off behind the shed? It is precisely what sociobiologists maintain should clearly characterize the nature of social interaction: nepotism and reciprocity. It is not just sociobiologists who confirm this observation. Howard Becker maintained reciprocity to be a defining feature of human social interaction, dubbing our species *Homo reciprocus* (Becker 1956). In his analysis of stabilizing mechanisms in social systems, Alvin Gouldner characterized reciprocity as the virtually universal "cement" that holds societies together, functioning as a culturally non-relative common denominator of interactive expectations, "no less universal and important an element of culture than the incest taboo" (Gouldner 1960:171).

Marshall Sahlins' sweeping anthropological survey elaborates variations on the underlying theme of reciprocity, noting the inverse relationship between kinship distance and flexibility in terms of exchange. Distant relationships are associated with explicit reciprocity based on clearly specified expectations; closer relationships have more casual accounting. Citing an extensive array of cross-cultural data, he concludes that "close kin tend to share . . . and distant and non-kin to deal in equivalents or in guile" (Sahlins 1965:149).

Sahlins's generalizations of universal cultural emphasis on kinship and reciprocity are highly congruent with the major tenets of sociobiology. He later criticizes the sociobiological use of such data by pointing out that culturally variable kinship categories do not demonstrate genetic relatedness (1976). But the fact is that the categories themselves are universally operative. They are undeniably reflective of genetic relationship even though not invariably predictive of it. And even where "kin" are minimally related, family units promote reciprocal benefit en lieu of kin selection. Moreover, behavioral plasticity in primates is in keeping with, rather than inconsistent with, evolutionary theory. These facts rob Sahlins's objections of any lasting impact (Fox 1989).

Sahlins's generalizations about kinship and reciprocity are virtually recycled in E. O. Wilson's later notions of "hard core" and "soft core" altruism, which Wilson relates causally to kin selection and reciprocal altruism (Wilson 1978). For Wilson, hard core altruism "expresses no desire for equal return and performs no conscious actions leading to the same end" (Wilson 1978:155). While they seem quite "unselfish," such actions are invariably directed to close kin, whose survival, even at great personal cost to the individual, will nevertheless result in a net enhancement of the individual's inclusive fitness. It is "genetic selfishness" being promoted by kin selection, and the worst carnage and immorality may be perpetrated on *non*-kin at its behest.

In contrast, soft core altruism extends the domain of cooperation outside the group of nearest kin, but the individual "expects reciprocation from society for himself or his closest relatives. His good behavior is calculating, often in a wholly conscious way" (Wilson 1978:156). True to Sahlins' notions, soft core altruism broadens the scope of social organization via behavior that entails more explicit accounting, being both genetically and motivationally self-interested. Moreover, it usually does not even aspire to genuine reciprocity, seeking instead to get something for nothing by "lying, pretense, and deceit, including self-deceit, because the actor is most convincing who believes that his performance is real" (Wilson 1978:156).

Thus, for Wilson, there no such thing as genuinely self-sacrificing human altruism. There cannot be, not only for the ultimate reason that a "leash principle" (Lumsden and Wilson 1981) constrains us, but for the proximate reason that we are caught between two poles of selfish impulse. Hard core altruism can be "unilaterally directed at others," but it subjects relationships (outside a small kin group) and it enslaves reason itself (a la Hume) to the passions – "the imperatives of blood and territory." It is therefore the "enemy of civilization" and contractual social cooperation, not to mention unconditional love. On the other hand, soft core altruism trades a narrow domain of unselfishness for a larger domain of self-interested, hypocritical cooperation. As such, it is "the key to human society" (Wilson 1978). The necessity of genetic self-interest yields the inevitability of motivational selfishness.

The view of society that most readily emerges from such a model resurrects the specter of "the problem of goodness." In an abundantly quoted phrase. Ghiselin declares: "No hint of genuine charity ameliorates our vision of society, once sentimentalism has been laid aside . . . scratch an altruist and watch a hypocrite bleed" (1974:247). Wilson does not contradict this perspective, but attempts to counterbalance the pessimism it represents by assuring there is reason to be "optimistic" based on his estimate of the ratio between hard and soft core altruism. While we cannot achieve social stability through unselfish love, he believes we are "sufficiently selfish and calculating" to overcome the divisiveness of rigid hard core drives. This will enable our social interactions to achieve, via the plasticity of soft core interactions, "indefinitely greater harmony" (1978:157).

Ironically, the possibility of indefinitely greater harmony was precisely what Malthus had set out to refute, when he broadcast the notion of an all-pervasive struggle for existence and linked it with "inevitable misery and vice" a century ago. In his *Essay on Population,* Malthus confidently declared "the argument against the perfectibility of mankind is decisive" But Spencer used the explanatory alchemy of social Darwinism to spin social perfectibility from the straw of Malthusian competitive conflict (Oates 1988). In response to a homologous pessimism, sociobiology can weave a similar cloth to cover our woe: "True selfishness, if obedient to the other constraints of mammalian biology, is the key to a more nearly perfect social contract" (Wilson 1978:157).

In this context sociobiology functions as not only a scientific theory but also an interpretive myth – "the best myth we will ever have" (Wilson 1978:201). That does not make it false or true. But if it *is* to function as a scientific theory, we must seek to verify it empirically. The problem is that in the above analysis of altruism, Wilson shifts the descriptive focus away from fitness, which is the theoretically relevant, operationally definable variable, back to the elusive area of motivations. In other analyses, fitness is addressed, though primarily by mathematical modeling or comparative argument (Lumsden and Wilson 1981; Alexander 1987). Like any idea in science, sociobiology may merit theoretical status by its ability to provide conciliatory explanation of diverse observations (Hull 1978). But at this point in the theory's development, the crucial question is whether reproductive sacrifice *is actually* part of the human behavioral repertoire.

This is so, because according to evolutionary principles it is quite possible for individuals to exhibit behaviors that reduce reproductive success, without having to posit group selection or biologically transcendent causation. Natural selection would not eliminate such a behavior, so long as one condition is met: the phenotypic variance in behavior (upon which natural selection operates) must be randomly related to genotypic variation in individuals exhibiting it. The behavior itself could still be biologically mediated, but the variation in the behavior would be associated with environmental and not genetic heterogeneity. (Lightning-struck trees, under some circumstances, would be an analogous anatomical phenotype.) Natural selection would not operate on this trait, for, by definition, to have differential reproduction of genotypes we must have phenotypes that are genetically inherited.

There is nothing shocking in this, for all sorts of variation in human behavior have nothing at all to due with genetic differences. Wilson himself assumes that virtually all the behavioral variation associated with cultural evolution over the last 10,000 years is *un*associated with genetic change (1978:34). Such a tremendous amount of genetically unfettered plasticity in not just the behavioral repertoire of individuals. Rather, even the social structures that contain and create them may provide testimony more for immense biological potential than for non-negotiable biological constraints (Sahlins 1976; Gould 1977; Lewontin, et al. 1984). And if the interaction of biotic potential, environmental influence, and cultural variability *does* enable the emergence of biological altruism, the "genetic leash" of sociobiology has effectively broken.

Regrettably, in the case where it would be most helpful (but as pointed out above, most difficult) to have empirical studies available, there is the most dogmatic argumentation. Speculative assertions abound on the tensile strength of leashes and the contractile force of canine teeth, but we just don't know how far the real dog gets from the post of self-interest, let alone whether it is constrained by the genetic leash or the cultural lash.

The controversy is often viewed as another incarnation of the nature/nurture debate, in the form of environmentalist and hereditarian determinisms. While some of this no doubt exists as a function of disciplinary rivalry, professional boundary work, or academic egos (which occasionally break their "intellectual leashes"), the literature persistently seems to pay the *least* attention to the most exclusivistic assertions of determinism. Barash's contention (that humans raised in isolation from culture would develop their own language) has been largely ignored. I suspect this reflects a virtually universal recognition that not only is individual behavior a multivariate function of biology, culture, and physical environment, but the developmental interactions among all three "independent" variables make it meaningless to speak of a single factor being ultimately determinative.

Rather than representing competing determinisms, then, the arguments more accurately represent "rival fatalisms" (Midgley 1980): antagonistic postures that differ less in their observations of what *is* than in their pronouncements of what *must be*. For some sociobiologists the world *must be* devoid of altruism. Ghiselin claims you get hypocrite blood when scratching an altruist, not because he has distinguished the former by comparative hemodynamics, but because he is convinced that if "natural selection is both sufficient and true, it is impossible for a genuinely disinterested or 'altruistic' behavior pattern to evolve" (Ghiselin 1973:967). The truth of natural selection is not in question, but its sufficiency as a comprehensive explanation of social behavior is. We need to verify the consequent. But, because the initial premise is taken as a given, the conclusion is assured. Sociobiologists therefore, and only therefore, emphatically claim, "Real, honest to God altruism simply doesn't exist in nature" (Barash 1977:135).

The other pole maintains, not so much that altruism exists, but that whether or not it exists, sociobiology *must be* false. These arguments, which go beyond questioning sociobiology's validity to demanding its falsity, take one of two forms. One claims that the social consequences of biologically deterministic theories are morally unacceptable (Science for the People 1976; Lewontin et. al. 1984). Though social injustice has indeed been justified by biological determinism with regrettable frequency (Chase 1980; Gould 1981; Sayers, 1982), I would think it more warranted and more helpful to speak of moral responsibility for the uses to which we choose to put an idea, rather than the moral consequences inherent in an idea itself.

In fact, there are a number of non-sociobiologists, even critics, who claim that sociobiological perspectives on cooperation can contribute to the expansion of social justice by helping us understand the impediments to it (Hull 1978; Midgley 1980; Singer 1981; Konner 1982; Degler 1991). Moreover, Midgley (1980) argues that to suggest biological determinism is more dangerous than environmental determinism, or that any determinism necessarily limits human freedom, betrays an ambivalence about both causal explanation and the contingent nature of freedom itself.

In any case, to argue the theory one way or another on the basis of moral outcome is to again fight the battle of natural theology. We may or may not legitimately extract a moral *ought* from an empirical *is*, but surely it is invalid to specify an empirical *is* from a moral *ought* (Hull 1978; Irons 1991).

The second anti-sociobiological fatalism asserts that the ideological foundation of sociobiological interpretation is unacceptable (Bock 1980; Schwartz 1986; Kaye 1986; Greenwood 1989). There is room to argue this for the strongest sociobiological claims. But to conclude that this makes sociobiology untrue, or even unhelpful, is to commit the genetic fallacy. Moreover, if we seek alertness to the influence of ideologically conditioned perspectives, then we must be willing to cut with the deconstructionist sword in both directions: distorted or not, the interpretive mirror of any theory can clear up the blind spots of our own. For my part, I am convinced that sociobiological perspectives on moral altruism – adequate or not – are heuristically invaluable.

At this point, then, two things must be acknowledged. First, we have not observed any behavior in non-human animals that clearly qualifies as altruistic. Williams (1989) and anthropological observations of human behavior are sociobiologically consistent. Second, definitional ambiguity, methodological complexity, and ideological bias have served to obscure further resolution of whether humans evidence altruism.

There are three final domains of evidence. First, over the last decade, there has been an explosion of sociobiological analyses and predictive studies in the areas of mating behavior, parenting strategies, family structure, crime and homicide. In all of these areas, sociobiological explanations have been consistently born out by and successfully applied to patterns observed (Irons 1991). Even though altruism itself has been less well studied, nothing in the literature is at all suggestive of broadly distributed, socially stable patterns of interaction involving even apparent reproductive sacrifice.

Second, the significance of the above is justly debatable, since developing sociobiological theory may be sufficiently totipotent to make sense of anything. For example, Symons (1979) explains the lack of sexually selected male ostentation in human gender dimorphism, by suggesting that the unusually protracted and demanding care required by human infants makes it advantageous for females to be most attracted to males whose conservative appearance suggests the restraint necessary to honor a provisional pairbond! This and other explanations like it have been criticized as "just so stories" or "parlor games" that generate no verifiable predictions, and even when they do, neither demonstrate maximization of fitness nor rule out alternative hypotheses (Gould and Lewontin 1979; Baldwin and Baldwin 1981; Bock 1980; Breuer 1982; Kitcher 1985). Instead of being able to claim "nothing in human behavior makes sense except in light of sociobiology" it may merely be true that "anything in human behavior can be made to make sense in light of sociobiology."

In his fascinating analysis of sociobiological theorizing, David Hull (1978) disagrees with little of the above. Comparing the discipline to both Darwinism and phrenology at early stages in their development, Hull concludes that such fluidity is characteristic of newly emerging theories and is not sufficient in itself to differentiate between which will, or which "should," be established as valid theory and which should be rejected as bad science. He also notes that the methodological and ethical objections to sociobiology were raised against both Darwinism and phrenology as well. The two types of concerns interact, for when theories are believed to have ethical implications, they may be subjected to more stringent methodological expectations than other theories. Special caution on issues of ethical sensitivity is understandable, but a methodological double standard may be scientifically counterproductive.

This paves the way for the third area of evidence: anecdotal data. There is nothing scientifically "illegitimate" about non-experimental observation (Hull 1978). Though they cannot simply be strung together to furnish global generalizations, anecdotal observations can serve as pointed anomalies, cognitive "speed bumps" that disrupt the rush toward a favored explanatory destination. I have already indicated that genetic altruism has not been demonstrated to exist. However, there are a number of specific behaviors, and typological individuals, that demand attention because of significant sacrifices that do not appear readily explainable by kin selection or reciprocal altruism.

Breuer (1982) cites well-documented behaviors that are directed toward neither kin nor social group, such as giving refuge to fleeing (enemy) prisoners during war, risking life to provide sanctuary for Jews – often total strangers – under the Third Reich, and global relief efforts on behalf of distant strangers who will never return the favor (e.g., Amnesty International, disaster and famine assistance). Other ostensibly problematic behaviors include voluntary blood donations on behalf of strangers (Singer 1984) and voluntary assistance programs to the homeless (Wenegrat 1990). Larger-scale examples include pacifist-abolitionist movements in America and England. Sociobiologists themselves add to the list, citing elaborately wasteful funerals (Campbell 1991), noblesse oblige (Irons 1991), adoption, homosexuality, asceticism, suicide, and falling in love with strangers (Alexander 1979). Along with behaviors, typological individuals may be frequently cited: Socrates, Jesus Christ, Albert Schweitzer, Theresa of Calcutta, Francis of Assisi (Sahlins 1976; Mattern 1978; Wilson 1978).

Thomas More, whose life recommended itself to Robert Bolt for dramatic consideration by virtue of its very oddity, provides a fitting illustration. More sacrificed himself neither for kin, nor for kindred, nor for any person at all, but for a conviction. Bruno poses the same problem, as do all those voluntarily martyred for science, religion, or other convictions across the ages. "Across the ages" is an especially apt phrase, for when More was asked if he was so arrogant as to dispute the judgment of all the learned men in the realm, he answered he was rather in humble agreement – with the learned men of all other realms in all other ages.

It is precisely this ability that causes Breuer to maintain that "man[sic] – *and only man* – can identify with any conspecific. We do it far too seldom, but when doing so we put at least the tip of a toe beyond a threshold that is unsurpassable for animals . . . that cannot be explained or even dealt with within a system of genetical cost-benefit relations" (Breuer 1982:139, 259). I suspect he may both overstate and understate the situation. We do more than identify with; we die for. We do this for more than conspecifics, but also for animals or spirits or ideas. However, whether this can be dealt with by sociobiological models remains to be seen. The ability to relate sympathetically to any other human confers a potency to love that makes little biological sense. But it also could bestow an ability to sense when others are deceiving or deceivable, that would lead to reproductive advantage (Alexander 1987). Yet certainly, the ability to establish radically sacrificial affiliation with a group – or a mere abstraction – from which no material benefit is remotely possible or even conceivable, is of singular importance in characterizing human behavior and requires sociobiological explanation.

Can Theory Explain Data?

There are four explanations that sociobiological theorists have to the behaviors cited above, only three of which are strictly sociobiological. First, one would seek to ask, "is the behavior likely to lead to reproduction via an unusual route?" (Alexander 1979:203). For example, in several cultures the adoption of unrelated children facilitates cooperative alliances between adopting and birth groups, which may increase parental fitness by promoting reciprocal altruism. Or falling in love, which can involve the extension of radical altruism to a genetically unrelated stranger, could nevertheless still contribute to fitness by facilitating the advantages of both outcrossing and "long-term commitment."(Alexander 1979). And regarding many of the helping behaviors enumerated above, while they are not directed toward individuals from whom a compensatory response is possible, they are nevertheless often performed in the context of a group from which a return benefit is completely possible (e.g., Red Cross, Amnesty International, the local church, etc.). Other behaviors, like suicide, homosexuality, asceticism, and martyrdom, can all result in increased resources to kin, either through diminished consumption by the individual or compensatory accrual to family. And the individuals whose behaviors appear most sacrificial may possess the greatest power to manipulate others through hypocrisy. Altruistic-appearing behavior can exert a profound influence. Witness the very facts that this volume was written, and that most people have such a great interest in "altruism" (Alexander 1987; Irons 1991).

But there are rejoinders to these explanations. Of all the adoptions in cultures all over the world, many, presumably most, involve no unusual alliances. And falling in love is notoriously fickle: the experience is usually not long term, and it frequently involves people already pairbonded to others. Thus, it is not clear whether being able to fall in love ultimately facilitates or disrupts stable pairbonding, nor do we know that pair bonds themselves are always contributory to maximum fitness. Clearly we need many more empirical studies involving the above circumstances.

The second explanation acknowledges that occasionally organisms may behave in ways that help others at reproductive expense to themselves, but it is not because of altruism: help is "taken" rather than "given" in a sense. Predation, herbivory, endoparasitism, interference competition, and even rape are common forms of unilateral exchange that involve no contradiction of sociobiology and no suggestion of helping behavior. But more ambiguous interactions – manipulation of other organisms, including conspecifics by the use of directive force or intimidation, subtle or overt coercion, stealth, or deception – may result in an asymmetric exchange that can appear to be altruistically cooperative, but is in fact "manipulated" (Dawkins 1982; Williams 1988).

The third explanation is addressed to behaviors that may reduce fitness without manipulation by others. Behaviors that could be in this category include asceticism, homosexuality, suicide, voluntary martyrdom. One explanation for such behavior is "genetic lag": the assumption that the behaviors may have been adaptive in the environments in which they originally evolved, but that the human genome has not kept up with culture-induced environmental change (Irons 1991).

Thus, it is claimed, the ultimate meaning of human nature is decipherable only by the authority of the genetic text, which *was* optimal in a long past era that is no longer accessible. This notion sounds much like another, competing explanatory paradigm. The ultimate meaning of human nature is decipherable only by the authority of the biblical text, which was inerrant in the original autographs, but these autographs have all disappeared. Here are two ambitiously fundamentalistic attempts to explain absolutely everything by a comprehensive system, the key elements of which are omitted by nature, required by reason, and supplied by imagination! Of course, this does not make either explanation false, but surely difficult to test.

Another explanation in this third category involves the extraordinary plasticity of human behavior. Rather than being based on rigid behavioral responses within set roles, human social cooperation involves normative cognitive goals that both facilitate group coherence and allow enough flexibility to preserve the substantial genetic investment represented in each individual (Ruse 1986a,b). That flexibility can allow humans, unlike ants, to occasionally manifest reproductively pathological behaviors. That's the "price you pay for a first class social facilitating mechanism like morality" (Ruse 1986b: 244).

Like Ruse, Wilson also is convinced plasticity is important, so much so that "genes promoting flexibility in social behavior are strongly selected at the individual level" (Wilson 1975). (It is not clear how it strengthens the sociobiological argument at this point to posit the existence of something unseen and undemonstrated that promotes wide variability, rather than just saying there is no evidence for significant restraint) Though Wilson maintains "mental hypertrophy" has "distorted" our most fundamental traits (1975:548), unlike Ruse, he avoids the notion of pathology as an explanation of altruism. Rather he argues the very opposite: "Sainthood is not so much the hypertrophy of human altruism as its ossification. It is cheerfully subordinate to the biological imperatives above which it is supposed to rise" (Wilson 1978:166). Thus altruism is not biologically deviant but fully assimilated.

For Wilson, of course, there are two deep biological imperatives. The first is soft-core altruism, which involves calculation of net gain. "Lives of the most towering heroism are paid out in the expectation of great reward, not the least of which is a belief in personal immortality" (1978:154). The second is hard-core altruism, which involves selfless giving to a restricted group, but territorial hostility outside the group. "There lies the fountainhead of religious altruism . . . pure in tone and perfect with respect to ingroup altruism . . . All have contended for supremacy over others"(Wilson 1978:165). Religious altruism is ultimately ingroup love; outgroup hostility. Mother Theresa, for example, is a member of one ingroup, "secure in the service of Christ." Lenin, another example, was a member of a different ingroup, and he "called Christianity a contagion of the most abominable kind, a compliment that has been returned many times by Christian theologians" (Wilson 1978:165). There we have it: Theresa, Lenin, black panthers, evangelical Christians – "the substance matters little, the form is all" (1978:164).

There are three problems with Wilson's explanation. First, typical of the most extremist behaviorism, it compresses virtually all differentiating content out of the social institutions, the cultural values, and the human personalities referred to. For a theory that is to make sense of social reality, that is a bit of a shortcoming. But, one might claim, the ultimate goal of the theory is to predict behavior, not cognitive content. In so doing, we make human behavior "far less complex and difficult to understand than contemporary social theory leads one to believe" (Lumsden and Wilson 1981:350).

That is the second problem: its predictions and descriptions are factually wrong and empirically unhinged. Sister Theresa, Albert Schweitzer, citizens who hid Jews, and abolitionists have not "contended for supremacy over others;" they have contended for the dignity of others. The very absence of a stratifying contentiousness is what we are seeking explanation for. Nor, contrary to Wilson's claim, has such supremacy been "urged by the seers of every major religion." The followers, seers, and founders themselves may all be utter hypocrites, ruled at every step by manipulative selfishness cloaked in impenetrable self-deception, but the tradition to which Wilson refers *urges* the disciples to "let this mind be in you, which was in Christ Jesus, who took upon himself the form of a servant . . ." And the most significant empirical fact that completely contradicts the description, is the behavioral transgression of ingroup boundaries. Gifts were given, sacrifices made, lives risked – and lost – by Catholics for Hindus, whites for blacks, Germans for Jews, Jews for Germans. Surely, this behavior is not "perfect with respect to ingroup altruism."

Third, and most important, the explanation simply fails utterly as a scientific theory. Wilson has not just slipped back into the analysis of motivations; he has taken up residence there. Even that would not be fatal, if there were some way of connecting his notions to fitness. Unfortunately there is – but the connections yield *negative* fitness results. The ingroup description entails a group identity with no genetic component, the social character of which typically *denies* familial attachment altogether. Even if Wilson were right and individuals restricted their altruism to the group (which I argue above they do not), it would result in no genetic returns on sacrificial investment by the individual – the very opposite of what sociobiology predicts. The reciprocity argument is even more deficient, for at least the ingroup behavior involved real human beings, even if they *did* violate Wilson's own kinship criteria for ingroup composition. But now he is suggesting that the sociobiological explanation for Mother Theresa's lifetime of celibacy is that she was swapping reproductive success for personal immortality. However, that is precisely the kind of exchange that sociobiologists argue does *not* happen. According to sociobiology, those genes that calculate the return rate in heavenly currency will lose their seat on the reproductive exchange.

All the above explanations attempt to demonstrate that apparent human altruism isn't characteristically altruistic, or isn't characteristically human (i.e., either it is self-serving or manipulated, or pathological or transient). The fourth explanatory tradition (not sociobiological) affirms the existence of altruism within the context of several non-selectionist perspectives. One perspective maintains that aspects of cultural evolution proceed largely independent of genetic restraints, through genetic independence or culture-gene synergy (Burhoe 1979, 1988; Cavalli-Sforza and Feldman 1981; Singer 1981; Boyd and Richerson 1985; Wenegrat 1990). Fitness-reducing behaviors are therefore free to arise. They will not be eliminated because there is no connection to any particular genotype. Or, though there is genotypic association, the rise and maintenance of the behavior is possible because altruism is not reproductively detrimental in the emergent cultural environment. A second perspective is that the altruism is rooted in a specific genetic capacity, which arose via group selection or other non-Darwinian processes (Campbell 1975a,b, 1991; Richards 1986a,b). Altruistic inclinations may be in conflict with other genetic impulses toward selfishness, and culture involves the attempt to tip the balance toward greater altruistic cooperation.

A final non-sociobiological view, is that altruism is not characteristic of humans, yet we must still seek and hope to attain it. For while we are genetically programmed against it and culturally swept against it, with intelligence and strength of will we might be able to press toward it – to "set man to subdue nature to his higher ends" (Huxley 1894:141), to "save humanity from human nature" (Williams 1988:402), to "rebel against the tyranny of the selfish replicators" (Dawkins 1976:215). Stent's objection (1980:12), that the notion of fighting against our genes is a "biological absurdity," incites Williams to respond that he has "apparently missed the significance of major technologies (hair dyeing, tonsillectomy), based on such rebellion" (Williams 1988:403).

But Stent is right. Truly resisting the force of our genes would require a genetically transcendent fulcrum (such as Christian dualism might provide in its notion of spirit versus flesh), which has no place in any biological theory. The "major" technologies Williams mentions represent not rebellion against our genes, but the mere interaction between one set of genes that determine unconscious developmental processes and another set of genes that enable behavioral inclinations – neither of which represents insurrection against phenotypes we would expect natural selection to allow. Unlike hair dyeing, however, radical sacrificialism gives every appearance of running counter to genetic self-interest. If such exists, either we admit to non-Darwinian agency, or we find that the most truly unilateral acts of human sacrifice, while altruistic in motivation, are not fitness-reducing in consequence.

This is precisely what I would like to propose in a final account that is sociobiologically consistent yet altruism-affirming. Let us start with what we *don't* know:

we don't know if genetic altruism exists. We *do* know that history is full of myriad examples of the most extraordinary sacrifices in the name of all conceivable persons and abstractions. But, for all our guessing, we don't know if such behaviors generally result in an enhancement or reduction of fitness. Nor do we even know, though most of us have our intuitions, if such actions are motivationally unselfish.

If we leave aside group selection or biologically transcendent processes, the three most complete, evolutionary treatments of apparent altruism are that of Ruse (1986a,b, 1988), Alexander (1979,1987) and Irons (1991). Ruse views radical sacrifice and the exhortations toward it as genuine. But they are fitness-reducing, and are pathological in their deviation from the golden mean of humane concern for kin and a meaningfully restricted group of mutually cooperating comrades. Alexander and Irons see apparent sacrifice as part of image management, and exhortations to sacrifice as not at all pathological, but completely hypocritical. This is because as human group size increased and likelihood of intimate personal knowledge between interactors decreased, there was more need for common, codified morality and negotiated contracts to establish germinal trust. There was also more opportunity to lie and get away with it. Thus there was an increase in interpersonal sensitivity, so that lies might be discerned without knowledge of past behavior. The most convincing lie would be from one who espoused a morality of radical love;, who demonstrated a flair for convincing, ostensibly sacrificial acts; and who was self-deceived into thinking his/her own behaviors and attitudes were really other-oriented.

Both views have in common that although they are fully evolutionary, they are "functionally" almost nonbiological. Human actors are viewed as black boxes of fitness, resource accounts into and out of which deposits and withdrawals are made – with net profit or loss tallied in *resources* but converted seamlessly into *reproduction*. Consequently, the only way to survive is to get more resources from others than you give to them. But they leave out the fact that living things, especially humans, are not passive, static tally sheets. They are dynamic systems capable of generating interest, as it were, on what comes in. They enjoy a greater or lesser return, based on homeostatic integration, psychological or immunological processes, learning, stress, etc. I propose that securing favorable terms of exchange with others – making sure one deals in equivalencies or better – is not the only route to genetic solvency, for biologically efficient utilization of what one takes in is also important, and may be reproductively compensatory.

Specifically, it is possible that a strategy of authentic generosity and honest concern for others could do equally well or better than one of manipulative exploitation, *not* because resource flow would maintain parity with other strategies, but because it could yield more successful reproductive output per unit resource. Self-aware, relationally genuine, psychologically integrated, caring, other-oriented individuals (according to a wide variety of clinical, psychotherapeutic, religious, and folk-wisdom traditions) may be more emotionally balanced, physically healthy, relationally stable, and cognitively robust – all of which may directly translate into reproductive advantage.

In the words of Darwin, "if we choose to let conjecture run wild," (Degler 1991:7), then the scenario proposed by both Irons and Alexander could establish this strategy. As size of social group increases, intimacy decreases and reliance on rules and contracts increase. Lying, relational ambiguity, and stress increase beyond the levels and types that the organism's integration system had evolved to handle optimally – genetic lag. Interpersonal sensitivities increase, distinguishing deception and safeguarding self-interest. But that further augments psycho-physiological stress, through heightened recognition of the guile of others, of personal vulnerability to exploitation, and of deep longings for hard core altruism, evolved to be met and expressed in a social matrix that no longer exists. This might even be compounded by the autonomic effects of intentional or self-deception (Trivers 1985).

This scenario reduces to a "tragedy of the commons," where each individual's pursuit of self interest makes it more necessary for the next one to participate, but creates a social environment that degrades health and well being for all. "We have lacked a vocabulary to express what is really happening: the negative interaction of species level disadvantage and individual advantage" (Gould 1982:385).

The most adaptive response is neither group selection nor increasingly vigorous pursuit of individually favorable terms in the reciprocity equation, but rather letting go of that pursuit. It entails extending traditional, hard core (unilateral) altruism, or something very close to it, to a larger group of soft core altruists. This amounts to genuinely self-forgetful preoccupation with the good of another (typical of kin groups), and may well result in a net cost in the individual's exchanges. But such costs can be offset by an increase in individual vigor, resulting in maintenance or a net increase in fitness.

As wildly speculative as the above scenario is, it nevertheless does in substance follow the case Darwin makes for the development and furtherance of sociality in the process of "civilization" (1871). Darwin, however, posited group selection and inheritance of acquired characteristics. In this scenario, something like pleiotropic interaction may be operating.

An interesting upshot of the above involves the biological function of morality. While sociobiologists affirm that "the only demonstrable purpose" of morality is the perpetuation of the genome (Wilson 1978), it is usually assumed that the *means*, the distinctive contribution of morality toward accomplishing this, is its contribution to social cohesiveness (Campbell 1975a; Wilson 1978; Irons 1991). (Whether or not this requires the need to invoke group selection is debated.) Moral norms are sociobiologically understood as rules, put forward with the illusion of absolute and external legitimacy, which extend and stabilize social interaction by subjugating individualistic behavior (Ruse 1986b).

This may be true. It may also be true that morality involves something far more simple and straightforward: axioms for achieving, not cultural stability, but behavioral homeostasis within each individual: advice about what seems to make life work, based on the kind of organisms we are. Although Ruse (1986b) sees traditional religious teaching as a set of moral rules that assert absolute, externally legitimized truth, he is not completely correct. "Man was not made for the Sabbath, but the Sabbath for man." Here, Jesus reflects the view that divine law is not written in heaven so much as decoded from the deepest needs of human nature. Proverbial wisdom and moral exhortation abound with aphorisms that are not ethical *rules* at all, but embodiments of value judgments or prescriptions for fulfillment that are consistent with the above suggestion that genuine, sacrificially motivated behavior may be part of the human design: "Better is a little where love is than a house full of feasting with strife;" "he who clings to his life will lose it;" "If I have not love, it profits me nothing;" "To give is more blessed than to receive."

Conclusion

"The licentious tell men of orderly lives that they stray from nature's path, while they themselves follow it; as people in a ship think those move who are on the shore . . . We must have a fixed point in order to judge. The harbor decides for those who are in a ship; but where shall we find a harbor for morality?"

Pascal, Pensee #383

What can be said of the necessity, sufficiency, and relevance of sociobiological theory to our understanding of human altruism?

Necessary for moral understanding?

Surely we must conclude that sociobiology is a *necessary* ingredient in understanding the major structural features and limitations of human sacrifice as socially expressed. It is not that the virtual universality of kinship categories and reciprocity requires belief in their innateness; nor would innateness require biological causation. Universality may suggest but does not require genes. However, these particular universals are given a compelling rationale by the process that influences genes: natural selection.

Having said that, it is *not* true that sociobiology is necessary to understand particular inter-cultural variations in general patterns of behavior, or significant individual deviations from normal patterns of behavior, including highly irregular but not altogether uncommon sacrifice. Darwinism may be necessary to understanding systems at the biological level of integration, because of its vast power to integrate previously disparate observations under one, unified explanatory rubric. Sociobiology, however, is not (yet) able to readily integrate such a variety of behavioral phenomena, nor does it have anything close to a unified explanatory scheme when dealing with those most significant human behaviors: morality, interpersonal intentionality, and asymmetric (sacrificial) exchange.

At a deeper level, is sociobiology necessary to understand the human nature, if any, that is both formed by and formative of moral behavior? Greenwood (1989) claims that on this very point sociobiology is both most pernicious and least Darwinian, for in its imputation of "human nature" at all, it fails to understand Darwinian species as dynamic interactions, without fixed natures. But he is only partially correct. A species, though evidencing significant variation over ecological space and evolutionary time, may, and especially in animals, usually does, evidence functional boundaries. Evolutionary theory describes the nature and development of such boundaries, while at the same time affirming that the concept is descriptive and not prescriptive, extending just so far as everything a particular species does. Therefore one could never say, on evolutionary grounds, that any human behavior was contrary to human nature. But one could offer an explanation of why observed behaviors were in the human behavioral repertoire, and proffer speculation on which *un*observed behaviors were most within reach.

The political implications of the last statement notwithstanding, sociobiology becomes absolutely necessary to any informed and resilient understanding of human nature. But it in its stronger forms, it also becomes inhibitory. For evolution can explain the origin or interpret the function of specific traits we see. But "human nature," especially as it entails a suite of disputable motivations, is unseen. There are only two options. One, we can infer what human nature would have to be, were a particular evolutionary scenario true. Or, two, we can assume a version of human nature, and construct an evolutionary explanation. Although neither process can justifiably result in anything other than the most tentative "explanations," sociobiology makes the most dogmatic assertions, particularly concerning human selfishness.

Moreover, it does so under the auspices of pursuing route one, when there is ample evidence that the theory's development has been covering its tracks along route two. To suggest that any human behavior, *any* behavior no matter how sacred it is considered, may have selfish roots, and to suggest why, is really tremendously helpful. But to assert that *every* human behavior must have selfish roots, and in proportion to the professed unselfishness, deceptive roots as well, makes one wonder whether the destination all along may have been a sort of "slapdash egoism . . . a natural expression of people's lazy-minded vanity, an armchair game of cops and robbers that saves them the trouble of real inquiry and flatters their self-esteem" (Midgley 1980:132). The cops and robbers analogy calls to mind Victor Hugo's protagonist thief in *Les Miserables*, who is transformed by the bountiful extension of undeserved love. The policeman who hounds him can never fathom its existence, for he never sees beyond his conception of "the law," that merciless process that is ultimately a reflection of his own experience. So, too, may a distorted understanding of the law of natural selection result in the imprisonment of others within the confines of loveless, interpretive bias.

It is necessary to hear sociobiology, for it helps us to see, using Voorzanger's (1987) exquisite analogy, how selfishness is in human nature as Michaelangelo's David was "in the marble." Another marble would have given another David. Yet it is necessary to disregard sociobiology when it suggests that only David is in the marble, for there is also a Jonathan, or a thousand other figures as well.

"We cannot simply do away with ideology. The question is, whether evolutionary biology furnishes a good stage for the debate on the most appropriate conception of man. I think it does not . . . Instead of using evolutionary history to get to learn ourselves, we have to know ourselves in order to give an evolutionary reconstruction of our behavior" (Voorzanger 1987:265).

Sufficient for moral understanding?

Logically, sociobiology is sufficient to explain nearly everything. This is not, however, because it is able to integrate all things, but because it is adequate to accommodate most anything. Though gainsaid by sociobiology's critics, this explanatory resilience may develop into potent sufficiency, if the theory's advocates acknowledge and work on areas of weakness rather than over-inflate the theory's strengths.

While sociobiology is ripe with speculation on the function of moral systems, it has not begun to assess how human beings experientially interact with those systems. Aside from Alexander (1992) noting the need to examine moral development theory from a sociobiological perspective, there is virtually no attempt to address the wide variety of scholarly analyses and rich, cross-cultural accounts of personal moral and religious experience.

The human moral domain is not comprised only of rules and behavior. It is characterized by subtle and profound perceptions of motivational state (accurate or not), which evidence developmental regularity. These feed back into moral rules, and themselves require explanation. John Wesley had already given all he had to the poor when he underwent motivational reconstruction on his transatlantic voyage (Wesley 1909). From a different tradition in a different era, Dag Hammarskjold was already a committed, "moral" citizen when he sensed, and yielded to, the moral imperative on his celebrated carriage ride through the snow (Hammarskjold 1964). Darwin's notion of conscience may be true: that which causes us to feel regret after we have indulged transitory passions (1871). The sociobiological notion of conscience may be true: the alarm that tells us when our cheating behaviors are likely to get us into trouble (Alexander 1987). But these fail to explain or even note the manifold dimensions of the human moral impulse.

This results in a truncated notion of what morality itself really entails. On one level Ruse is correct in suggesting that the reciprocal altruism of mere contractual fidelity – paying a fair price in exchange for a bag of potatoes – is not "moral" behavior

134

(1986b). But paying, or not paying, becomes a profoundly moral act when the potato money is all there is for a man to buy his wife's life-sustaining medicine (Gilligan 1982; Kohlberg 1984). Furthermore, human perspectives on the moral dimensions of that act evidence documented variability across the biologically relevant categories of both age and gender. If sociobiology is to attempt explanation, it must start with recognition of the experiential fountainhead – affective and cognitive – of human morality.

Perhaps it does not yet do that job well because its methodological paradigm has been rather contortedly behaviorist. In his original popularization of ethology, Conrad Lorenz invoked the detached, scientific metaphor of looking at human beings as if he were on Mars, viewing them through a telescope (1966). Wilson advances a virtually identical image, suggesting we might examine human beings as though we were visitors coming to earth on a spaceship from another planet (1975). But of course we cannot do this, for we are not extra-terrestrials but participants in humanity. We *must* not do this, for the sake of recognizing rather than concealing our own biases, and for the sake of understanding rather than denying our deepest humanity.

"If only it were all so simple!," Wilson quotes Solzhenitsyn, right after he describes the ingroup supremacy he believes characterizes the religious tradition to which Theresa of Calcutta belongs. "If only there were evil people somewhere insidiously committing evil deeds, and it were necessary only to separate them from the rest of us and destroy them. But the line dividing good and evil cuts through the heart of every human being. And who is willing to destroy a piece of his own heart?" (Solzhenitsyn 1973, in Wilson 1978:167).

In this fascinating apposition of two Nobel laureates is contained the nexus of sociobiology's claim to explanatory sufficiency. As Theresa's religious exclusionism is contrasted with Solzhenitsyn's literary insights into the common human condition, so, Wilson goes immediately on to observe, "sainthood . . . subordinate to the biological imperatives above which it is supposed to rise" is eclipsed by "the *true* humanization of altruism," which "can come only through a deeper scientific examination of morality" (Wilson 1978:166; italics added).

But the distinctions drawn are false and contrived. Theresa and Solzhenitsyn are, almost literally, from the same fold, sharing similar experiences of deprivation and social marginality, convictions of common humanity, moral exhortation of the international community, and even the same religious tradition. Moreover, Solzhenitsyn's notion of the line cutting through every human heart, though rhetorically useful to Wilson, is never really treated again as a theme of a work, entitled, *On Human Nature*. Instead, Wilson takes the line *out* of human nature, and attempts to put it between disciplines that are, in reality, no less of the same fold than the two human protagonists. Ironically, the sociobiological account began on a spaceship of aliens coming to objectively observe the curiosities of human behavior. Now the aliens are convinced that it is "only through" *their* understanding that we can come to "true humanization."

The aspiration toward total sufficiency (revealed as not just sociobiology but full blown scientism) culminates in a rhetorical response to God's questions of Job regarding the ultimate mysteries of death, human finitude, and the nature of the universe (Wilson 1978:201):

God:

> Have the gates of death been revealed to you? Have you ever seen the doorkeepers of the plane of darkness? Have you ever comprehended the vast expanse of the world? Come, tell me all this, if you know.

Wilson:

> Yes, we *do* know and we have told. Jehovah's challenges have been met and scientists have pressed on to uncover and to solve even greater puzzles.

Some of the solutions he mentions include understanding "approximately how and when" life began, "most of the knowledge" necessary to produce elementary life forms, and "the results of chemical soil analyses" from another planet. How science has solved the fundamental religious questions and in what way it has raised and answered greater ones, is taken as apparent. Yet with all our vast understanding, at least one great puzzle remains. "Astonishingly," western culture still seems to give preference to the thought of "those who work in the prevailing mode of the social sciences and humanities." And regrettably, the perceived accomplishments of scientists continue "to be evaluated in an ethos extraneous to science" (Wilson 1978:203).

It is tempting to suggest that the answer to Wilson's quandary, and the root presumption of sociobiological sufficiency, is a lack of humility. Such a sense of humility, or awe, does not derogate the thrilling attainments of science but magnifies the wondrous object of scientific study. It elevates the mysterious through "a rapturous amazement at the harmony of natural law, which reveals an intelligence of such superiority that, compared with it, all the systematic thinking and acting of human beings is an utterly insignificant reflection. This feeling is the guiding principle of [a scientist's] life and work. . . ." (Einstein 1954:50).

But the problem is not just a failure to appreciate mystery. It is a refusal to recognize that the mystery contains both questions of *mechanism* and questions of *meaning*. Of course the two are related. If sociobiology could someday explain the activity of moral philosophers, it would be of monumental moral import. But it would still be the task of moral philosophy, and not sociobiology, to make *sense* of the situation. At this point, sociobiology claims right to the throne of all sufficient explanatory myth, as "the only mythology that can manufacture great goals from the sustained pursuit of pure knowledge" (Wilson 1978:207). However, such claims do not rest on its ability to inform questions of meaning, much less to answer them, but rather on its attempt to banish such questions to the provinces of remote obsolescence.

Irrelevant to moral understanding?

The above does not in the slightest bit diminish the importance of sociobiological understanding to the moral quest. It only helps distinguish pretensions of significance from true relevance, which exists in four respects.

First, sociobiological insights into how we got here and who we are – what *is* – may bear implications for what *ought* to be. Especially in light of the teleonomic aspects of living systems, there has been renewed discussion of the is/ought question and the so-called naturalistic fallacy (Flew 1978; Rottschaefer 1984, 1990; Gewirth 1986; Richards 1986a,b,c; Ruse 1986a,b; Ball 1988; Bateson 1989; Williams 1990; Geiger 1992, 1993). However, even if we do attempt to extract an *ought* from an *is*, that does not mean, as Midgley jibes, that "we should all run out and become astrophysicists." Science may provide us with bushels of raw *is*-ness; we will still need the apparatus of ethics to perform the extraction of *oughtness*.

Second, sociobiological (and all) attempts to understand the proximate and ultimate causes of human behavior can help us in the effort to expand the effective domain of human cooperation (Midgley 1980; Singer 1981; Konner 1982; Ayala 1987; Williams 1988; Rachels 1990). And within domains that are traditionally described as cooperative, sociobiological insight might contribute to understanding failures such as child abuse, sexual harassment, battery of women, and intergenerational conflict. Of course, associating the existence of a problem with human nature may be used by some as a legitimation of the behavior. But this reflects the character of those who use it, and not the truth or utility of the theory. It remains true that "to admit a weakness is real is not to increase it, but to put oneself in a position to resist it" (Midgley 1980:32).

Third, biological explanations may enable us to evaluate more knowledgeably our own moral feelings and impulses. As true for any aspect of self discovery, "discovering biological origins for our intuitions should make us skeptical about thinking of them as self-evident moral axioms" (Singer 1984:70). It obviously does not require sociobiology to point out the limitations of naive, romantic intuitionism: Nathaniel Hawthorne knew the adulteress, Hester Prynne, would be less than convincing when she exclaimed, "What we did had a consecration of its own; we *felt* it to be so!" But understanding that moral legitimacy is not wrought by emotional intensity only gets us out from under the dictatorship of intuitions and feelings; we must still decide how to count their vote. For this more difficult task, it can be helpful to understand both the functional origin and common consequences of our moral feelings and intuitions. Sociobiology has something relevant to say.

Last, and perhaps most importantly, sociobiology may help us assess actions in the same way it helps us examine intuitions. For just as feelings and intuitions may take on moral authority through a kind of *personal* intensity, so behaviors may be viewed as morally normative through a kind of *social* intensity. Certain religious, interpersonal, or political behaviors can be so reified that they are uncritically accepted as virtual icons of love or selfishness, moral integrity or degeneracy. Biological explanations can correct the stereotypic interpretations of such behaviors by revealing they are not intrinsically special, just as Singer (1984) argues that naturalistic explanations can result in "debunking the lofty status" of moral intuitions.

In the past this task was performed by certain expressions of religion. The prophetic tradition challenged the self-assured complacency of routine expressions of justice. The contemplative tradition, from the perspective of the one burning love, perceived the charisma of normal human loves as ultimately carnal and selfish. To some extent, the teachings of Jesus represent both traditions. He invites us to the uncommon love of our enemies, warning us that even the evil give good things to their children, and the wicked are good to those who are good in return.

"It is now sociobiology that points out that there is nothing unique or necessarily transcendent about caring for kin or reciprocating benefactors. A number of studies, none particularly sympathetic to religion, have even recognized that the sociobiological interpretation of human nature is consistent with, moreover suggestive of, the traditional notion of original sin (Huxley 1894; Campbell 1975b; Kaye 1986; Williams 1988). This is surely true in the strong assertions of sociobiological egoism, "all acts are selfish." Yet the really significant claim is not that all human acts are, but that *any* act may be selfish, the result of genetic defaults or biosocial autopilot. We are not allowed to hide behind the vain moral assurance of reified expressions of sacrifice or love:

> "Hypocrisy, artifice, wiliness, and seduction stretch unconditionally as far as love does, and they can imitate true love so strikingly that there is no absolute criterion, because in every expression of truth or of true love there exists the possibility of deception that corresponds to it exactly" (Kierkegaard 1847:215).

The above passage, with its emphasis on the way in which manipulation and deceit and connivance may take on the appearance of genuine love, could almost have been written by Wilson, Alexander, or Irons. This is morally relevant, because sociobiology reminds us (and not just reminds but furthers our understanding) of this phenomenon. But sociobiology could have only *almost* concocted the above. For while sociobiology debunks false love, it denies, or is ambivalent about, any alternatives. "Having slain the theological enemy," it demonstrates itself as having "little to offer as a replacement" (Oates 1988:452).

Thus in its cautions against the sentimentalist deceit of self-interest in sacrificial clothing, sociobiological "realism" may exalt a complimentary deceit by asserting that the fundamental longings of the human heart must be relinquished with a mature commitment to facing the truth: "The yearning to be loved 'for one's self alone' is perfectly normal, but it is unwise to fashion one's expectations by this yearning once the years of childhood are past . . ." (Hardin 1977:25). There is, of course, an alternative vision of maturity, which understands the far side of disillusionment, having known but not quit at either the false comfort of sentimentality, or the false safety of cynicism: "When I was a child, I used to speak as a child, think as a child, reason as a child; when I became a man, I did away with childish things . . . Still, now abide faith, hope, love, these three; but the greater of these is love" (I Cor. 13).

"To cheat oneself out of love is the most terrible deception; it is an eternal loss for which there is no reparation . . ."

Kierkegaard (1847:23)

References

Alexander, R.D.
> 1979 *Darwinism and Human Affairs*. Seattle and London: University of Washington Press.
> 1987 *The Biology of Moral Systems*. Chicago: Aldine-de-Gruyter.
> 1992 Biology and the Moral Paradoxes. In *Law, Biology and Culture*. M. Gruter and P. Bohannan. McGraw-Hill, Inc.

Alper, J.S.
> 1978 Ethical and Social Implications. In *Sociobiology and Human Nature*. Michael S. Gregory, Anita Silvers, and Diane Sutch, eds. Washington: Jossey-Bass Publishers. Pp. 195-212.

Ardrey, R.
> 1966 *The Territorial Imperative: A Personal Inquiry into the Animal Origins of Property and Nations*. New York: Atheneum.

Ayala, F.J.
> 1987 The Biological Roots of Morality. *Biology and Philosophy* 2: 235-252.

Baldwin, J.D. and J.I. Baldwin
> 1981 *Beyond Sociobiology*. New York: Elsevier.

Ball, S.
> 1988 Evolution, Explanation, and the Fact/Value Distinction. *Biology and Philosophy* 3: 317-348.

Barash, D.P.
> 1977 *Sociobiology and Behavior*. New York: Elsevier.
> 1982 *Sociobiology and Behavior,* 2nd edition. New York: Elsevier.

Bateson, P.
> 1989 Does Evolutionary Biology Contribute to Ethics? *Biology and Philosophy* 4: 287-301.

Becker, H.
> 1956 *Man in Reciprocity*. New York: Prager. Cited in Gouldner, 1960.

Bock, K.
1980 *Human Nature and History: A Response to Sociobiology*. New York: Columbia University Press. (Quotes from paperback edition, 1982.)

Boyd, R.L. and P.J. Richerson
1985 *Culture and the Evolutionary Process*. Chicago: University of Chicago Press.

Breuer, G.
1983 *Sociobiology and the Human Dimension* (translation of *Der Sogenannte Mensch*). Cambridge: Cambridge University Press.

Burhoe, R.W.
1979 Religion's Role in Human Evolution: The Missing Link between Ape-Man's Selfish Genes and Civilized Altruism. *Zygon* 14: 135-62.
1988 On "Huxley's Evolution and Ethics in Sociobiological Perspective" by George C. Williams. *Zygon* 23: 417-430.

Campbell, D.T.
1975a On the Conflicts Between Biological and Social Evolution and Between Psychology and Moral Tradition. *American Psychologist*. 30: 1103-26.
1975b The Conflict Between Social and Biological Evolution and the Concept of Original Sin. *Zygon* 10: 234-49.
1991 A Naturalistic Theory of Archaic Moral Order. *Zygon* 26: 91-114.

Cavalli-Sforza , L.L. and W.W. Feldman
1981 *Cultural Transmission and Evolution: A Quantitative Approach*. Princeton: Princeton University Press.

Chase, A.
1980 *The Legacy of Malthus: the Social Costs of the New Scientific Racism*. Urbana: University of Illinois Press.

Daly, M. and M. Wilson
1983 *Sex, Evolution, and Behavior*, 2nd Edition. Belmont, CA: Wadsworth

Darwin, C.
1967[1859] *On the Origin of Species by Means of Natural Selection: Or, the Preservation of Favored Races in the Struggle for Life*. Cambridge: Harvard University Press.
1981[1871] *The Descent of Man and Selection in Relation to Sex*. Princeton: Princeton University Press.

Dawkins, R.
1976 *The Selfish Gene*. Oxford: Oxford University Press.
1982 *The Extended Phenotype*. Oxford: W.H. Freeman and Co.

Degler, C.N.
1991 In *Search of Human Nature: The Decline and Revival of Darwinism in American Social Thought*. Oxford: Oxford University Press.

Dewey, J.
1951[1910] *The Influence of Darwin on Philosophy, and Other Essays.* New York: P. Smith.

Dobzhansky, T.
1973 Nothing in Biology Makes Sense Except in the Light of Evolution. *American Biology Teacher* 35: 125-129.

Einstein, A.
1954 *Ideas and Opinions.* New York: Dell Publishing Company.

Flew, A.
1978 From "Is" to "Ought" in Evolutionary Ethics. In *New Studies in Ethics.* W. Hudson, ed. New York: St. Martin's Press, Inc.

Fox, R.
1989 *The Search for Society: Quest for a Biosocial Science and Morality.* New Brunswick: Rutgers University Press.

Geiger, G.
1992 Why There Are No Objective Values: A Critique of Ethical Intuitionism from an Evolutionary Point of View. *Biology and Philosophy* 7: 315-330.
1993 Evolutionary Anthropology and the Non-Cognitive Foundation of Moral Validity. *Biology and Philosophy* 8: 133-151.

Gewirth, A.
1986 The Problem of Specificity in Evolutionary Ethics. *Biology and Philosophy* 1: 297-305.

Ghiselin, M.T.
1973 Darwin and Evolutionary Psychology. *Science.* 179: 964-968.
1974 *The Economy of Nature and the Evolution of Sex.* Berkeley: University of California Press.

Gillian, C.
1982 *In a Different Voice: Psychological Theory and Women's Development.* Cambridge: Harvard University Press.

Gould, S.J.
1977 *Ever Since Darwin.* W.W. Norton. New York.
1981 *The Mismeasure of Man.* Norton, New York.
1982 Darwinism and the Expansion of Evolutionary Theory. *Science.* 216: 380-387.

Gould, S.J. and R.C. Lewontin
1979 The Spandrels of San Marco and the Panglossian Paradigm: A Critique of the Adaptationist Programme. *Proceedings of the Royal Society of London.* 205: 581-598.

Gouldner, A.J.
1960 The Norm of Reciprocity: A Preliminary statement. *American Sociological Review* 25: 161-178.

142

Greenwood, D.J.
1989 *The Taming of Evolution*. Ithaca and London: Cornell University Press.

Hamilton, W.D.
1964 The Genetical Evolution of Social Behavior. *The Journal of Theoretical Biology* 7: 1-16.

Hammarskjold, D.
1964 *Markings*. New York: Knopf

Hardin, G.
1977 *The Limits of Altruism: An Ecologist's View of Survival*. Bloomington, IN: Indiana University Press.

Himmerlfarb, G.
1968 *Darwin and the Darwinian Revolution*. New York: W.W. Norton.

Hrdy, S.B.
1981 *The Woman That Never Evolved*. Cambridge, Massachusetts: Harvard University Press.

Hull, D.
1978 Scientific Bandwagon or Travelling Medicine Show? In *Sociobiology and Human Nature*. M. S. Gregory, A. Silvers, and D. Sutch, eds. San Francisco: Jossey-Bass Publishers.

Huxley, T.H.
1989[1894] *Evolution and Ethics*. Princeton: Princeton University Press.

Irons, W.
1991 How did Morality Evolve? *Zygon* 26: 49-89.

Kaye, H.L.
1986 *The Social Meaning of Modern Biology: From Social Darwinism to Sociobiology*. Yale University Press.

Kierkegaard, S.
1962[1847] *Works of Love*. Howard and Edna Hong, translators. New York: Harper Torchbooks.

Kitcher, P.
1985 *Vaulting Ambition: Sociobiology and the Quest for Human Nature*. Cambridge, Massachusetts: MIT Press.

Kohlberg, L.
1984 *The Psychology of Moral Development: The Nature and Validity of Moral Stages*. San Francisco: Harper and Row.

Konner, M.
1982 *The Tangled Wing: Biological Constraints on the Human Spirit*. New York: Holt, Rinehart, and Winston.

Lewontin, R.C., S. Rose, and L.J. Kamin
1984 *Not in Our Genes: Biology, Ideology, and Human Nature*. New York: Pantheon Books.

Lorenz, K.
1966 *On Aggression*. Harcourt Brace Jovanovich.

Lumsden, C.J. and E.O. Wilson
1981 *Genes, Mind, and Culture: The Coevolutionary Process*. Cambridge, Massachusetts: Harvard University Press.

Mattern, R.
1978 Altruism, Ethics, and Sociobiology. In *The Sociobiology Debate*. Arthur L. Caplan. New York, Hagerstown, San Francisco, London: Harper and Row, Publishers.

Midgley, M.
1980 Rival Fatalisms: The Hollowness of the Sociology Debate. In *Sociobiology Examined*. A. Montagu, ed. Oxford University Press. Pp. 15-38.
1982 Foreward. In *Sociobiology and the Human Dimension,* by G. Breuer. New York: Cambridge University Press.

Morris, D.
1967 *The Naked Ape*. New York: McGraw-Hill Book Company.

Oates, D.
1988 Social Darwinism and Natural Theodicy. *Zygon* 23: 439-454.

Pascal, B.
1958 *Pensees*. (T. S. Elliot, commentator). New York: E.P. Dutton.

Rachels, J.
1990 *Created from Animals: The Moral Implications of Darwinism*. Oxford, New York: Oxford University Press.

Richards, R.J.
1986a *Darwin and the Emergence of Evolutionary Theories of Mind and Behavior*. Chicago: University of Chicago Press.
1986b A Defense of Evolutionary Ethics. *Biology and Philosophy* 1: 265-293.
1986c Justification Through Biological Faith: A Rejoinder. *Biology and Philosophy* 1: 337-354.

Rottschaefer, W.A.
1984 Singer, Sociobiology, and Values: Pure Reason Versus Empirical Reason. *Zygon* 19: 159-170.

Rottschaefer, W.A. and D. Martinsen
1990 Really Taking Darwin Seriously: An Alternative to Michael Ruse's Darwinian Metaethics. *Biology and Philosophy* 5: 149-173.

Ruse, M.

1979a *The Darwinian Revolution: Science Red in Tooth and Claw.* Chicago: University of Chicago Press.

1979b *Sociobiology: Sense or Nonsense?* Dordrecht, Holland: D. Reidel Publishing Company.

1986a *Taking Darwin Seriously.* New York: Basil Blackwell Inc.

1986b Evolutionary Ethics: A Phoenix Arisen. *Zygon* 21: 95-112.

1988 Response to Williams: Selfishness is not Enough. *Zygon* 23: 413-416.

Sahlins, M.D.

1965 On the Sociology of Primitive Exchange. In M. Banton, ed. *Relevance of Models of Social Anthropology.* New York: Praeger.

1976 *The Use and Abuse of Biology.* The University of Michigan Press.

Sayers, J.

1982 *Biological Politics.* New York: Tavistock Publications.

Schwartz, B.

1986 *The Battle For Human Nature Science, Morality and Modern Life.* W.W. Norton and Company, New York, London.

Science for the People, Sociobiology Study Group

1976 Sociobiology: Another Biological Determinism. *BioScience.* Vol. 26: 3.

Singer, P.

1981 *The Expanding Circle.* New York: Farrar, Straus and Giroux.

1984 Ethics and Sociobiology. *Zygon* 19: 141.

Solzhenitsyn, A.I.

1973 *The Gulag Archipelago, 1918-1956: An Experiment in Literary Investigation,* I-VII. New York: Harper and Row.

Stent, G.S.

1980 *Morality as a Biological Phenomenon.* Berkley, Los Angeles, London: University of California Press.

Symons, D.

1979 *The Evolution of Human Sexuality.* New York: Oxford University Press.

Tiger, L. and R. Fox

1971 *The Imperial Animal.* New York: Holt, Rinehart, and Winston.

Tobach, E.

1978 The Methodology of Sociobiology from the Viewpoint of a Comparative Psychologist. In *The Sociobiology Debate: Readings on the Ethical and Scientific Issues Concerning Sociobiology.* A. C. Caplan, ed. 411-423. New York: Harper and Row.

Trivers, R.L.

1971 The Evolution of Reciprocal Altruism *The Quarterly Review of Biology* 46: 35-39.

1985   *Social Evolution*. Menlo Park: Benjamin Cummings.

Voorzanger, B.
1987   No Norms and No Nature – The Moral Relevance of Evolutionary Biology. *Biology and Philosophy* 2: 253-270.

Wenegrat, B.
1990   *The Divine Archetype*. Lexington Books, Massachusetts/Toronto.

Wesley, J.
1909   *The Journal of the Rev. John Wesley*. Vol. I and II. R. Culley. London.

Williams, G.C.
1966   *Adaptation and Natural Selection*. Princeton University Press. Princeton.
1988   Huxley's Evolution and Ethics in Sociobiological Perspective. *Zygon* 23: 383-407.
1989   A Sociobiological Expansion of *Evolution and Ethics*. In *Evolution and Ethics*. T. H. Huxley. Princeton University Press. Princeton.

Williams, P.
1990   Evolved Ethics Re-Examined: The Theory of Robert J. Richards. *Biology and Philosophy* 5: 451-457.

Wilson, D.S.
1992   On the Relationship Between Evolutionary and Psychological Definitions of Altruism and Selfishness. *Biology and Philosophy* 7: 61-68.

Wilson, E.O.
1975   *Sociobiology*. Harvard University Press, Cambridge, Massachusetts.
1977   Biology and the Social Sciences: Discoveries and Interpretations. *Studies in Contemporary Scholarship* 2: 106: 127-140.
1978   *On Human Nature*. Harvard University Press. Cambridge, Massachusetts.

Chapter 7   The Human Brain, Religion, and the Biology of Sin

Timothy J. Shaw

Introduction

The human brain is an amazing, yet largely mysterious instrument of human nature. Among the members of the animal kingdom, Homo Sapiens is most distinguished by a complex brain. As one compares organisms ascending the phylogenetic ladder, increasing complexity can be observed in both the structure and function of the brain. Although some abilities of central nervous system function such as vision, auditory sense, or olfactory sense, may show some decrease in acuity at different points in this ascension, we place the human brain at the top of animal phylogeny. This superior position among the animals is based largely on the unmatched human ability to integrate, remember, communicate, and assign meaning to significant amounts of sensory stimuli while directing complicated and purposeful behavioral responses to these stimuli. In this paper, I will discuss the implications of human cerebral complexity for human morality, religion, and especially the concept of sin.

Comparative animal studies

We can learn a great deal about the workings of the human brain through comparative studies with the brains of animals. Behavioral capabilities are directly linked to physical structures in the brain and when animal brains are compared phylogenetically, a linkage can be made between characteristic animal behaviors and levels of structural complexity. Phylogenetic brain comparisons attempt to explain the evolution of behaviors observed in both animals and humans.

A quick and simplified survey of the phylogeny of vertebrates places fish at the bottom of the ladder, followed by reptiles, and then a divergence to birds and mammals (Torrey and Feduccia 1979:27-31). When one compares our brain to the brains of other vertebrates, a generalized progression is observed in the development of the cerebral hemispheres which corresponds to increases in the complexity of behavior and the ability to make thoughtful choices. For example, when one examines the brain of fish at the bottom of the vertebrate phylogenetic ladder, the cerebral hemisphere accounts for only a small portion of the total brain mass. When one considers the degree of conscious thought necessary for survival of the fish, it becomes obvious why greater intellectual ability is not necessary among the fish populations. When fish are hungry, they eat from the available food supply, and when there is not an abundance of food, they starve. When the conditions or the season is right to allow maximum offspring to survive, fish are automatically hormonally stimulated to engage in reproductive behavior. For fish, planning, understanding, or social cooperation are not important qualities for survival. As one ascends the phylogenetic ladder, however, there is a need for increased behavioral complexity. Comparative anatomy reveals substantial increases in the structural complexity of the vertebrate cerebral hemispheres. These increases correspond to the increased complexity of behavioral abilities characteristic of the species, abilities necessary for survival (Torrey and Feduccia 1979:475-492). Mammals are at the top of this comparative ladder, and of the mammals, humans are clearly superior. Contrary to common perception, when the brain of humans is compared to the brains of other mammals, it is not the largest, or even the largest in proportion to body size. The human brain is, however, the most complex in relation to the cerebral hemispheres and their internal connections with the rest of the central nervous system (Nolte 1988:15).

We should be aware that many portions of our brains remain very similar to the brains of animals. Areas that govern physiological activities show great similarity among all the vertebrate species. In phylogenetic comparison of the animals, it is frequently assumed that evolutionary improvements in the brain were caused by newer structures replacing older structures as the species of vertebrates became more complex in brain function. However this is not always the case. Although new capacities are realized in the more advanced brain, the apparatus governing more primitive responses often remains intact. While the potential for more sophisticated behavioral responses is present, this potential may not be exercised in every case, and more advanced vertebrates will at times exhibit behaviors characteristic of organisms lower on the phylogenetic ladder.

Human uniqueness

Although comparative studies can provide interesting insights into behavior, they are incomplete in their explanation of certain human behaviors, most notably those linked to unselfishness and religion. Among the characteristics that separate human behavior from the behavior of animals are those which involve more complex integration (thinking) associated with an area of the brain known as the neocortex. Portions of this area of our brains are clearly superior to our animal counterparts. When we examine the behavior of organisms in the animal kingdom, it is only among humans that we observe:

1. Morality – conscious and intentional behaviors directed by individuals based solely on the motivation to do what is "right." These behaviors are often, but not always, self-sacrificial or altruistic in nature and are based on strong beliefs.

2. Empathy – the ability to consider, and imagine in our mind, the feelings associated with another's experience. It is our ability to feel empathy that allows us to show mercy, or to experience sorrow for the misfortune of another.

3. Religion – we are unable to observe any human cultures that do not exhibit religious behavior. Conversely, we observe no behaviors in animals that we attribute to religion. Although atheists may exist as individuals, people in all cultures attempt to describe God, gods, or the non-empirical.

4. Altruism – although unselfish and self-sacrificial social behaviors exist in certain colonies of insects and other invertebrates, these can primarily be explained as instinctual behaviors that insure reproduction of the genes of the colony. Many species of animals among the vertebrates show altruistic behaviors toward their offspring; however, these are also can be explained as largely instinctual behaviors that preserve one's genes into future generations. Only humans make conscious and rational decisions resulting in self sacrifice for individuals outside of their own gene pool.

5. Language – Many animals have forms of communication. However, we see a formalized spoken and written language among humans that is unmatched in the animal kingdom.

6. Aesthetic Appreciation and Creativity - Among animals we do not observe significant energy invested in activities that are purely aesthetic. Among humans, however, artistic expression and the appreciation of art are found in all cultures.

Other than the debatable possibility that the perception of beauty among humans may serve as a potential guide in selection of a "genetically fit" mate, appreciation of beauty in people, nature, or objects provides no reproductive advantage and is very difficult to explain as a product of natural selection.

It could be said that the human brain contains within it an animal brain. The regions of our brains that are similar to animals are primarily those regions which are involved in visceral or physiological activities, plus those activities classified as more primitive, including more primal drives and survival-based activities. Although the more primitive areas of the human brain are surpassed by more sophisticated regions of the neocortex, these more primitive areas still hold great influence on human behavior. For example, all mammals show a similar set of behavioral responses to stimuli that are important for survival and maintenance of the species: a basic fear of danger and caution concerning the unknown, irritation or motivation at the cry of infant progeny, repulsion by spoiled food, aggression against a challengeable threat, and sexual drive for propagation. Humans tend to produce these more primitive automatic behavioral responses to stimuli unless the neocortex intervenes to override them. Intervention to avoid these natural behaviors requires some type of conscious "choice," whether this "choice" takes the form of simple adherence to a learned custom or an original action directed by calculated consideration of all the options. In either case, the ability to override these primitive or natural behaviors is a characteristic of the human brain.

Triune brain theory

Paul MacLean summarizes an interesting theory of the relationship between structure and function of the human brain in his recent book, *The Triune Brain in Evolution* (MacLean 1990). This picture of the human brain suggests that the evolutionary development of the brain has produced a forebrain (telencephalon and diencephalon) which has retained three basic formations representing different levels of physiologic complexity that were formed one on top of the other. In each case, these structures represent the highest centers regulating brain function and behavior in reptiles, more primitive mammals, and the highest mammals, respectively. It is suggested that this neural hierarchy is overlapping rather than exclusive, resulting in three brains in one, or "The Triune Brain." Of these different levels of brain function, none is silent, but rather each has its own anatomical components and responds to sensory input according to its own subjectivity. This may result in three corresponding, but potentially different, prescriptions for behavior in response to specific stimuli.

The lowest of the three areas considered as directive components of behavior is called by MacLean the "Protoreptilian Formation" or "R-Complex." This term describes an area of gray matter nuclei and their associated structures at the base of the forebrain, or cerebrum, that are common to reptiles, birds, and mammals. In the mammalian brain this area corresponds to a region referred to as the "striatal complex" and includes the "basal ganglia" that have traditionally been considered to be important structures in the coordination of movement, rather than behavior. In reptiles however, the cerebral hemispheres are composed of little more than these R-Complex structures, and together with their primitive cortical connections they appear to play a significant role in reptilian behavior. Behaviors important to the life of the reptile include the regulation of daily routine and subroutine, and certain types of non-verbal communication. The types of behaviors generated by the reptilian brain include:

1. Struggle for power or dominance

2. Adherence to routine

3. Imitation

4. Obeisance or submissive behavior

5. Deception

The next hierarchical component of the Triune Brain is called the "Paleomammalian Formation" (Maclean 1990). Structures of this formation surround the more primitive Protoreptilian portions, and include many of the structures considered to be analogous to those of the "Limbic System" in the human brain. The term "Limbic System" is really more of a functional term than an anatomical term, but it is generally considered to include more primitive portions of the cerebral hemispheres that, because of their commonality to all mammals, are viewed as phylogenetically older. Regions of the cerebral cortex included in this formation are referred to as "old cortex" or "archicortex," and these older cortical regions together with related subcortical cerebral structures compose the "Limbic Lobe" of the brain. The term "Limbic System" really describes this "Limbic Lobe" and all of its connections throughout the brain. Phylogenetically new behaviors that must be accounted for in the mammalian brain include: Nursing and maternal care-giving behavior, audiovocal communication with offspring, and play (MacLean 1990).

Although some portions of the limbic system may be present in reptiles and fish, portions linked specifically to these behaviors are found primarily in mammals. Functions generally associated with the limbic system include emotional responses to stimuli, basic physiologic drives, deep- seated perceptions of what is pleasure and what produces emotional pain, and what constitutes reward and punishment (Guyton 1987). In lower mammals, it is this structure together with the Protoreptilian Formation that rules behavior (MacLean 1990:247-411).

MacLean suggests a third level of ruling complexity in higher mammals: the Neomammalian Formation. In the brains of higher mammals, sophisticated components have been added to meet new behavioral challenges. These regions of the cerebral hemispheres are not seen in lower mammals and therefore are considered phylogenetically more recent. Portions of the cerebral cortex unique to higher mammals are referred to as the "neocortex" (MacLean 1990:519-563). The Neomammalian Formation consists primarily of the neocortex and the subcortical structures with which it is directly connected. These added areas are mostly involved with the increased analysis of stimuli and with decisions directing the most appropriate responses to those stimuli. The neomammalian formation allows for an increased ability for problem solving, learning, and for the memory of details. It is the neomammalian formation that provides the substrate on which can occur the generation and interpretation of more detailed audible communication characteristic of higher mammals. The brain of humans however, is unmatched among even the highest mammals in its ability to generate spoken and written language.

On simple examination of the mammalian brain, one takes note of a parietal lobe involved in perception of pain, temperature, and tactile sense; an occipital lobe responsible for the perception of our visual sense; a temporal lobe related to our learning and auditory sense; and a very large frontal lobe that primarily directs our actions in response to these perceptions. In the most simplistic analysis, this frontal lobe controls our responses to perception of stimuli, and represents the essence of what determines behavior and personality. These frontal lobe areas are also intimately connected with the deeper more primitive structures of the R-complex and the limbic lobe, which have significant influence on the actions directed.

The prefrontal cortex

The triune brain theory provides useful and interesting insights concerning functional relationships of the brains of reptiles and most mammals, but does not by itself explain the complexity of human behavior. The human brain must be placed in a category above the most intellectually sophisticated of the other mammals. Our brain is distinctly different from the brains of even our closest animal relatives, and certain portions of the human brain have no analogous structures in any other species. When comparing the human brain to the brain of other mammals, even to our closest relatives among the primates, one can note a number of modifications. Perhaps the most striking anatomical difference observed about the human brain in comparison to other primates is the large frontal lobe and specifically the relative size devoted to the "prefrontal" areas of this lobe.

The prefrontal cortex is a fascinating portion of the brain that is directly involved in the control of behavior and contains the origin of some functions that we would view as uniquely human. Prefrontal functions might also be seen in other mammals, but the human brain is clearly superior in the degree to which the prefrontal portions can control behavior. Functions attributed to interactions of the prefrontal cortex with other parts of the brain include:

1. Problem solving

2. The ability to focus on a specific task or question

3. Anticipation of, and reaction to, unpleasant stimuli

4. Planning and goal setting ability

5. Motivation to action. The ability for unique or non-imitative behavior (spontaneous behavior)

6. Insight and Empathy

7. Sense of "self" in relation to perceptions of others

8. Social inhibition of behavior

9. The ability to predict and to expect the results of actions

10. Integration of all sensory data (visual, auditory, olfactory, gustatory, and somesthetic)

11. Purposeful decision making

12. Cooperation with the limbic system to assign priority of attention to different sensory stimuli

13. Control of the limbic system's behavioral urges and drives

Sociobiological explanations for behavior

Sociobiologists argue that in the analysis of the behavior of all animals, including humans, the dominant determining factor that controls behavior is increased reproductive "fitness" (Wilson 1975). Behaviors occur to maximize the potential for an organism's genes to be passed on to subsequent generations. This means that behavioral characteristics that are observed among animals are those which have been able to withstand the test of natural selection. For this to be possible, behavioral tendencies must be either reproductively neutral or produce a reproductive advantage for the organism's genes if they are to avoid being weeded out of the population over time. Throughout the animal kingdom, one sees a priority of behaviors that would appear to be "hard wired" or instinctual to accomplish this end. The natural order of importance generally places the interests of self at the center. Of next greatest importance are interests of one's offspring, followed by those of related kin. In some cases this order can be extended to include as a lower priority the concerns of a social group of which one is a part. These levels of priority correspond directly to the proportion of genes one shares with each of these groups. The greater the potential for enhancing the survival of copies of the organism's own genes, the greater the vested interest. Of course, the organism is not aware of the sociobiological reasons for these priorities.

Behaviors expected as a result of natural selection are those which would enhance the genetic fitness of the individual. These behaviors are normally seen among humans and other mammals of the world and include the following:

1. Struggle for dominance or social power – an organism's fitness is best enhanced through maximizing its ability for control of its own destiny

2. Aggression – this provides a mechanism for establishing dominance

3. Obeisance – the yielding to another's dominance when it is advantageous

4. Selfishness – fitness is maximized by maximum devotion to self, or in some rare cases to another close kin better capable of passing on one's genes

5. Fear – avoidance of pain or unpleasant stimuli, and the ability to recognize danger

6. Physiological drives for survival and propagation

    a. Drives to satisfy needs of hunger and thirst, warmth, and rest

    b. Drive to satisfy desire for reproductive activity

7. Preference for routine – there is security in a lack of deviation from the norm

8. Desire for "pleasure" – "pleasure" here means that mysterious part of the human and animal brain that motivates; the built-in reward system that causes one to pursue behaviors ranging from gaining control of one's surroundings, to quenching a thirst, to sexual activity

The keys to the motivation of behavior involve what could be called "pleasure centers" of the brain. Not that these centers necessarily always generate strong euphoria within the organism, but they produce a preference for certain activities over others based on some internal reward. A good question to ask concerning behavior is, "What makes any animal do anything?" Is there a conscious decision in most cases, carefully weighing all possibilities and considering all possible outcomes of a given action? Of course there is not. In fact, most members of the animal kingdom possess a very limited ability to project into the future an understanding of the consequences of their actions. One would have to say that there are probably few actions taken even by human beings that involve a calculated assessment of all potential consequences. Most actions are motivated naturally "from within" and correspond to behaviors expected of an organism trying to increase its survival or reproductive fitness. The majority of human behavior are in accord with the explanations of the sociobiologists based on the idea of the "selfish gene."

Human behavioral control

We must remember that the same basic structures of the brain responsible for motivating behaviors in animals are also present in the human and exert similar influences. Control of the expression of an emotion or an inner drive may at times be very difficult, if not impossible, even when an individual deeply wants to be in control. Yielding to inner physiological or emotional drives is often in keeping with the goals of our animal brain and produces strong internal "reward" from the limbic or reptilian portions. Denial of these deeply motivated behaviors would be contrary to our human nature. The expanded neocortex and associated structures of the human brain gives yet another level for the understanding and regulation of behavior. The human brain has a superior ability to assess the consequences of actions for one's self as well as for others. In the human, urges and drives generated by the limbic system and lower centers of the brain can be consciously modified or denied based on decisions of higher centers. There are four basic conditions suggested where humans may exhibit apparent self-denial or unselfish behavior:

1. When temporary denial will provide protection from danger or risk, or will accomplish a predicted greater reward in the foreseeable future

2. In some cases when risk-taking or self-denial will enhance the chances of offspring or close kin survival (Hamilton 1964:1-52)

3. When limited self-denial produces a benefit for another that later may result in reciprocal benefit from the other member (Trivers 1985:361-394)

4. In a social system where altruistic-appearing behavior is done so that it can be noted by other members of the social group. This enhances the reputation of the originator of the behavior as a good reciprocator. The behavior will then increase the probability of receiving the benefit of unselfish actions from other group members also seeking trustworthy reciprocal relationships (Alexander 1987:93-94).

It should be noted that in all of these examples, any sacrifice by the originator is only temporary or useful in exchange for the increased potential for survival of self and the genes. In explaining selfless behaviors among humans, these four explanations are largely incomplete. Unselfish behavior toward non-genetically related individuals occurs frequently among humans. This behavior often cannot be explained as the avoidance of risk, increased potential for reciprocity, or enhancement of reputation. Of course it could be argued that humans need not always have a conscious awareness of ultimate selfish ends for these ends to be the true motivators of behavior. After all, most birds and mammals are not consciously protecting their offspring in order to promote their genetic fitness. They are intensely committed to offspring protection, however, and we see gene survival as the ultimate biological explanation. In the same way, it could be argued that humans may be unconsciously motivated by behavioral tendencies that have evolved to produce success of the species. However, unselfishness in a social context creates a disadvantage in genetic fitness unless it is directed toward close kin, or increases the chance of reciprocal unselfishness. Selfless behavior that does not accomplish these ends should not evolve unless "by accident," and in this case, if it produces a negative effect on genetic fitness, it should be eliminated from the gene pool over a period of generations. Humans frequently practice unselfish behavior and self denial. Therefore, natural selection is an insufficient explanation for this behavior.

Religious behavior

Self-denial and unselfish behavior are often tied to religious commitment. For example, a 1990 Gallup survey reported that the 24 percent of Americans who attended church weekly accounted for 48 percent of all charitable giving. Numerous other surveys show that this group has a nearly doubled rate of participation in service of philanthropic causes, when compared to the general population (Myers 1992:23-26). Almost any discussion in the literature of altruistic behavior will include examples of behavior in the context of religion. If altruism is caused by the genes, then it is not surprising that some humans may express this characteristic more than others. It is interesting, however, that altruism correlates with religious behavior. This suggests that either behavioral tendencies toward religion and altruism have a genetic relationship, or that there is something unique about religion which enhances this behavior. The latter of these two possibilities is strengthened by considering that significant changes regarding selfish and unselfish behavior can occur in individuals following a religious experience. How, then, would one account biologically for religious behavior? I limit my arguments to teachings and practices of the Christian religion with which I am most familiar. However, I feel that humans in every culture manifest religious needs, and some of my examples from Christianity will be applicable to other religions as well. Since religious behavior is uniquely human, the sociobiologist must believe that the superior brain that has evolved to serve humans has added, rather than a clearer perception of reality, a clouded or deceptive picture of reality that deeply affects man's religious behavior. It is very difficult to imagine a biological evolution of brain structure that would create such an altering of reality necessary to imagine the supernatural. Indeed, for humans to be motivated to protect offspring and kin and to practice reciprocity, this self-deception is not required. Belief in the supernatural is not a necessary element of successful social behavior, and it does not seem logical to insist that religion is a necessary part of man's social evolution. From a purely biological perspective, religious behavior is a tax on the efficiency of the human organism. Of what reproductive advantage could it possibly be to believe strongly, expend energy, and alter behavior in pursuit of a fictitious supreme being? Why do human beings experience a love for, and a sense of communication with, a nonexistent entity? Why do so many humans experience such a strong desire for spiritual fulfillment, and why do so many aspects of their lives, including often their motivation for life itself, revolve around this preoccupation?

E. O. Wilson acknowledges that religious behavior is unique to humans, and among humans it is a universal social behavior that is present in all societies (1975:169-193). He describes religious practice as the "consecration of the group" and believes that religion evolved as a sort of tribalism between competing groups of early humans. Wilson suggests that the evolution of religious behavior occurred through influences on three successive levels. The first level of influence was "Ecclesiastic" selection, where religious leaders laid down rules and guidelines that were required of other more subordinate members of the group. The second level was "Ecological" selection where the ecclesiastic guidelines were tested by the success of the group in the environment. If the religion weakened the society or interfered with its procreation, the religion would decline. Religions that increased the stability of the society would grow. The third level of influence involved the genes themselves, whose frequency would be constantly changing in the midst of social influences. Genes producing behaviors more consistent with success in these religiously dominated groups would be favored. Wilson believes that religious people seek the supernatural for "purely mundane rewards" that include "long life, abundant land and food, averting of physical catastrophes, and the conquest of enemies" (Wilson 1978:174).

The idea of natural selection increasing the frequency of certain religious-like behaviors within religious groups is logical, and probably occurs to some degree. One cannot deny that many religions, including Christianity, have been used by some groups or individuals as vehicles to obtain selfish gain. However certain aspects of religious behavior remain very difficult to explain in these sociobiological terms, for example, the type of "hard-core altruism" (Wilson 1978:174) demanded by Jesus that a follower "deny himself, and take up his cross and follow"

(Matthew 16:24[1]) suggests that the faithful will be required to endure significant sacrifice and persecution in a social context.

Numerous other biblical texts point to significant social persecution, even to the point of death, against those who become believers and associate themselves with this religious group (see Matthew 5:10-12, Matthew 5:44, Matthew 10:39, John 15:20 and Romans 12:14 for a few examples). When considering the ideas of "ecclesiastic and ecological selection" as described by Wilson, these texts appear to represent the antithesis of what one would expect to increase genetic fitness. Although it may be difficult for modern Americans to imagine, the devoutly religious have suffered persecution historically and globally. Over the years, persons of the Christian faith have endured severe persecution and produced uncounted religious martyrs. However, this religion seems to flourish rather than perish in the face of persecution.

Humans often pursue religion for more than purely selfish motivations of perceived reward. For example, it would be difficult to imagine that Christians who hid Jews in their homes during the reign of Nazi Germany did so with the intent of receiving some reward that they perceived they might miss if they did not engage in this behavior. In the same way, religious martyrs, foreign missionaries, and certain other "saints" of the faith go far beyond what they may believe is required to obtain heavenly reward. The biological cost of these activities on genetic fitness is obvious, and any reproductive advantage passed is clearly questionable. Consider for example the well-known missionary, Mother Teresa. Her life's commitment to philanthropic aid to the sick and needy does not require anything of those who receive the benefit of her actions, nor is it selectively based on her or her group's relationship to the recipients of the aid. From a sociobiological perspective, there is no possibility for her genes to be passed on to subsequent generations, and her sacrificial actions do not enhance the chances for survival of the genes of her relatives. Something, however, motivates her to expend her time, energy, and resources in this way, rather than in ways that would prove to be more profitable to her personally and to the genetic fitness of herself or her kin. It is difficult to imagine how the brain that produces this type of unselfish behavior could evolve from the selfish animal brain. One could argue that the benefit this type of behavior produces for the group overshadows the effect of any reduced

---

[1] All biblical quotations are from the New American Standard Version.

genetic fitness of the individual caregiver. The genes that allow this type of unselfish behavior would only survive, however, if members of the recipient group shared the same genes. This is probably not the case in this example, because, if the recipient group shared the same genes as the caregiver, why would the caregiver be unique, and why would the recipients not practice the same types of behavior?

Sin and the brain

The idea of sin is at the very core of Christian beliefs about behavior. In a general sense, sinful behavior can be described as the transgression against ecclesiastical laws and principles of a religious group. These laws and principles are assumed to have a divine origin and to be mandated by God. Within Christianity, one can categorize sinful behavior into one of three categories:

1. Rejecting the existence, or discounting the importance, of God and creation

2. Discounting the importance, or infringing upon the basic rights of another individual

3. Causing inappropriate or purposeless harm to oneself

Great insight can be gained into the nature and biology of "sinful" behavior by consideration of the phylogeny and functional organization of the human brain. In the animal brain we see altruistic behavior limited to kinship relatedness and reciprocity only. However, we have suggested that in the human brain there exists a unique potential for truly unselfish behavior.

Humans struggle between their natural animal brain tendencies for selfish behavior and the motivation to rise above these tendencies. For instance, throughout his biblical writings, St. Paul refers to struggles with the desires of the "flesh" and the tendencies of the "natural man." We might infer that he refers to the strong inner directives of our animal brain. Natural biological drives are important for survival. Our limbic system is set up to reward us for those behaviors that increase our genetic fitness, and genetic fitness is best enhanced through behavior that is ultimately selfish. However, sinful behavior is defined as an inability to control these drives, or a tendency to assign greater importance to them than to spiritual goals.

As already noted, all humans and animals tend to view self as the central priority. Second, humans and higher vertebrates show concern for the well-being of their offspring. Third, individuals show concern for other kin, and perhaps for other members of a special group or clan. They show less concern for those outside this group. This hierarchical arrangement of priorities is consistent with the genetic fitness of the organism. On the other hand, the Christian call to moral behavior seeks to rearrange this hierarchy of priority, placing God at the center and the needs of self subordinate to the needs of others. From a biological perspective this new arrangement would seem to create a fitness disadvantage, yet it is fairly common and seen as necessary among followers of the Christian faith.

One may argue that religiously motivated moral behavior is not different from any moral behavior witnessed among humans, whether religious or not, and is tied to commitments of kinship relatedness or agreements of reciprocity. The words of Jesus recorded in the Bible, however, seem to address these very points. He makes it very clear that commitment to the principles of Christianity must take priority over the natural focus on related kin. The motivation to religious moral behavior must come from a source other than what would be considered natural. Jesus warned, "He who loves father or mother more than Me is not worthy of Me; and he who loves son or daughter more than Me is not worthy of Me. And he who does not take up his cross and follow after Me is not worthy of Me. He who has found his life shall lose it, and he who has lost his life for My sake shall find it" (Matthew 10:37-39*). These certainly do not seem like actions to increase either genetic fitness. Jesus prescribes a moral behavior that transcends kinship relatedness. Jesus also suggests that unselfish behavior only toward one's offspring is not of itself redemptive, when he states, "If you then, being evil, know how to give good gifts to your children . . ." (Luke 11:13 and Matthew 7:11). He also speaks strongly against good deeds that are intended only to enhance reputation building (an important aspect of sociobiological explanations for moral behavior based on reciprocal benefit). In the Sermon on the Mount, Jesus spends much time criticizing those he sees as hypocrites, who do their good deeds in ways that ensure that they will be seen by others (Matthew 6:1-8). Christian moral behavior requires unselfish actions to others beyond kinspeople and potential reciprocators. The capacity for this behavior must come from a source outside the animal brain.

Conclusion

Thus, if unbridled selfishness results in sin, and our natural tendency is to selfishly increase our own genetic fitness, what motivates us to behave unselfishly and avoid sinful behavior? Although the capacity exists in the human brain to override the natural tendencies of behavior from the limbic and reptilian portions of the brain, the question remains: why would an individual ever want to do this? It seems that in almost all cases the best genetic interest of the individual is served through behavior with an ultimate selfish motivation. The limbic system is arranged to reward those behaviors that enhance genetic fitness, and true unselfish behavior should not produce a biological advantage. No clear biological explanation exists for:

1. a motivation to avoid limbic system rewards of behavior without ultimate selfish purpose.

2. the existence of true unselfish religious altruism observed in many people of faith, in spite of the obvious reduction in genetic fitness which should result from this type of behavior.

3. the sense of guilt and need of redemption or divine approval felt among many humans.

4. the energy spent by many in the relentless pursuit of a supernatural God.

I feel that the only answer to this question is that the desire to rise above selfish animal behavior must come from a "spiritual side" of humankind. All humans must ask, "Is it possible that a source of motivation exists for behavior that is outside the human mind?" Although the lack of a biological explanation should not of itself demand a supernatural explanation, at this point a better explanation for these phenomena is difficult to imagine.

References

Alexander, RD.
   1987 *The Biology of Moral Systems*. New York: Aldine De Gruyter.

Guyton, A.C.
   1987 *Basic Neuroscience: Anatomy and Physiology*. Philadelphia, PA: W.B. Saunders Co.

Hamilton, W.D.
   1964 The Evolution of Social Behavior. *Theoretical Biology*. Vol. 7. Pp. 1-52.

Holy Bible
New American Standard Version.

MacLean, P.D.
1990   *The Triune Brain in Evolution: Role of Paleocerebral Functions.* New York: Plenum Press.

Myers, D.G.
1992 (November 23)   Who's Happy? Who's Not? *Christianity Today.* Pp. 23-26.

Nolte, J.
1988   *The Human Brain: An Introduction to its Functional Anatomy.* St. Louis, MO: The C.V. Mosby Co.

Torrey, T.W. and A. Feduccia
1979   *Morphogenesis of the Vertebrates.* New York: John Wiley and Sons Pub.

Trivers, R.
1985   The Evolution of Cooperation. In *Social Evolution.* Melano Park, CA: The Benjamin/Cummings Pub. Co. Pp. 361-394.

Wilson, E.O.
1975   *Sociobiology: The New Synthesis.* Cambridge, MA: Harvard University Press.

Chapter 8 Implications of The Human Genome Project for Views of Morality

V. Elving Anderson
and
Bruce Reichenbach

We are now well into the Human Genome Project, a massive 15-year program designed to map and sequence human genes. Emphasis in the first years was placed on designing faster and more efficient methods for mapping and sequencing than have already been used to locate over 6,000 genes on specific chromosomes. As the main goals of the project are reached, research efforts will shift to the even more complex task of determining the functions of the gene products and the ways by which the genes are regulated (turned on and off).

The decade of the 1990s has also been designated by the U.S. Congress as the Decade of the Brain. The human brain, which is perhaps the most complex structure in the universe, has until recently been the most unknown. Researchers generally lacked the sophisticated instrumentation and computer-assisted conceptual models to conduct research on the scale needed to understand its functions. Now the brain is the subject of intense and sophisticated investigation, and its structures and processes are gradually revealing their secrets.

We can expect these broad-scale research efforts, individually and where they significantly intersect, to provide much new information and to generate significant issues well into the next century. Our concerns in what follows, however, are limited to the moral implications that will arise from this research. In particular, we will focus on the potential impact that genetic research will have on issues having to do with human morality and ethics (Reichenbach and Anderson 1995). In this task we extend the discussions by Cole-Turner (1994) and Anderson (1994).

166

Genes

The goals of the Human Genome Project are to map all human genes and eventually to sequence all the human DNA. Each human cell with a nucleus contains 60,000 to 70,000 genes (Fields et al. 1994) that guide development from conception to adulthood and that are passed on to our children. These genes are made of DNA, a slender twisted thread composed of four different nucleotides (bases) arranged in pairs. One full set of human DNA (the "genome") contains about three billion pairs of bases strung end to end.

To comprehend the sheer magnitude of the project, imagine trying to decode and print 24 volumes of an encyclopedia (for the X and Y chromosomes and 22 other pairs). At the outset all that we know is that the books use only four letters (A, C, G, and T), representing the four kinds of bases, and are printed without any punctuation or spaces. Figuring out the order of the letters on one page would be equivalent to sequencing a very short segment of the DNA molecule. A certain sequence of this DNA provides the information for making a specific protein (such as an enzyme). If we can find out which volume and which page contains this DNA sequence, we would have mapped the gene for that enzyme.

When genes are mapped and sequenced, attention will turn to efforts to understand the message conveyed by the genes. This involves determining how the genes express themselves, so as to assemble amino acids into various kinds of proteins which, in turn, affect the development of cells and of the entire body.

In the light of other recent research our concept of genes has shifted from seeing them as fixed units having clearly predictable effects to a more dynamic view. For example, the changes in type of hemoglobin from embryo to fetus to adult is now understood to result from developmental programming that "reads" first one gene and then others in a series along a specific chromosome. Master genes control sets of other genes to lay out the segmental pattern of the early embryo from head to tail. The expression of some genes depends on whether the gene was transmitted from the mother or father (genomic imprinting). A growing number of disorders (such as Huntington disease and fragile X syndrome) result from an increase in the number of three-base sequences (trinucleotide repeat expansion), which represent a new type of mutation. Furthermore, the expression of genes within specific cells can be modified or tuned by protein signals which are transmitted within and among cells (signal transduction).

In summary, genes are now known to be less stable and more subject to regulatory factors than had been realized earlier. Thus the pathways from genes to expressed traits are more complex and less predictable than has been assumed in the past. The history of an organism becomes important, with each step dependent on prior developmental events that continually alter the internal environment. The effect of individual genes must be described in terms of probabilities rather than rigorously determined outcomes. "In ontogenesis, genetic and nongenetic factors interact in producing successive stages, each of which is the prerequisite, and determines the conditions, for the next one to follow. In this interplay, genes are a necessary, but not sufficient, component. The structures already present, gradients, threshold values, positional relationships, and conditions of the internal milieu, are equally essential" (Wolf 1995:127).

Genes and the brain

Meanwhile, the "Decade of the Brain" has focused attention on the most complex and highly organized organ of the body. Until recently the brain has seemed to be a "black box" that is not accessible to study except upon autopsy. Recent advances in technology, however, have produced new, non-invasive methods for brain imaging which yield sharply defined views of brain *structure*. These methods can be modified to analyze normal brain *functioning* (to determine brain centers for complex tasks such as hearing, speaking, and writing) as well as pathology.

At the biochemical level it has become clear that the pathway between genes and behavior is not in one direction only. Genes may indeed influence certain behaviors, but behaviors may also affect how genes are expressed. Seizures, for example, can induce the selective expression of "immediate early" genes, which in turn may have a critical role in long-term synaptic plasticity. Also, hormones released during stress can change the relative expression of a number of genes.

Another dramatic fact is that about half of our genes are expressed exclusively or mainly in the brain. The reasons why such a large portion of the genome is devoted to the brain are still a matter of conjecture. Furthermore, even though all cells in the brain presumably have the same genetic information, a given gene may be expressed only in a specific brain area or a specific cell type, and then only within a limited time during development. If brain functioning were controlled by a computer, a part of the program would be devoted to organizing and scheduling the rest of the data base.

The development of the brain is not fully pre-programmed, however. The early steps involve genes that lay out the basic segmentation of the early brain. In the migration phase the neurons follow cues, both structural and biochemical, which are partly under genetic control. Some areas generate too many neurons and the extra ones are removed by genetically programmed cell death. The final differentiation of neurons into subtypes relies mainly on signals from the immediate environment surrounding the neurons.

Cell to cell communication is made possible by chemical messengers (neurotransmitters) that interact with channels and receptors on the surface of neurons. Some of the receptors contain channels which open or close to control the flow of specific ions (calcium, sodium, potassium or chloride), while others trigger secondary biochemical changes within the cell. Taken together, the neurotransmitters, receptors and channels control excitation and inhibition of neuronal activity, and thus provide a fine-tuning control that has been likened to the balancing effect of accelerator and brake in a car. Receptors also are primary targets for drugs used in the treatment of various disorders. Furthermore, some receptors are constructed from subunits which are produced by different genes. The various combinations of subunits permit an amazing receptor diversity. This mix can be altered in response to changes in the local cellular environment, thus providing a major mechanism for brain plasticity.

The rapidly growing inventory of "brain genes" with identified functions permits direct tests of hypotheses concerning brain function. Once a specific gene for an ion channel has been identified, the messenger RNA for that gene can be introduced into experimental cells. The functioning of the ion channel now can be tested in its new setting, and the response to a variety of drugs can be checked. Furthermore, site-directed mutagenesis makes it possible to change a small section of a channel gene in order to determine which parts are critical for a given function.

By the end of the 1990s we should be able to recognize many genes that are active in the brain, identify their chromosomal locations, and analyze the structure and function of their protein products. But more research questions remain. How are the genes regulated (turned on and off)? How does each gene affect behavior?

Genes and behavior

Our concern is not with the brain *per se* but with the effect of genes on the behaviors that reflect the brain's activity. At the outset it must be noted that heredity is not to be equated with inevitability. To be sure, there are rare circumstances in which a gene has such a strong effect that it may appear to determine one's destiny. The same may be said for environmental events that can swamp genetic potential. On the whole, however, few behaviors are completely without genetic influence, and few behaviors are completely without environmental influence.

The pathways from genes to behavior are necessarily indirect, since they involve complex physiological systems and are affected by experience throughout development. The analysis may be relatively simple in some genetic syndromes in which significant alterations in a single biochemical process account for the main behavioral consequences. Most behaviors, on the other hand, appear to involve many genes, each with a small effect (a multifactorial system). In the latter situation mathematical models can be used to partition the observed variability, or phenotypic variance (V_P), into its components: genetic (V_G), shared environment that is common to relatives reared together (V_{SE}), and nonshared environment (V_{NE}). The relationship among these components is expressed in the following formula:

$$V_P = V_G + V_{SE} + V_{NE}$$

The proportion of phenotypic variance which is due to genetic factors (the heritability) *is neither constant nor immutable*, but only describes the situation in a population sample at a given time. The heritability may be quite different in different circumstances at a different time. Both of these perspectives may be informative (Turkheimer and Gottesman 1991:19): "In some contexts, it is perfectly reasonable to ask how individuals in their natural environment come to vary as they do; in others, it is reasonable to ask how they might vary if the environment were to be altered radically."

In general, it is easier to specify the genetic contribution since the transmission of genes from parents to offspring follows predictable rules. It is much more difficult to assess environments that are relevant for a kind of behavior. As a result, the environmental contribution to the variation in behavior may include factors that would be better described as experience or development.

As a matter of fact, development is as important for human behavior as for the human brain, since later stages are conditioned by prior experience. Furthermore, there may be critical time windows during which specific genetic and environmental factors may be particularly influential. These considerations may help to explain the common observation that "individuals get stuck in diverging ruts as they age." (Turkheimer and Gottesman 1991:20)

Sociobiology and morality

We have briefly how genes, along with environment, significantly influence behavior. Now we must move on to the role genes play in explaining *moral* behavior.

The claim that genes do affect moral behavior is not novel. Its most notable advocate is E. O. Wilson (1975), who gave the first chapter of his book *Sociobiology: The New Synthesis* the provocative title: "The Morality of the Gene." His thesis was that we cannot understand morality and ethics until we understand the brain that is involved in these tasks. Furthermore, we will not know the brain until we know the genes that specify the development and function of that brain. Only then can we envision a scientifically correct and appropriate ethical system.

Wilson's presentation was considerably more sophisticated than earlier views of social Darwinism that justified ruthless competition (and even warfare) as an inevitable and desirable form of natural selection. He reviewed the studies of social behavior in a number of animal species and concluded reasonably that genetic factors must have contributed to the possibility of such behavior. (The extrapolation to human behavior, however, was not as carefully documented and analyzed in that initial volume.) The sociobiology paradigm, as developed by Wilson and others, involves four major themes:

1) Biology is the key to human nature, and social scientists cannot afford to ignore its principles.

2) Understanding biological and cultural evolution is the central issue of sociobiology.

3) Natural selection is the major mechanism for maintaining behavioral variation.

4) Altruism is one of the main theoretical problems.

Lumsden (1989:90) summarized the impact of this approach as follows:

"Moreover, contemporary research in human sociobiology proposes a specific mechanism to explain both the origins of human nature and its unique properties. This is the causal circuit of interactions that runs from our genome to innate rules of brain development and culturally mediated learning, through individual decision-making to social action and social form. As sociobiology's grip on the connections among genes, mind, and culture becomes firmer, the science-religion dialogue will acquire an improved method to predict and explain the key attributes of human nature."

The widespread interest in sociobiology (now called evolutionary psychology by many in the field; Barkow et al. 1992) cannot be ascribed only to these bold claims. The conceptual approach established a connection between human and animal studies of social behavior in a manner parallel to that already seen in psychology for individual behavior. In turn, this juxtaposition generated many new hypotheses that are being tested at the experimental and theoretical (mathematical) levels. Research workers were enlisted from fields that earlier may have been thought unrelated, and their combined efforts represent a significant "paradigm shift."

Theories and research in sociobiology have depended heavily upon evolution, with emphasis on the role of natural selection. Mutations (changes in DNA) are essentially random, but natural selection can bring about directional change, either positive (selecting for a phenotypic trait) or negative (against a trait). The current status in a natural population is taken to represent a balance between the forces of mutation and selection acting over many prior generations. Using this assumption, changes in gene frequencies can be analyzed or predicted through the use of formulas and equations. Alterations in medical practice (an aspect of culture) can affect gene frequencies, thus illustrating the interactions between cultural and genetic evolution. These matters are treated more fully in other chapters of this book.

Thus we are connected, both to the past and to the future, by genes and by culture, and consequently must consider both cultural and genetic transmission, and both cultural and genetic evolution. Furthermore, the brain is "the yoke that binds genes and cultures" (Burhoe 1981:157). This linkage can be used to analyze the development of individuals and societies, both on the evolutionary time scale and at the present time.

Evolutionary explanations are not ultimate or final, however, but they can generate hypotheses which then must be tested in current populations. It is our view that the effect of genes upon behavior, including moral behavior, cannot be understood without considering the development and function of the brain and the role of trait-relevant environmental factors (both internal and external). We are now entering a period in which some of the related hypotheses of psychology, sociology, and sociobiology might be tested by the newer methods of genetics and neuroscience. This process, however, will require new levels of interdisciplinary collaboration.

Genes and moral behavior

In the remainder of this paper we will consider whether genes affect moral behavior and, if they do, how this causal connection can be properly understood and ethically cultivated for human benefit. To explore these issues we should attend *first* to the question, What abilities and traits does moral behavior presuppose? That is, in order to determine what effect genes might have on moral behavior, it would be helpful to identify beforehand at least some of the abilities and traits that may be thought to underlie moral behavior. The task is not easy, for moral behavior clearly involves an integrated nexus of human abilities, both cognitive and volitional, as well as traits of personality or temperament. Not only is it unlikely that we can delineate all of these abilities and traits, but any listing necessarily will be confronted by the ambiguities facing any attempt at categorization. Yet some progress is essential if one is to use current methods of analysis to ascertain genetic influence, since one cannot start with the genes themselves, but must commence by measuring their phenotypic effects.

Among the cognitive abilities is the ability to be aware of alternatives, both in terms of the desired outcomes and in the possible means to realize them. Without the comprehension that there are alternatives or what they might be, *oughts*, which rely on the imperative to do one thing rather than another, have no significance. The moral agent likewise must possess the ability to understand and predict outcomes, for the inability to realize that actions have particular consequences or to anticipate those consequences impairs the rationality of the decision-making process that is required by moral considerations. Further, the person must be able to determine what information is relevant to the decision-making process, for moral judgments invoke both moral principles or rules and empirical, factual claims about the specific situations faced. Ethical principles alone cannot form moral judgments. Finally, persons must also be able to understand and store moral rules so that they can be recalled at appropriate times, and to engage in moral reasoning (e.g., be able to see how moral rules or principles apply to cases and be able to justify the decisions and actions taken).[1]

Volitional abilities also are diverse, including the ability to make decisions, to withstand pressures from various sources so as to make one's own decisions, to defer immediate gratification for the attainment of a higher or greater good, and to implement the decisions taken. A person, for example, might come to a moral decision but be unable to act on it, due to some type of volitional paralysis.

In addition to these cognitive abilities, personality traits seem to be involved in some aspects of moral behavior. Bouchard (1994), for example, reviewed the evidence that genetic factors contribute to variation in the five main dimensions of personality, listed here with some of the trait subscales of interest for the present discussion in parentheses – extraversion, neuroticism (emotional stability), conscientiousness (conformity and dependability), agreeableness, and openness. In a similar manner Eaves et al. (1989) analyzed the dimensions and traits assessed by the Eysenck test – psychoticism (aggressive, impulsive, antisocial), extraversion (assertive, sensation-seeking), neuroticism (irrational, moody), and a "Lie" scale (social desirability, cheating, greediness).

Even beyond the understanding that these represent only a partial list, it is obvious that any attempt to apply experimental procedures and genetic analysis to moral behavior will be difficult at best. One hope is that, since these abilities and traits may function conjointly in moral decision making, researchers might be able to determine the interaction of sets of factors.

This introduces the *second* consideration: the need to develop operational methods for assessing individual variability in the possession of each of these abilities and traits. Several questions arise. Can the abilities and traits be quantified? What tests will distinguish among related attributes? Do they interact with each other? Are the several abilities and traits causally connected, or are they merely correlated in a statistical manner?

Initially, consideration can be given to the factors that have been identified in other studies of human behavior. A wide array of cognitive tests are available, some of

---

[1] Classically, morality involved certain dispositional dimensions, most notably captured in the notion of virtue. Virtue is the quality of character that disposes the person to act for the good. The virtues themselves are not so much abilities as the state of character from which actions flow.

the pencil-and-paper type, but others that involve instrumentation. Such measures can distinguish between verbal and performance skills, or between short- and long-term memory. Tests of attention (or vigilance) have been shown to be sensitive to biochemical changes such as those seen in some genetic disorders. Personality tests commonly are composed of self-report items which contribute differentially to the trait subscales. A similar format has been used to develop inventories to evaluate the stability, responsibility, and dependability of potential employees.

The main issue will be to select or devise measures that appear to have some relevance to the abilities and traits that have been postulated to be involved in moral capacity. It may be possible to estimate the contribution of such factors to the overall level of moral reasoning ability, if in fact the latter could be measured. We could not readily determine, however, if any abilities or traits are unique to moral reasoning and thus not shared with other behaviors. The design of a measurement protocol will require thoughtful multidisciplinary collaboration and appears to be a major problem in this type of research program.

Thirdly, to what extent is it possible to trace these abilities back to their genetic roots? To test the claim that our genes affect the abilities that lie behind moral action, one has to design appropriate studies. A first step is to analyze family or twin data to estimate heritability and test for evidence of specific inheritance patterns. Then, in order to gain a more detailed picture of the behaviors, one can use methods that have been developed for quantitative genetic analysis of specific cognitive abilities (Plomin et al. 1994).

a) *Developmental genetic analysis* examines the changes in genetic effects over the lifetime of the individuals. In the case of cognitive abilities, for example, genetic factors become more important with increasing age.

b) A second strategy, *multivariate genetic analysis* goes beyond individual traits to assess the genetic contribution to the covariance among traits. This examines the possibility that abilities may overlap. Genes associated with one trait may affect others, both in beneficial characteristics as well as psychiatric disorders.

c) A third approach, *extremes analysis*, could compare the behavior of individuals who display nexuses of ability so radically different that their moral decision-making and behavior present obvious divergences between the "normal" and the seriously impaired. Even though some behavioral variations appear to form a continuous distribution, the extreme cases may result from different causes.

All of these three methods could be used to study specific families like the one from the Netherlands, described below. The syndrome involves *extreme* behavioral changes which result from a genetic mutation, and thus presents a special case of the third approach. It is still not clear how the genetic deficiency leads to the behavioral manifestations, nor has the variability in signs among the affected males been explained; yet these questions could be explored by a form of *developmental* analysis. A modified *multivariate* analysis of behavioral data would disentangle the relationship between the violence and the aggressivity that has been observed in those expressing the syndrome.

Finally, supposing that we can identify the abilities, devise methods for assessing individual variation in the abilities, and trace the genetic contribution, is it meaningful to think about genetic methods that could be used to modify the effects of, or directly alter, the genes responsible for these abilities? It is true that genetic technologies are proving very effective in *understanding* the pathogenesis of diseases (such as cancer), in *diagnosing* the subtypes of conditions (such as muscular dystrophy), and in developing more effective means of *therapy* using gene products (such as human insulin). These advantages, however, require considerable prior knowledge of the pathogenetic mechanisms involved.

The criteria for the use of *gene insertion therapy* are even more stringent. (1) This treatment must be *necessary*, in the sense that other types are not available or not effective. As a result, gene-insertion therapy is usually reserved for serious, often life-threatening, conditions. (2) There must be evidence that the treatment is *effective*, first in animal studies if possible, and then in pilot tests in humans. (3) The therapy must be *safe*. There is concern, for example, that the retroviruses often used as carriers for the inserted gene might undergo genetic recombination and produce harmful variants. As of this writing, these three criteria have been met only for a few patients suffering from a single rare disorder, an enzyme deficiency which causes severe immunodeficiency.

At the present state of research, phenomena such as alcoholism and schizophrenia are simple compared with moral behavior. It is extremely unlikely that one or a few genes could be isolated as being responsible for any of the abilities tentatively identified above, let alone when these abilities work in concert. Thus it appears that genetic intervention will be applicable mainly for severe disturbances which can be diagnosed clearly, and would not be appropriate for variations within the normal range of moral capacity.

Three examples

How might the considerations noted in the previous section be brought to bear on the issues related to moral behavior? We will examine three areas, with increasing degrees of complexity.

Genetics and Impulsive Aggression. In 1993 a large family was identified in the Netherlands that had 14 males affected with a syndrome manifested as aggressive behavior, often in response to anger, fear, or frustration. The social manifestations included aggression toward family members and strangers, arson, attempted rape and murder, and exhibitionism. The "aggressive behavior tended to cluster in periods of 1-3 days, during which the affected male would sleep very little and would experience frequent night terrors." (Brunner et al. 1993a). All affected persons were related through unaffected females, and gene mapping studies provided additional clear evidence of an X-linked recessive pattern of inheritance.

Further studies (Brunner et al. 1993b) showed a complete and selective deficiency of the activity of monoamine oxidase A (MAOA), an enzyme that metabolizes serotonin, dopamine, and noradrenaline. DNA analysis demonstrated a point mutation in the MAOA gene itself, which introduced a stop codon and hence a truncated gene product. These findings provide a likely explanation for the low levels of 5-HIAA that were found in these affected males. (Low levels of 5-HIAA have been observed in other cases of impulsive, rather than premeditated, aggression and violence.) Appropriate therapy to control the enzyme deficiency has not yet been tested in this family, and other families with the same enzyme defect have not yet been identified.

What is important to consider here are the consequences of the conclusion that a biochemical, and ultimately a genetic, mechanism may contribute significantly to the impulsive, aggressive behavior in this multigenerational family. The study clearly indicates that a borderline to mild mental retardation and also a tendency toward aggressive behavior can be inherited, though confirmation must be sought in other families. Further testing in this family would be required, however, to determine if the retardation, aggressiveness, and impulsivity provide a sufficient explanation for the wide range of behaviors or if other abilities and traits are involved as well.

What is of particular interest are the implications that this genetic etiology has for the study, treatment, and understanding of the moral accountability of the family members. Simply raising the possibility of a genetic basis for violent behavior has precipitated passionate discussion in the past, notably in the study of XYY males that was initiated in the late 1960's. The resulting controversy ultimately did little to slow the pace of research on whether there are genetic links behind violent behavior, although it has altered the way in which the studies are conducted.

Diverse ethical considerations arise from such studies. For one thing, attention must be given to the *conduct of the studies* themselves. It is possible that such studies might negatively affect those being studied. What does it do to persons to have researchers tell them that they have a certain risk of engaging in aggressive or violent behavior, or to tell parents that their child has a certain risk of growing up to be aggressive or impulsively violent? Does this stigmatize the persons studied, categorizing them as deviant in the eyes of those privy to the study and its results? Can the studies clearly differentiate between the genetic factors and the social-cultural influences that also affect the development of violent behaviors?

Apart from the studies themselves, a second set of concerns involve potential *treatment* of individuals identified as having some genetic disorder that predisposes toward impulsive aggression. How serious must the behavior be before treatment is justified? Is a tendency enough to warrant therapy, or must the symptoms have already appeared? To treat for tendencies toward behavior suggests that the environmental and volitional factors can be ignored, or at least minimized, in explaining the behavior. Yet if moral behavior is biopsychosocial in nature, such oversimplification is unwarranted.

In the future might this and similar conditions be treated with some form of gene therapy? Pharmacological treatment provides a fairly effective way to help some persons control their aggressive behavior, but the effects of drugs wear off during the day and can have serious side effects. Therapy directed at the underlying genetic problem would hold out the promise of greater effectiveness and fewer side effects. Gene insertion therapy, however, would tend to be reserved for use when other methods are ineffective and would have to meet the strict criteria outlined above.

The third aspect of the Netherlands case involves assessing the *moral account-ability* of those who manifest genetically-conditioned aggression. Only one of the affected males was convicted for a criminal offense (the rape of his sister). It is possible that some actions of the others would have been adjudged criminal if the familial nature of the problem had not been recognized. To what extent can their behavior be morally excused? One way to understand the issue is to place moral responsibility on a scale of freedom. At one end lies pure freedom, without any causal determinants or influences; at the other lies complete causal determination. The first extreme is probably not found in humans; biological (including genetic) and environmental factors always influence the basis from which we operate in decision making. The opposite extreme (determinism) would exist when there is behavior but no agency. The person moves or behaves in some way, but has not performed an action. In such cases there can be no moral accountability.

Most behaviors do not fall close at either extreme; the above case, however, indi-cates that some impulsive, aggressive behavior can lie closer to the deterministic end. In such cases, moral responsibility for the action would be lessened. The point here is that certain persons might have genetically-impaired cognitive or vo-litional abilities. Since these abilities are involved in moral behavior, genetically-related deficiencies reduce their ability to act morally, and hence reduce their moral responsibility for their actions.

An interesting implication is that, should genetic therapy be used successfully to alleviate the drive to perform impulsive aggressive acts, it would mean that moral responsibility could be restored (or created) through genetic treatment. This should not be surprising, if we grant that genetic causes can reduce moral respon-sibility for actions. But it does raise the provocative question whether there might be some cases where the individual might not want the therapy, that is, might not want increased moral responsibility. In such cases what actions toward these pa-tients are legitimate for researchers or physicians? The issue of paternalism may become significant.

Genetics and Criminality. This discussion leads naturally to the controversial is-sue of the relationship between genes and criminal behavior in general. In August 1992 a controversy arose about a conference that had been planned on the theme "Genetic Factors in Crime: Findings, Uses, and Implications" (Palca 1992). The list of invited speakers, reflecting a wide range of expertise and points of view, seemed to promise a reasonably balanced discussion. The advertising brochure, however, went well beyond the current state of knowledge: "Genetic research holds out the prospect of identifying individuals who may be predisposed to certain kinds of criminal conduct, of isolating environmental features which trigger those predispositions, and of treating some predispositions with drugs and unintrusive therapies."

The term "criminality" introduces a new factor into the discussion. Whereas the Netherlands family can be described in terms of a range of behavioral manifestations, in the case of criminality the legal/social factors which help to ascertain an action as a crime enter the discussion. This produces a host of new considerations.

First, it requires a careful analysis of what is meant by a "crime," and correspondingly by "criminal behavior." What is considered criminal behavior in one jurisdiction might not be the case in another. In addition, criminal behavior encompasses a wide scope, from misdemeanors like speeding and writing graffiti on walls to violence directed against property and persons. Hence, to lump all these together in a search for genetic factors for criminal tendencies is far too simplistic an endeavor.

Second, ascertaining those with a "criminal tendency" for genetic studies is fraught with danger. Sociocultural factors and volition play significant roles in affecting behavior, so that it is difficult to determine what – the genetic, the sociocultural, or the volitional – is the primary cause. For another, predictors of future behavior are notably inaccurate since they produce a sizable proportion of "false positives" – individuals who meet the criteria but do not later manifest the predicted behaviors.

Despite this, some who study violent behavior believe that we are coming closer to the time when we can predict (with reasonable accuracy) such antisocial behavior.

> "As sociologists reap the benefits of rigorous long-term studies and neuroscientists tug at the tangled web of relations between behavior and brain chemistry, many are optimistic that science will identify markers of maleficence. 'This research might not pay off for 10 years, but in 10 years it might revolutionize our criminal justice system,' asserts Roger D. Masters, a political scientist at Dartmouth College. 'With the expected advances, we're going to be able to diagnose many people who are biologically brain-prone to violence,' claims Stuart C. Yudofsky, chair of the psychiatry department at Baylor College of Medicine" (Gibbs 1995:101).

Such optimism appears unwarranted. It overlooks not only the complexity of behavior, but also the fact that the biological causes themselves are rooted in the brain, which (as we noted above) is probably the most complex thing in the universe.

Altruism. Manifestations of aggressive behavior (as described above) are counterexamples to the altruism emphasized by most ethical systems. (It is of interest that evidence for a genetic influence on both altruism and aggressiveness was obtained in a large-scale twin study by Rushton et al. 1986.) Altruism seeks the good for the others concerned, even at the expense of the agent. "Altruism"[2] has also been a major issue for sociobiology because of the intriguing theoretical problems involved. The major difficulty is that, in statistical models of natural selection, widespread "altruism" cannot endure. Organisms are constrained by epigenetic rules, innate predispositions that are not only shaped by evolutionary development, but which "generally serve as guides to action, and help us to organize our thoughts and desires, and to make sense of the information from without" (Ruse 1987:423). The predispositions that evolutionary theory seeks to interpret are egoistic in character. Natural selection works for the survival of individuals, who "seek" to pass their genes on to future generations. Selfishness, not altruism, works for preservation. Sacrificing oneself does not lead to the continuance of one's genes. As Michael Ruse (1987:424) puts it, "'Nice guys finish last' and for that reason evolution has seen to it that we are not nice."

Ruse attempts to resolve the problem by suggesting that it is the epigenetic "rules which make us 'altruistic.'" They can do this because, as innate dispositions, they make "us think that we *ought* to help each other!" That is, biology predisposes us to be altruistic, and it does this by "imbuing us with thoughts of right and wrong, good and bad." We learn that acting altruistically is more effective than acting egoistically. The altruism here is more than "altruism," it is moral altruism, the intentional seeking of the good of others. Thus the *ought* derives biologically from the *is* of the predisposition. Or, as Hefner (1991:127) expressed it, "Although we may not derive our *oughts* from our experience of the *is*, the *ought* would have no real substance if it were not rooted in the *is*."

---

[2] We adopt here a convention suggested by Michael Ruse (1987:440), who recognizes that "altruism" might be used in various ways. Without quotes, the term refers to the distinctively moral use of the term, where the agent intentionally seeks the good of other concerned. When used in quotes, the term is used in an amoral, metaphorical sense to indicate the biological phenomenon of acting for another's good, without necessarily realizing that one is, or ought to be, doing so.

Biology becomes involved in views of the moral by showing us that being altruistic is actually in our interest. That is, altruism is preserved because it works, not only in general, but for individuals as well. Whereas "altruistic" animals like bees and ants can sacrifice large numbers and survive, humans cannot afford this luxury. Hence, the disposition is affirmed in our experience when we realize that our greater good is bound up with the good of the whole.

In effect, contrary to those who contend that natural selection can endow us with a kind of "altruism" that acts contrary to our own interests, Ruse (1987:424) bases altruism on psychological egoism which in humans is transformed into ethical altruism. "Morality can now be viewed as a natural outgrowth of the evolutionary process." The result is that morality is not so much justified as explained. It just is the case that nature dictates that we ought to act altruistically.

But if we are predisposed to "altruism," how does one account for nonaltruistic acts? Is it that psychological egoism can give rise to either ethical egoism or ethical altruism? But then what is called for in any given situation? Why *ought* one be altruistic and not egoistic? Only the former is morally recommended, yet both might be predispositional, and it is unclear in any case that the former will get us farther than the latter. The problem is that Ruse denies any justification for morality. He only gives an explanation of it. Hence, if both ethical altruism and ethical egoism are based on the same biology of psychological egoism, one is not *morally* better than the other. But then in what sense *ought* one be altruistic rather than egoistic? If the basis is survival only, altruism loses all notion of *oughtness* as a moral concept. It is reduced to a matter of biological expediency.

Summary

In this brief treatment of such a broad topic it has not been possible to give the related issues the in-depth treatment that they deserve. Nevertheless, we have reached some tentative conclusions that may help to stimulate further consideration.

1) Evolutionary explanations of the biological basis for morality are incomplete and inadequate. However, they have generated some interesting hypotheses which now must be examined in terms of the present development of individuals and societies.

2) The methods of behavioral genetics, molecular genetics, and neurogenetics can begin to make important contributions to our understanding of moral capacity. Earlier, simplistic views of heredity vs. environment have been replaced by the realization of the biopsychosocial nature of human behavior. The recognition of environmental components is essential for analysis of the genetic contribution; likewise, recognition of possible genetic factors is needed for adequate determination of environmental risk factors for behavioral problems.

3) Any attempts to intervene in antisocial or immoral behaviors must be multidimensional in recognition of their biopsychosocial nature. The criteria for any treatment should include the removal of limitations and the restoration of the ability to make free choices.

4) A major limitation to progress is the present inability to identify the cognitive and volitional abilities and personality traits that form moral capacity. Studies of the dimensions of cognition and personality can provide the background for developing more appropriate assessment measures. Care must be taken, however, to guard against the use of such assessment to provide new labels for stigmatization.

5) The recognition that moral capacity may involve a set of abilities and traits may bring the need for a more nuanced view of moral responsibility. An intuitive feeling of degrees or kinds of responsibility may be reinforced.

6) Genetic research has been most effective in analyzing extreme deviations from "normal" functioning, and this is likely also to be true for moral capacity. The identification of other families of the type reported from the Netherlands would facilitate such studies.

7) This discussion has been limited to moral capacity. Enhancing moral capacity, however, does not assure improved moral behavior. Increasing freedom does not guarantee responsible behavior.

References

Anderson, V.E.
  1994 Genes, Behavior and Responsibility: Research Perspectives. In *The Genetic Frontier: Ethics, Law, and Policy*. Mark S. Frankel and Albert H. Teich, eds. 105-130. Washington: American Association for the Advancement of Science.

Barkow, J.J., L. Cosmides and J. Tooby
1992 *The Adapted Mind: Evolutionary Psychology and the Generation of Culture*. Oxford: Oxford University Press.

Bouchard, T.J., Jr.
1994 Genes, Environment, and Personality. *Science* 264: 1700-1701.

Brunner, H.G., M.R. Nelen, P. van Zandvoort, N.G.G.M. Abeling, A.H. van Gennip, E.C. Wolters, E.C., M.A. Kuiper, H.H. Ropers, and B.A. van Oost.
1993a X-linked Borderline Mental Retardation with Prominent Behavioral Disturbance: Phenotype, Genetic Localization, and Evidence for Disturbed Monoamine Metabolism. *American Journal of Human Genetics* 52: 1032-1039.

Brunner, H.G., M. Nelen, X.O. Breakefield, H.H.Ropers, and B.A. van Oost.
1993b Abnormal Behavior Associated with a Point Mutation in the Structural Gene for Monoamine Oxidase A. *Science* 262: 578-580.

Burhoe, R. W.
1981 *Toward a Scientific Theology*. Ottawa, Canada: Christian Journals Limited.

Cole-Turner, R.S.
1994 The Genetics of Moral Agency. In *The Genetic Frontier: Ethics, Law, and Policy*. Mark S. Frankel and Albert H. Teich, eds. 161-174. Washington: American Association for the Advancement of Science.

Eaves, L.J., H.J. Eysenck, and N.G. Martin
1989 *Genes, Culture and Personality: An Empirical Approach*. San Diego: Academic Press.

Fields, C., M.D. Adams, O. White, and J.C.Venter
1994 How many Genes in the Human Genome? *Nature Genetics* 7: 345-346.

Gibbs, W.W.
1995 Seeking the Criminal Element. *Scientific American*. March. Pp.100-107.

Hefner, P.
1991 Myth and Morality: The Love Command. *Zygon* 26: 115-136.

Lumsden, C. J.
1989 Sociobiology, God, and Understanding. *Zygon* 24:83-108.

Palca, J.
1992. NIH Wrestles with Furor over Conference. *Science* 257: 739.

Plomin, R., M.J. Owen, and P. McGuffin
1994 The Genetic Basis of Complex Human Behaviors. *Science* 264: 1733-1739.

Reichenbach, B.R. and V.E. Anderson. *On Behalf of God: A Christian Ethic for Biology*. Grand Rapids: William B. Eerdmans.

184

Ruse, M.
1987   Darwinism and Determinism. *Zygon* 22: 419-442.

Turkheimer, E. and I.I.Gottesman
1991   Individual Differences and the Canalization of Human Behavior. *Developmental Psychology* 27: 18-22.

Wilson, E.O.
1975   *Sociobiology: The New Synthesis*. Harvard University Press: Cambridge.

Wolf, U.
1995   The Genetic Contribution to the Phenotype. *Human Genetics* 95: 127-148.

Chapter 9   When Psychologists Speak of Good and Evil

Lucie R. Johnson

When psychologists and sociobiologists speak of good and evil, it is often reluctantly, and with the desire to tame these mystical terms into acceptable positivist categories such as gene preparedness or reinforcement history. In their reductionistic efforts, psychology and sociobiology face some predictable hurdles, such as how to account for the development and maintenance of altruism, a category of behavior that is personally useless, possibly harmful, and beneficial to someone else's genes. Much has been written about this, and it seems doubtful that the issue will be resolved any time soon.

Let us however suppose for a moment that it was satisfactorily demonstrated that altruistic behavior does exist, and that it can be reduced to a combination of DNA, rewards, punishments, contiguous stimuli, and species survival benefits. Have we then explained all of moral reality in terms of psychological and biological categories, or will transcendence, like the mythical hydra, rear its persistent head in a new place?

We could venture an answer to this question by looking at theorists of morality: the moral pondering and the sometimes incidental comments they make, the themes of moral inquiry they pursue in their work, the moral insights they achieve, and the directions of inquiry they persistently pursue, sometimes even against the advice of their contemporaries. These phenomenological observations would give us some sense of the intuitive moral landscape of the theorists, and we might become aware of this valley, or that mountain, which does not fit the mold cast by the logic of the theory. We might even find a neglected rift providing us with a new context for our understanding.

This paper is a journey through the moral universes of three people: Sigmund Freud, Edward O. Wilson, and Vladimir Lefebvre – two evolutionary theorists, and one builder of computer models of ethical behavior. What are their intuitive theories of ethics and morality? Are they in any way similar? Are there unsolved recurring themes? Besides altruism, are there other dimensions of moral behavior that might be difficult to explain within the bounds of psychological theory? Those are some of the questions we will pursue.

Sigmund Freud

Freud entered his quest following the medical route, having been passed over for a career at the university of Vienna. His quest stemmed at first from curiosity about hysteria, which at the time was considered to be an unexplainable medical condition. Progressively, however, Freud's pursuits shifted to an interest in the human condition in general, then to the understanding of culture, of civilization, and of larger phenomena, such as religion. However, as Freud's interests moved from the individual to the societal, they also moved from explanation to interpretation (Ricoeur 1970), and became increasingly concerned with ethical issues and morality.

Perhaps Freud's first question was: Why do proper and wealthy young women from wealthy Viennese families develop hysterical symptoms with obvious sexual undertones incompatible with their outward morality? Initially, Freud suggested that traumatic events might have disturbed the normally moral behavior of the patients. However, Freud's clinical work eventually led him to a very different, almost opposite question: how does an individual full of wild, unconscious, primitive instincts become a moral human being? Thus, the puzzle shifted from how to explain pathology to how to understand normality, from how to account for moral aberrations, to how to understand why all of us are not morally perverted. He moved from a homeostatic energetic model that explains symptoms through the inadequacy of various channels of tension release, to a hermeneutic model interested in deciphering behaviors, cultures and civilizations in terms of the moral forces that move them. The question shifted from a clinical puzzle to a general ethical one.

Some of Freud's later interests were of course also present in the beginning of his work, but his major ideological shift probably occurred in 1900, with the publication of *The Interpretation of Dreams*. Dreams, indeed, are definitely not pathological: everyone dreams three or four times a night. Of course, people with psychological disturbances also dream, and in searching for the key to their problems, Freud, looking for access to unconscious motives, started to analyze their dreams. He discovered that dreams were one place where the struggle between untamed instinct and moral behavior became more transparent. But Freud also dreamed, and he knew that his dreams were not very different from those of his patients, and he knew that he was also engaged in the moral struggle. Perhaps Freud's most exceptional contribution is the idea that dreams may be a place where moral dilemmas become unveiled. Freud's question had been: "How can the energy blocked in this traumatized individual be discharged appropriately?" Now he asked, "How, with all these wild motives and drives, do we manage to be human beings that are decent (and not all that neurotic)?" Thus, he switched from a medical model, to one whose impetus was moral.

Also at this time, Freud shifted from the strictly individual to the collective. Ricoeur points out that Freud proposed that dreams are the dreamer's private mythology while myths are the waking dreams of peoples. Therefore, Sophocles' Oedipus and Shakespeare's Hamlet are to be interpreted in the same ways as dreams. This opens the way for Darwinian interpretations of behavior, especially the theory of recapitulation, which is evident in Freud's later writings such as *Totem and Taboo* (1955[1913]). It also opens the way to consider the effects of moral forces on society.

By 1915, in a letter to J. J. Putnam, a New England physician, Freud admitted to a lack of understanding of social (in contrast to sexual) morality, a morality that he defines as justice, care and compassion even in the face of personal disadvantage (Sagan 1988:3-4). It is not surprising that people should be afraid: there are many natural causes for fear. Neither is it surprising that they should be vengeful and malicious: after all, they too have been hurt, and it is only natural that they should be motivated by their self interest. But that so many of us should be decent, honest, and kind -- that is a mystery.

After this, Freud continued to work at resolving this problem. Using intricate lines of reasoning, psychoanalysis attempted to resolve the mystery by tying altruism to sublimation mechanisms, decency to the workings of the superego, and strivings toward good, to the ego-ideal (Freud 1961a, 1964), thus making the development of moral good to be one of the tools in the service of a basic life force, sexual in nature.

It is noteworthy that, while Freud speaks a fair amount about "morality," he never analyzes (beyond his basic intuition), the content of "moral good." Freud, otherwise so analytical, does not offer much here because, for him, one's conscience is a form of immediate knowledge, in the manner of Kant's moral imperative. The German word for conscience is *Gewissen*, while the word for "know" is *Wissen*. Conscience thus, literally means: "what is known," and can be defined as the internal perception of a command (generally, a command to refrain oneself from acceding to an unconscious wish). The origin of this imperative, for Freud, lies in the emotional ambivalence resulting from the Oedipal conflict (Ricoeur 1970:203-204). Freud was not interested so much in the content of that imperative than in some of its dynamics.

For instance, one of the more puzzling characteristics of the superego (the agency that, in the Freudian model, is the carrier of the moral imperative), is the cruelty that it sometimes exerts upon the ego. Why is moral conscience at times so wrathful? Why can the superego overwhelm the ego with self hate, as in melancholia? Why does it happen that self-righteousness turns into violence? How can it be the case that the superego, an agency connected to the maintenance and propagation of life, becomes an agent of death? Why is it that the more a person tries to be "good," the more s/he becomes prone to compulsive evil? Why is there resistance to healing? The examination of the paradoxical relationship between good and evil led Freud to conclude that it was not possible to reduce all behavior to the workings of one basic life instinct, but that there appeared to be another principle as well, also imbued with some dynamism: the death instinct, or instinct toward destructiveness (Freud 1955, 1964). Like the sexual drive, the death instinct can be repressed and sublimated, and can thus invade the levels of personality organization, especially the superego.

Freud hypothesizes that the superego, permeated with sublimated death drives, can become a "pure culture of death" that serves destruction rather than life (Ricoeur 1970:301). Of course, all of this does seem somewhat vague. Unfortunately, the origin, nature, and modes of operation of the death instincts did not easily yield to Freud's analytical acumen, and have remained one of the more nebulous parts of his theory. Yet, while he did not understand them well, and often against the advice of his professional colleagues, Freud persisted in making them a very important part of his understanding. In *Civilization and its Discontents* (one of his later works), he writes: "The fateful question for the human species seems to me to be whether, and to what extent, their cultural development will succeed in mastering the disturbance of their communal life by the human instinct of aggression and self-destruction" (Freud 1961b:145).

Thus, starting with a self-evident moral imperative, and an interest in explaining the puzzle of non-self serving virtue, Freud first attempted to explain moral behavior in terms of general sexual life energy. In the process of doing so, he discovered the need for his explanatory scheme to assume the existence of an independent force oriented toward death and destruction. One could say that Freud's quest starts with the puzzle of virtue and ends with the mystery of evil.

While psychoanalysis asks questions of ontogenesis ("How does moral behavior arise?" or, "How does an individual's moral conscience become destructive?"), Freud frequently asks phylogenetic questions as well. He is interested in understanding not just the individual, but also, and perhaps even mostly, the process of the psychological and cultural evolution of the species. One could even say that Wilson's sociobiology, in its ambitious effort to bring all of human behavior into a tight evolutionary scheme, is a child of Freudian psychoanalysis. Had Freud and Wilson been contemporaries, they might have been friends, perhaps even colleagues.

Edward O. Wilson

When did Wilson become a psychologist? Perhaps sometime between 1975 and 1978, between the 26th chapter of *Sociobiology* and the writing of *On Human Nature*, a book that, in Wilson's words is "about how far the natural sciences can penetrate into human behavior before they become something new" (Wilson 1978). Wilson's work, however, has always been multidisciplinary. In his book, *Sociobiology: The New Synthesis*, while introducing the "new" research and conceptual tools of population biology, Wilson demonstrated interests very similar to ethologists who also study the biology of behavior, such as Konrad Lorenz and Niko Tinbergen (Bateson 1987). Wilson, thus, has well-established psychological credentials.

Wilson describes his starting point as " . . . the central theoretical problem of sociobiology: how can altruism, which by definition reduces personal fitness, possibly evolve by natural selection?" (Wilson 1975:3). This question is not very different from Freud's puzzlement with human justice and kindness in the face of personal

loss. Besides being similar in content, Freud and Wilson's morality are also contained within the realm of nature. Both of them argue for the lack of existence of a
transcendent reality as a moral referent, although Wilson makes that point more
clearly and decisively. We are not able, says Wilson, to transcend our own brains;
they are the product of evolution. We and our moral theories are thus captives of
the dynamics of our own species survival (Wilson 1975:563). There is no way to
get out of the "species" box.

Because of his "scientific" approach to ethics, Wilson does not see himself as an
ethical intuitionist. Nevertheless, this paper places him in that category because,
while Wilson's method is scientific, his questions are based on intuition. Why is it
for example, that altruism is held to be the central problem to be explained? Why
not reflectivity or esthetics, issues the theory also finds problematic? Or pacifism,
which it does not mention? Wilson's choice of the issue of altruism as central to
the moral discourse reflects the intuitive content of his own moral universe; and his
decision to use the scientific knowledge he has acquired to pursue ethical questions
seems to indicate that in his eyes the ability to be moral, and when being moral, to
also be kind, are important human distinctives. Wilson's intuitive value system
leads him to his interest in ethics and altruism. Studying insects, and re-labeling
intuition as "genetic preparedness" does not alter this ethical interest. An example
of his intuition can even be found in the prologue of *Biophilia*, a rather passionate
and thoughtful work on conservation ethics: "I will make the case," wrote Wilson,
"that to explore and affiliate with life is a deep and complicated process in mental
development. To an extent still undervalued in philosophy and religion, our existence depends on this propensity, our spirit is woven from it, hope rises on its cur-
rents" (Wilson 1984:1). It is good, says Wilson, to affiliate with life. It is difficult.
It must be done, because it must. For Wilson, also, there is a moral imperative. Is
it written in our genes? Perhaps . . . in our genes or in our soul. Who truly
knows? Is it not a matter of faith either way?

Also like Freud, Wilson became aware of deeply destructive human impulses, and
he too considers them to be somewhat of a mystery. "The audaciously destructive
tendencies of our species run deep and are poorly understood," writes Wilson.
"They are so difficult to probe and manage as to suggest an archaic biological origin." Like the characters of Greek tragedies, we could be brought to our ruin by a
fatal flaw (Wilson 1984:118). Thus, for Wilson also, the journey started with the

question of altruism, and somewhere along the way met an unexplained destructiveness. Unlike Freud, however, Wilson is still pondering the puzzle.

Vladimir Lefebvre

In going from Wilson to Lefebvre, one moves from organisms to computers, and from observation of living organisms to the mathematical modeling of possible intelligences. Lefebvre's work is rooted in social psychology, and especially in the approach followed by George Kelly in his analysis of human personality. Kelly developed an instrument, the Role Construct Repertory Test, in which subjects rate persons who fulfill important roles in their lives, on a set of bipolar constructs they have chosen. All judgments are all-or none (only the positive or negative pole can be chosen). Contrary to Kelly's expectations, the subjects did not choose positive and negative poles equally often; they made positive choices 62% of the time. This finding was replicated a number of times in Addams-Webber and Benjafield's research, in different cultural settings, and along a variety of dimensions. Always, the .62 value showed up (Lefebvre 1985, Rapoport 1987).

For mathematicians, .62 (.618 to be more precise) is a special number. It is the golden section ratio. If a line is cut at 61.8% of its total length, then the ratio between the total length of the line and its longer segment is equal to the ratio between the longer segment and the shorter one. The persistent re-appearance of the golden section value in evaluative judgments led Lefebvre to research the possibility of the existence of a mathematically precise inner computer that would predict these results. This led to his further experimentation in that area (Lefebvre 1985).

Lefebvre, however, was not just interested in any bipolar dimension; he was mostly interested in ethical choice: evaluation of people and situations along the dimensions of "good" and "bad." According to Lefebvre, when human beings function as evaluative mechanisms, they are actually making choices on a number of bipolar dimensions and they include in their evaluations a number of levels of reflection (analogous to what psychologists have often called "meta-perspectives," but they are not linguistic in nature. In this process, they also behave as if good = 1, and evil = 0. Calculations using Boolean algebra predict that, when people evaluate objects and persons, the positive pole is chosen, on the average, 62% of the time (Lefebvre 1985, 1987). A very exciting result. Imagine, being able to say: "the answer to ethical choice in human beings is .62." It is probably even true, under certain conditions.

But what conditions? Well, only if good = 1, and bad = 0; that is, if one's inner computer agrees with the moral philosophy of Augustine, who defines evil as the lack of good. While Augustine might be pleased with this unexpected affirmation, he probably would have preferred that the default option of this inner computer not be quite so unconscious. After all, it just may be possible that good = 1 and bad = -1, with a neutral point at 0, and then the predictions would not work, and the real world analogies that Lefebvre constructed would not hold. The discrepancy between Lefebvre's ethical intuitiveness and his mathematical sophistication is perhaps unfortunate, but, like both Freud and Wilson, he centered upon an idea of the good in his theorizing.

Morality as an independent category?

Within an evolutionary mindset, it is of course life that evolves in complexity, not death. Death is only the soil from which a better adapted life grows. Death is in the service of life, or at least in its background. At first, this was Freud's intuition as well.

For Freud, the libido is a life force directed toward creation and the propagation of life. In itself, the libido could be called good in the sense that its overall direction is positive. It is however amoral because it does not consider the needs of others or the demands of society. Morality, of which the primary agency is the superego, is a mechanism that has evolved to achieve a balance between individual and societal needs. This balance, while sometimes uncomfortable, optimizes the functioning and thus the survival of the individual. We may not be allowed to devour, but neither shall we be devoured.

This type of understanding of morality which would explain all altruism in terms of this balance is quite compatible with the sociobiological viewpoint. While one might not agree with this explanation of morality in terms of adaptation, it would however seem impossible to demonstrate that it is false. Since good is oriented toward life, it lends itself naturally to a theoretical interpretation that uses life-oriented instincts as basic constructs.

However, a rift became apparent in both Freud's and Wilson's moral landscapes: Freud's death drive, and the deep destructiveness which Wilson mentions in *Biophilia*. How does one explain this destructiveness that exceeds the aggression an individual must demonstrate to gain reproductive advantage? Although they were primarily oriented toward life forces, both Freud and Wilson encountered this antagonistic, destructive side, not just briefly, but repeatedly and significantly. Freud, as a result, and despite pressures to give up his insistence on the death drive, spent the latter part of his professional life grappling with it.

Would it not be paradoxical if evil, not good, turned out to be the irreducible phenomenon, and the greatest support for the existence of transcendent moral categories?

References

Bateson, P.P.G.
>   1987   Ethology. In *The Oxford Companion of the Mind*. R. L. Gregory and O. L. Zangwill, eds. Oxford, England: Oxford University Press.

Freud, Sigmund
>   1953[1900]   The Interpretation of Dreams. In *The Standard Edition of the Complete Psychological Works of Sigmund Freud* (Vols. 4 and 5). Ed. and trans. by James Strachey. London: Hogarth
>   1955[1913]   Totem and Taboo In *The Standard Edition of the Complete Psychological Works of Sigmund Freud* (Vol. 13). Ed. and trans. by James Strachey. London: Hogarth.
>   1955[1920]   Beyond the Pleasure Principle. In *The Standard Edition of the Complete Psychological Works of Sigmund Freud* (Vol. 18). Ed. and trans. by James Strachey. London: Hogarth.
>   1961a[1923]   The Ego and the Id. In *The Standard Edition of the Complete Psychological Works of Sigmund Freud* (Vol. 19). Ed. and trans. by James Strachey. London: Hogarth.
>   1961b[1931]   Civilization and its Discontents. In *The Standard Edition of the Complete Psychological Works of Sigmund Freud* (Vol. 21). Ed. and trans. by James Strachey. London: Hogarth.
>   1964[1933]   New Introductory Lectures on Psychoanalysis. In *The Standard Edition of the Complete Psychological Works of Sigmund Freud* (Vol. 22). Ed. and trans. by James Strachey. London: Hogarth.

Lefebvre, Vladimir A.
>   1985   The golden section and an algebraic model of ethical cognition. *Journal of Mathematical Psychology* 29: 289-310.
>   1987   The fundamental structures of human reflection. *Journal of Social and Biological Structures* 10: 129-175.

Rapoport, A.
>   1987   Comment by Anatol Rapoport. *Journal of Social and biological Structures* 10: 192-204.

Ricoeur, P.

    1970 *Freud and Philosophy: An Essay on Interpretation.* New Haven, CT., and London, England: Yale University Press.

Sagan, Eli

    1988 *Freud, Women, and Morality.* New York, NY: Basic Books, Inc., Publishers.

Wilson, E.O.

    1975 *Sociobiology. The New Synthesis.* Cambridge, MA: Belknap Press, Harvard University Press.

    1978 *On Human Nature.* Cambridge, MA, London, England: Harvard University Press.

    1984 *Biophilia.* Cambridge, MA: Harvard University Press.

Chapter 10   Human Nature and Communicative Ethics[1]

Gary M. Simpson

How can a theological perspective on human biology enhance a promising, though theologically uninformed, approach to human morality? Jürgen Habermas's communicative ethics can make a significant contribution to Christian moral deliberation but his approach lacks a specifically theological grounding. My thesis is that Jürgen Habermas's communicative ethics, teamed with Wolfhart Pannenberg's theological anthropology, can provide the basis for an adequate contemporary moral theory that takes full account of sociobiological arguments. To make good on this thesis I will: 1) investigate Pannenberg's theological analysis of human biology which highlights two basic human characteristics ("exocentricity" and "centrality") and the tension between the two; and 2) sketch Habermas's moral theory, improving upon it by employing Pannenberg's insights on the religious dimensions of human biology.

The occasion for this volume is a discussion of sociobiological explanations of morality such as those of Edward O. Wilson. My inquiry, however, is an alternative proposal from the start. I will not, therefore, attend directly to the familiar issues that have surrounded discussions of Wilson's proposal, for instance. Both Pannenberg and Habermas depart from sociobiology because it fails to attend to the basic hermeneutical dimensions of human existence. Human behavior is always embedded within wider horizons of symbolic meaning and interpretation that remain inaccessible to the observation and explanation of only biological and behavioral factors (Pannenberg 1985:30-31, 160-161; Habermas 1990:21-29). Because

---

[1]I would like to thank the participants at the "Morality and Biology" conference at Bethel College, St. Paul, MN for their helpful conversation regarding an earlier version of this paper. I also have received particularly helpful criticism from James Hurd, Professor of Anthropology at Bethel College as well as from my assistant, Jeff Whillock.

sociobiological theories do not account for these specifically human phenomena, they cannot offer a moral theory adequate to human nature and reality.

Pannenberg on human nature

Pannenberg, in a manner uncharacteristic of most contemporary theologians, begins his theological investigation of human nature with the discipline of biology. He does so precisely to underscore the fundamental importance of the religious dimension of human biology. He challenges the anthropological disciplines to abandon their atheistic assumptions when investigating human nature. He also challenges theological disciplines to abandon their fear of, and sectarian isolation from, the natural and human sciences. In this paper we will focus on Pannenberg's theological analysis of human nature. We will pay particular attention to his reconstruction of the two traditional key anthropological themes of Christian theology – the image of God and sin – because both of these are relevant to our concern with morality.[2] In the process we will also follow his "story-line" that traces the modern intellectual history of these themes.

Exocentricity

Traditionally, Christian theology described the special place of human beings in relation to animals by appealing to the concept of an immortal soul that is united to an animal body. Western philosophy also traditionally held this same general orientation toward human uniqueness. During the seventeenth, eighteenth, and early nineteenth centuries Western philosophy continued the prior orientation by conceptualizing human nature from the internal perspective of consciousness. During the nineteenth century in particular this approach became increasingly dubious. The sciences began to understand human uniqueness in terms of how human bodies functioned. Since we know animals only from the outside, so to speak, from observing their behavior, this became the approach to understand the human creature as well.

Certain twentieth-century behaviorist psychologists made a break with previous approaches by seeking access to the human psyche through observable external

---

[2] Pannenberg's analysis in *Anthropology in Theological Perspective* begins with "The Person in Nature" as Part One, moves through Part Two, "The Human Person as a Social Being," and culminates with Part Three, "The Shared World." Due to our space restrictions, I will look only at Part One.

behavior. Three German philosophical anthropologists – Max Scheler, Helmut Plessner, and Arnold Gehlen – followed the lead of twentieth-century behaviorism. These philosophical anthropologists no longer sought to understand the human being as a creature in relationship with God. Rather they looked at humanity's place in nature and specifically in relation to the higher animals. They agreed with the behaviorist assumption of continuity between human beings and the higher animals and offered a philosophical interpretation of the empirical research of this continuity.

These philosophical anthropologists also departed from classical behaviorism. They noted that with humans the so-called stimulus-response pattern does not necessarily exhibit an observable cause and effect relationship. The same stimuli can elicit a variety of movements in response. Conversely, a variety of different stimuli can elicit the same response. Behavior, therefore, is always a "conducting oneself." It is the activity of a subject who interprets the surroundings, the environment, from the perspective of something unique to human beings. The philosophical anthropologists, therefore, also investigated that which elevates human beings beyond the higher animals. We can see here the evident fork in the road that separates the philosophical anthropologists (as well as Pannenberg and Habermas) from Wilson's sociobiological approach.

Pannenberg borrows an insight from each of the three philosophical anthropologists in order to make his theological analysis of human biology. Humanity occupies a special place in the animal world due to a central structural feature of the human form of life: human being's "openness to the world." Scheler had interpreted human "openness to the world" as the reality of "spirit" in the human form of life. While Pannenberg agrees with Scheler on this point, he also corrects Scheler. Scheler had thought of the human spirit as opposed to human biological life. Pannenberg, instead, follows Gehlen's understanding that "openness to the world" is connected with human biological structure and behavior. Pannenberg, however, disagrees with Gehlen's purely "activistic" understanding of humankind's unique "openness to the world." A purely activistic view of human nature would mean that human beings are self-created beings in the strict sense precisely by their action of gaining control over their world. Against this essentially atheistic view Pannenberg argues that human action is rooted within a human characteristic more basic than action itself. Pannenberg looks to Plessner's notion of "exocentricity" as the most basic and unique characteristic of the human creature.

Exocentricity means that humans have their center not only within themselves as do the higher animals – due particularly to the evolutionary development of a central nervous system – but humans also have their centers outside themselves.[3] Exocentricity means that humans can adopt an attitude toward themselves – self-reflection – which gives them the ability to stand back from things outside themselves and treat them as objects. This exocentric capacity to meet and be conscious of another as an other also includes perceiving the self as an other. Human self-objectivity grounds human objectivity. This exocentric capacity represents a structural modification of life itself at the stage of development that life has reached in humanity.

"The capacity of human beings for objectivity, for dwelling on the other as other, contains an element of self-transcendence, an element of disregard for their own impulses, and this element is specifically distinct from the ecstatic dynamism common to all living things. This element of self-transcendence is not yet achieved in the life of the higher animals, at least not as a way of life, even if there is a hint of it in the play of young animals. Even in humans this self-transcendence attains to its evolved form only in the course of the individual's development, and we may assume that in the development of the species too this human self-transcendence has not at all times been exercised with the same clear consciousness" (Pannenberg 1985:62).

Exocentricity as a human way of life is that human structure which is "the most generalized and to that extent fundamental characteristic of the properly human" (Pannenberg 1985:63). As such, exocentricity is the basis of those other human phenomena that have often been taken as most fundamental, such as subjectivity, consciousness, language, and action. In our later inquiry of Habermas's communicative ethics we will more fully press this insight as a basic warrant for linking language and moral action.

---

[3] Pannenberg correlates the notion of exocentricity with Martin Luther's theological understanding of faith as that which places human creatures "outside of themselves"– *extra nos* – either in God or in false gods. The *locus classicus* of Luther's nothin her is in his Large Catechism explanation of the first commandment (*The Book of Concord*, edited by T. Tappert (Philadelphia: Fortress Press, 1959), p. 365). Pannenberg profusely praises this notion of *extra nos* as "that excitingly profound idea of Luther's" (Pannenberg 1992:144).

Image of God

Despite their self-transcendence, humans do have limits. Our bodies limit us and we experience life "from our own point of view." Still, there are no definitive limits set for all time. Rather, these limits function as a point of departure for the development of individuals as well as of the species, a development that continues into the future.

Pannenberg argues that the biblical notion of the image of God means that human creatures are given a framework and a direction to their development toward a destiny, a process that also includes human participation and experience. Conceiving of the human creature as image of God represents an alternative vision to the Enlightenment's idea of purely human self-actualization and self-fulfillment. Furthermore, by conceptualizing the image of God as a process toward a destiny, Pannenberg also offers an alternative to various traditional Christian views of the image of God. These views understood the image of God as, in one way or another, an original state of affairs at the beginning of history but which was then lost through a Fall. Pannenberg notes that such Christian views no longer seem plausible in the face of an evolutionary view of the world and also in the face of the increasing importance assigned to history and especially to the future as the horizon of meaning for past and present history.

Pannenberg argues that exocentricity and its accompanying capacity to perceive other persons, as well as oneself, as an other, requires gaining an ever-expanding perspective or horizon that encompasses and embraces all others. Such a universal horizon, nevertheless, is always mediated to us through particular others. This step into the universal brings the self, of course, face to face with the question of God. Yet, because the universal is always mediated through particular others, this step into the universal also means that the self must become a self through social relations. This process of becoming a self through social relations is initiated through those relations that are closest to the self, that is, those relations defined by their distance from the self as center. Pannenberg notes a certain ambiguity in the structural tension between centrality and exocentricity. This tension within the human creature is the source of the moral predicament, as we will see below.

Sin

Pannenberg begins his analysis of this tension by discussing Augustine's classical description of sin. The ongoing illuminating power of Augustine's discussion of sin rests in two essentials: the empirical orientation of Augustine's psychological description and the relevance of sin to the relation of human beings with themselves. Only by faith can one acknowledge the radical meaning of sin as all-out hostility to God. Augustine, nevertheless, also looked to the empirical data for less radical manifestations of sinning that lead up to straight-out hostility toward God. Augustine often undertook his presentation of sin through an empirical analysis of concupiscence: the perverse desire which reverses means and end, *uti et frui*. Humans ought to use the transitory goods of the created natural world as a means to enjoy the imperishable blessings of God. This would be in conformity with the order of the cosmos. Humans, however, reverse the order due to their egocentric attitude toward the natural world. We fixate on the enjoyment of transitory goods at the expense of attending to higher heavenly things. We then instrumentally use God in order to secure our enjoyment of transitory goods.

Pannenberg notes that Augustine's psychological description of sin has the advantage of being close to the real experience of human life. "The distortion in human behavior does not begin with a conscious turning from God; rather, the estrangement from God takes place in an obscure manner and is for long periods more or less unnoticed, being simply implicit in the distortion of our relation to the world and ourselves" (Pannenberg 1985:94). Augustine's presentation of sin as the perverse reversal of means and end rests on the assumption of a God-given, fixed hierarchical order of nature that encompasses the whole created universe. Western modernity, however, no longer holds this assumption. Pannenberg argues, therefore, that a contemporary discussion of sin must look rather at the empirical data regarding human subjectivity. Subsequent to this analysis we ought to seek an understanding of sin by observing the relationship of human subjectivity to the natural environment.

A contemporary discussion of human subjectivity will in fact show a reversal of means and end. However, it will now focus on the concepts of centrality and exocentricity. "The central ego turns exocentricity . . . into a means in the service of its own ends" (Pannenberg 1985:106). This situation flows from "a structural element of the human form of life and its behavior, which is marked by a tension between the centralist organization which human beings share with all animal life and especially with its more highly organized forms, and the exocentric character, which is peculiar to human beings" (Pannenberg 1985:105). An analysis of self-consciousness demonstrates that this "tension" is always a "dominance" that centrality exercises over exocentricity.[4] Furthermore, this dominance precedes moral behavior and must therefore be said to have its origin in "the natural conditions of our existence" (Pannenberg 1985:107).[5] This structural dominance affects moral behavior.

Pannenberg does not specifically develop his theological analysis into a moral theory. Habermas can help us move in this direction. Two points from Pannenberg's analysis will help us to explore, evaluate, and strengthen Habermas's moral theory. First, the religious nature of humankind is rooted within the biological structure of the human creature's exocentricity. No moral theory, therefore, can be faithful to human existence that does not ultimately take into account the relationship of human beings to God. Second, an adequate moral theory must focus on the tension within the human creature between exocentricity and centrality and particularly the sinful dominance of centrality over exocentricity. This results in the dominance of humans over one another; it also results in hostility toward God. With this theological analysis of human biology in mind we move to communicative ethics.

Habermas and communicative ethics

This sketch of Habermas's communicative ethics concentrates on its basic moral intuitions and corresponding ideas. Habermas's prime concern is to counter moral and ethical skepticism, that is, the belief that normative statements offer no more than merely private opinion and individual taste (Habermas 1990:56, 98). Habermas believes that the resurgence of moral skepticism has "infiltrated" the everyday consciousness of many educated people. This infiltration has neutralized the moral intuitions that people usually acquire rather naturally through the socialization process. He begins his counter-argument by systematically clarifying the basic moral intuitions of everyday life. Habermas sets for himself the task of making

---

[4]Pannenberg at this point also touches base with Luther's notion of *homo incurvatus in se* (1985:107, 116-119). This would be a wonderful opportunity for Pannenberg to undertake a constructive dialogue with feminist criticisms and reconstructions of the doctrine of sin. Unfortunately, he does not even broach the subject.

[5]Pannenberg recognizes that locating the origin of sin within the natural conditions of human existence poses a number of difficult questions that must be addressed head on. He deals in particular with three: a) does this mean that human nature as such is sinful? b) since humans share centrality with the higher animals, why do we not ascribe sin to them? c) if sin lies in the natural conditions of human existence, what responsibility can we be said to have for this situation? In this latter question we also find Pannenberg confirming Luther's understanding of the bondage of the will (pp. 109-119).

explicit the norms embedded in the moral intuitions of everyday life (Habermas 1990:198). My task will be to indicate what those moral intuitions are, to understand how Habermas redeems them for a theory of ethics, and to suggest how the insights gained from Pannenberg's analysis offer a more adequate reason for pursuing the path toward communicative ethics.

Vulnerability

At the heart of the moral intuitions of everyday life is the sense that a "profound vulnerability" encompasses human life (Habermas 1990:200). "[M]orality," Habermas insists, "is a safety device compensating for a vulnerability built into the sociocultural form of life" (Habermas 1990:199). His account of the origins of human vulnerability follows closely the social dynamics resulting from the tension between centrality and exocentricity as analyzed by Pannenberg.[6] Modern societies intensify this tension. Because modern democratic societies are constituted by the consensus-oriented use of language, modern people need to become more and more individuated. Yet, our identities as individuals depend upon the social and cultural environments which morally nurture us from infancy on, starting with that form of the lifeworld which is closest to us, our families. In modern forms of life there arises a simultaneous growth of responsible individuality along with dependence on interpersonal relationships and bonds.

"The more the subject becomes individuated, the more he becomes entangled in a densely woven fabric of mutual recognition, that is, of reciprocal exposedness and vulnerability. Unless the subject externalizes himself by participating in interpersonal relations through language, he is unable to form the inner center that is his personal identity. This explains the almost constitutional insecurity and chronic fragility of personal identity – an insecurity that is antecedent to cruder threats to the integrity of life and limb" (Habermas 1990:199).

Habermas, therefore, tailors his moral theory "to suit the fragility of human beings individuated through socialization" (Habermas 1990:200). Pannenberg's analysis

---

[6]Habermas (1970) first undertakes to explicate the vulnerability of human existence in a critical dialogue with Arnold Gehlen (Habermas 1983:113-130). A fuller dialogue with Habermas on this issue would need to take into consideration what he means when he emphasizes that the unique root of ethics, rooted as it is in the reciprocity dynamics of the structure of speech as communication, "is certainly in no way a biological root" (1983:122). In a more sustained investigation than is possible in this format we could show how Pannenberg's analysis of the connection of exocentricity and biology would correct this assertion by Habermas without falling prey to biologistic behaviorism that both Habermas and Pannenberg want to overcome.

of sin as the dominance of centrality over exocentricity means that the fragility of human beings is further exacerbated by the presence of sin within social life.[7]

According to Habermas, moral theories that are adequate for modern life "must always solve two tasks at once . . . [They] must emphasize the inviolability of the individual by postulating equal respect for the dignity of each individual. But they must also protect the web of intersubjective relations of mutual recognition by which these individuals survive as members of a community" (Habermas 1990:200). Traditionally, ethicists who focus on equal respect and rights for the individual have formulated their moral theories around a principle of justice. Ethicists who focus on concern for the common good have constructed their theories around a principle of social solidarity. The history of moral philosophy in the West has been the development of these two contrary trajectories. Habermas claims that it is a misperception of the moral situation which leads to isolating the principles of justice and solidarity. He argues that the principle of justice and the principle of solidarity "have one and the same root: the specific vulnerability of the human species, which individuates through sociation" (Habermas 1990:200). Habermas's basic thesis emerges as he ponders the link between morality and vulnerability: "linguistically mediated interaction is both the reason for the vulnerability of socialized individuals and the key resource they possess to compensate for that vulnerability" (Habermas 1990:201). Habermas strives to redeem the connection between justice and solidarity by critically refashioning Immanuel Kant's moral theory.

Moral Truth

Kant took as his point of departure certain moral intuitions embedded in everyday life. Of first importance is that practical everyday moral questions admit of truth. (For example, "What ought I or we to do?") There is a general expectation in everyday life that norms of behavior could be backed up with good reasons if it became necessary to call forth those reasons.

Communicative ethics proceeds on the intuition that moral truth is possible. Habermas, therefore, points out the "ought" character of everyday moral norms. This represents a cognitivist approach to ethics. Noncognitivist approaches which reject in principle the possibility of moral truth rely primarily on two arguments

---

[7]Habermas comes the closest to the Christian understanding of sin when he analyzes the social dynamics of "systematically distorted communication" (Habermas 1970:205-218).

against the intuition that norms admit of truth. First, disputes about moral principles do not usually end in agreement. Second, cognitivist approaches have failed to explain what it might mean for normative statements to be true. Habermas takes up both of these challenges beginning with the latter.

The truth character of normative statements will be impossible to establish if normative statements must be seen as true in precisely the same sense as descriptive, propositional statements about the empirical world are said to be true. Habermas refuses to *equate* moral truth with propositional truth.[8] Rather, by means of a close exegesis and analytically thick description of both propositional statements and normative statements, he argues that moral truth is *analogous* to propositional truth. In order to secure this distinction Habermas substitutes the term "normative rightness" for moral truth. Statements of normative rightness and propositional truth are analogous because the validity of both statements is open to testing, though not in precisely the same way (Habermas 1990:48-62, 197). Cognitivist ethics aim, therefore, to specify precisely how normative statements are to be justified.

Impartiality and Reversibility

This brings us to another of Kant's basic moral intuitions: impartiality. Claims to normative rightness are to be tested impartially. For Kant this means that valid norms deserve to be recognized universally. Kant's universalizability principle, stated in the form of a categorical imperative – "Act only according to that maxim by which you can at the same time will that it should become a universal law" – functions within his moral theory both as a testing procedure and as a principle for discriminating between valid and invalid norms.

Like Kant's ethical approach, communicative ethics highlights the importance of the particular procedure for testing the truth claim of a moral norm. Precisely at this point, however, resides the greatest difference between Kant and communicative ethics. For Kant a norm would be justifiably valid if a rational subject could insist without self-contradiction that everyone else also follow this norm given the same circumstances. Kant's point here aims to capitalize on the moral intuition that the impartiality of moral judgment also requires the reversibility of moral per-

---

[8]Among Habermas's most basic theses is that "the fundamental intuition of every competent speaker [is] that his claims to truth, normative rightness, and truthfulness should be acceptable to all, under suitable conditions" (1990:31).

spectives. Reversibility means that if our places were reversed, I would still accept the rightness of the moral "oughts" that governed the relationship prior to the reversal. The Golden Rule – "Do unto others as you would have them do unto you" – and the Second Great Commandment – "Love your neighbor as yourself" – are both ancient expressions of this basic moral intuition.

Habermas argues persuasively that Kant's categorical imperative is a testing procedure formatted as a moral monologue. That is, the categorical imperative assumes that an individual on one's own can test the universal validity of a norm by descending into the loneliness of one's own soul. The categorical imperative mandates that a person ought first to look inwardly to determine if the norm would be acceptable and then to project that conclusion out onto all others. The Golden Rule and the Second Great Commandment both follow a similarly stylized procedure. Kant himself grounded this monologic procedure on a transcendental consciousness that took for granted a pre-established harmony of all relevant persons. Under the questionable presumption of a highly homogenous society, such a monologic moral procedure might seem adequate to the task.

Communicative ethics follows a different procedural path as it capitalizes on the everyday moral intuitions that impartiality and reversibility are necessary when testing a moral claim for its normative rightness. "True impartiality pertains only to that standpoint from which one can generalize precisely those norms that deserve intersubjective recognition" (Habermas 1990:65). Habermas, therefore, identifies a testing procedure that shifts the emphasis. In place of asking what each can will without self-contradiction to be a general norm, one must now ask what all can will in agreement to be a general norm. Such a shift also means that the intuitions of impartiality and reversibility are not sufficiently enacted when even many persons reflect individually on their yes or no positions regarding a norm and then register a vote or allow themselves to be polled. Habermas, therefore, states the distinctive idea of communicative ethics as follows: "Only those norms can claim to be valid that meet (or could meet) with the approval of all affected in their capacity as participants in a practical discourse" (Habermas 1990:66, 93).

Communicative ethics calls for real-life moral argumentation in which all affected by a decision are admitted and needed as participants. Within the conduct of everyday life the background normative assumptions of a particular family or neighborhood or even culture are not usually at issue. However, when someone raises a claim against the normative rightness of particular background assumptions, this,

then, convenes a practical moral discourse with all the limitations that actual everyday life and political realities place upon such discourses (Habermas 1990:105-
109).

Habermas presses his moral theory to an even more basic level. He contends that
the very norms which legitimate the kind of moral testing which he is describing
are "rooted in the structures of argumentation themselves and [do] not need to be
brought in from the outside as a supplementary normative content" (Habermas
1990:76).[9] In other words, "anyone who seriously undertakes to participate in
argumentation implicitly accepts by that very undertaking general pragmatic presuppositions that have a normative content" (Habermas 1990:197-198). In particular, the norms of reciprocity and equality are deeply embedded in the practice
of everyday communication. Furthermore, these norms surface emphatically in
moral discourses which function as "a more exacting type" of speech than everyday communication (Habermas 1990:201-202; 76-102, 21-29).[10]

We can now be more specific than in our earlier discussion regarding the analogous relationship between propositional truth and normative rightness. Normative
statements, like propositional statements, aim and claim to be true. The validity of
both must be demonstrated in a testing procedure. Furthermore, both tests em-
ploys a principle of induction as a bridging principle between the statement and its
demonstration of truth. The difference between testing propositional statements
and normative statements lies in the bridging principle. In the case of normative
claims (within a cognitivist ethical approach), the bridging principle is the principle

---

[9]I have undertaken an in depth analysis of the norms of reciprocity and equality (Simpson 1983).
Much of the debate among the proponents of communicative ethics centers around the status of
the attempts to justify the claim that the fundamental norms of practical moral discourses are
always already embedded within language pragmatics themselves.

[10]Karl-Otto Apel offers the strongest transcendental-pragmatic justification for the status of these
norms (Apel 1980; Apel 1987; Apel 1990). Habermas himself offers "a more cautious version"
of Apel's transcendental-pragmatic justification that gives up any claim to ultimate justification
without, however, capitulating merely to the ethnocentric fallacy (1990:76-98). He concentrates
on making explicit the moral intuitions of everyday life and then holding his reconstruction up
for cross-cultural and cross-gender empirical testing (1990:76-98). Seyla Benhabib argues for a
"historically self-conscious universalism" that justifies the norms of universal respect and egali-
tarian reciprocity as "culturally defined moral intuitions" presupposed within the "cultural horizon of modernity." Therefore, "these principles are neither the only allowable interpretation of
the formal constituents of the competency of postconventional moral actors nor are they une-
quivocal transcendental presuppositions which every rational agent, upon deep reflection, must
concede to" (Benhabib 1990:339). The most thorough critical and constructive presentation of
Habermas's communicative ethics is by William Rehg, *Insight and Solidarity: A Study in the
Discourse Ethics of Jürgen Habermas* (Berkeley: University of California Press. 1994).

of universalization (Habermas 1990:62-65, 76-77), meaning that: "All affected can accept the consequences and the side effects that a moral norm's observation can be anticipated to have for the satisfaction of everyone's interests (and the consequences are preferred to those of known alternative possibilities for regulation)" (Habermas 1990:65, 95).

Summary and conclusion

Habermas's proposal of communicative ethics essentially follows the correct path. However, it is my claim here that his position could be strengthened by attending more closely to Pannenberg's analysis of human nature. Habermas is right to focus on the fragility of human life due to the finite conditions through which humans are socialized. But the fragility of human existence is due also to the sinful dominance of centrality over exocentricity which in social life leads to the dominance of one person over the other. This issue goes to the very heart of moral life. People naturally view situations from their own perspective and, therefore, are in need of other perspectives (Habermas 1990:65). On the other hand, Pannenberg's analysis of the sinful dominance of centrality over exocentricity actually intensifies the need for a communicative approach to testing moral truth. Real face to face moral conversations and arguments founded upon the norms of reciprocity and equality insure the best counter-weight to the pressing dominance of centrality over exocentricity. Christian anthropology always attends to the blessings and limitations of human finitude but it also focuses on the destructive consequences of human sin.

Habermas's communicative ethics needs "no shared [universal] structures preceding the individual except the universals of language use" (Habermas 1990:203). Pannenberg, on the other hand, argues that universal to the human reality are the tension between exocentricity and centrality as well as the sinful dominance of centrality over exocentricity. Exocentricity as an expression of the image of God means that a more thorough theological analysis of human morality than we have offered here would have to assess how moral argumentation functions as an instrument of God's presence and activity in the world. The analyses of both Pannenberg and Habermas have taken us considerably beyond the inadequate assumptions of sociobiological approaches to morality. The pressing weight of centrality over exocentricity also requires moral theorists to give extensive thought to the relationship between morality and societal institutions. This dimension, too, is beyond the capacity of sociobiology.

References

Apel, K.
> 1987 The Problem of Philosophical Fundamental Grounding in Light of a Transcendental Pragmatics of Language. In *After Philosophy*. K. Baynes, J. Bohman, and T. A. McCarthy, eds. Cambridge, MA: MIT Press. Pp. 250-290.
> 1990 Is the Ethics of the Ideal Communication Community a Utopia? In *The Communicative Ethics Controversy*. S. Benhabib and F. Dallmayr, eds. Cambridge, MA: MIT Press. Pp. 23-59

Benhabib, S.
> 1990 Communicative Ethics and Current Controversies in Practical Philosophy. In *The Communicative Ethics Controversy*. S. Benhabib and F. Dallmayr, eds. Cambridge, MA: MIT Press. Pp. 330-369.

Habermas, J.
> 1970 Systematically Distorted Communication. *Inquiry* 13: 205-218.
> 1983 *Philosophical-Political Profiles*. Cambridge, MA: MIT Press.
> 1990 *Moral Consciousness and Communicative Action*. Cambridge, MA: MIT Press.

Pannenberg, W.
> 1985 *Anthropology in Theological Perspective*. Philadelphia: Westminster Press.
> 1992 The Doctrine of Justification in Ecumenical Dialogue. *dialog* 31: 136-148.

Chapter 11   Genetic Behavior and Moral Choice

Alfred Kracher

The investigation of human nature has become a legitimate topic of natural science. This raises the question of how "human nature" in the scientific sense relates to the older use of this term in moral discourse. The "classic" answer is, of course, that science deals with objective fact, which is somehow detached from "value judgments." Hence human nature in the scientific sense is seen, as it were, from the outside by traditional moral philosophy, as Iris Murdoch observes: "Science can instruct morality at certain points and can change its direction, but it cannot contain morality, nor [therefore] moral philosophy" (Murdoch 1970:27).

At the other extreme is the sociobiological view of morality as articulated by E. O. Wilson: "The genes hold culture on a leash. The brain is a product of evolution. Human behavior is the circuitous technique by which human genetic material has been and will be kept intact. *Morality has no other demonstrable ultimate function*" (Wilson 1978:167; my emphasis).

Morality is, on the latter view, simply one of many adaptations that ensure the survival of genetic patterns (Wilson 1975, 1978; Barash 1977; Alexander 1987). A scientific study of these adaptations is really all that is required for understanding human nature, including its moral dimension. In this sense sociobiology, as conceived by Wilson, does indeed make the claim to contain morality.

Those who want to avoid either extreme generally agree that the biological roots of human behavior are important, while maintaining the autonomy of moral choices. Arguments in favor of this view usually rest on the human capacity to benefit others without expecting a tangible return. In the first part of this paper I try to show that a stronger argument is available to refute the idea that morality is no more than a sociobiological exhibit piece. In the second part I suggest a way of understanding the relationship between human moral choices and genetically determined behavior.

To be clear about the problem we have to sketch the argument that leads to Wilson's view of morality. The idea of evolution necessarily entails adaptation. Fins evolve in aquatic animals (regardless of whether they are fish, bird, or mammal), because an animal having them is a better swimmer than one that does not. Genes have more chance to be passed to the next generation if the individual in which they reside is better adapted to its environment. This picture of inheritance can be reasonably extended to genetically determined behavior. Animal behavior, like animal morphology, is adaptive, and therefore one should be able to show how a certain trait increases the fitness of those carrying it. Selection does not work on an entire species, nor on single individuals. A genetic trait that leads an individual to risk its own life can survive if this risk increases the chances that the genes responsible for the trait survive. This is sometimes called the maximization principle (Lopreato 1984:20, who paraphrases the "Central Theorem of Sociobiology" of Barash 1977:63). If the death of one individual frequently leads to saving the life of several of its close kin (who carry some of the same genetic material), the genes leading to this sacrificial behavior can survive within the population. This is an example of inclusive fitness. Thus sociobiology gives a genetic account of what it calls, rather misleadingly, altruism.

When we want to extend this evolutionist concept of behavior to moral conduct, one further move is necessary. Human consciousness is also a product of evolution. Its adaptive value is obvious. Particular inherited behaviors in animals invariably work better in some environments than in others. This, too, is analogous to inherited morphology.

The specialization of organs has its price (fins are great for swimming, but clumsy on land). Inherited behavior has similar limitations. It greatly increases one's fitness to have some leeway in changing one's behavior in response to a changing environment. But the behavioral repertoire cannot exceed a certain level of complexity, as long as particular behaviors are called to action by purely instinctual triggers. Beyond this level of complexity, behavior has to be actually chosen; and if this ability works the same way other adaptations do, the "right choice" is the one leading to optimum inclusive fitness. If consciousness is an adaptation for flexibility of behavior (in the same sense that fins are an adaptation for efficient swimming), then it is possible to give a sociobiological interpretation of the idea of free will (Wilson 1978:71–77; Lumsden and Wilson 1983:174–184). Perhaps it would be more accurate, as well as more cautious, to say that sociobiology can investigate the biological conditions for the possibility of free will, which is rather less than claiming that the concept itself can be exhaustively explained by biological arguments.

Ethicists have attacked Wilson's view of morality primarily by trying to show that humans are capable of a kind of altruism that does not increase inclusive fitness, and therefore transcends the forms of altruism that can be explained by sociobiology (kin altruism and reciprocal altruism). An excellent example, cited by Singer (1981), is donating blood. This uniquely human form of altruism is sometimes called, not altogether felicitously, ascetic altruism (Lopreato 1984:207). In another example, humans can voluntarily forgo having their own children, and rather help people to whom they are not closely related. We will return to this example later. Ascetic altruism is distinct from both "soft-core" and "hard-core" altruism as defined by Wilson (1978). Both of these are the result of evolution, whereas ascetic altruism refers to behavior that cannot be the result of biological evolution only. It is thus by definition reserved for human behavior.

If some sociobiologists are largely unimpressed by arguments for the existence of ascetic altruism, it is because their view of morality as strictly subordinate to our genetic nature is rather impervious to arguments based on acts of altruism. The reason is simple. A species that is so highly social that it can develop consciousness has to have a strong genetic disposition toward reciprocal altruism, and hence can be expected to have, so to speak, "altruistic appetites." We normally want to be kind to others, and tend to satisfy this desire, as long as the cost is acceptable. Besides it is only natural that appetites do not always find their genetically appropriate objects. Just as songbirds will incubate the egg of the European cuckoo who lays its eggs into their nests, so our altruistic instincts can likewise be deceived into seeking the wrong object. It is unnecessary to debate genetic causes for every single example of apparently self-sacrificing behavior. For any such case there is always a possibility that it is simply a non-adaptive aberration.

If we want to show that morality is autonomous over genetics, altruism is not a good place to look for arguments. What we need is a situation where our natural appetites are in strong conflict with one another, and neither alternative is particularly desirable. In this case our consciousness should steer the choice in the direction of greater inclusive fitness. Conflicts between natural inclinations are, of course, a common occurrence in all higher animals. Which instinct is stronger, to flee from an enemy or to defend one's young? Since instincts are not infinitely flexible, the outcome of such conflicts is not in every case consistent with the maximization principle. Wilson's view of morality amounts to this: if consciousness evolved to solve such conflicts by the maximization principle, then "correct" morality should direct us to the side of greater inclusive fitness.

This is a hypothesis about the function of morality, and as such it can be tested by looking at actual cases. A drastic case in point is recounted by Josephus Flavius (*Jewish War* 6:199-215). During the Roman siege of Jerusalem in 70 AD a certain Mary, daughter of Eleazar, roasted her own infant son and ate part of him. The advantage of considering such a gruesome example is that the nature of the choice is exceptionally clear. The starkness of the alternatives would seem to leave little room for self-deception (a favorite explanation when actual human conduct causes headaches for sociobiologists; e.g., Lopreato 1984; Alexander 1987). Humans, like many other higher animals, have such a strong natural inhibition against eating their own young that it frequently overrides even their survival instinct. Of course, this is not the rational solution to the conflict between parental instinct and self-preservation. If the mother survives, she can have more children; if she starves to death, her baby will also die, and the genetic line ceases. From the perspective of inclusive fitness, parental inhibition leads to the "wrong" solution (e.g., starving to death), and one would therefore expect that we would have strong moral arguments in favor of overcoming our revulsion and supporting Mary's act.

In this regard, Josephus' own judgment of the situation is instructive. As a bystander he can, of course, feel the revulsion vicariously, but he is not the one who actually has to eat. At the same time, considering his own cultural background, continuation of a genetic line would be a rather more important duty to him than it is to us. He would therefore seem able to articulate the "morally correct" choice. Yet he writes that Mary's act has "no parallels in the annals of Greece or any other country" (6:199). This makes it quite clear that for Josephus morality is not on Mary's side, and we can hardly claim that he simply made a mistake in this. Whatever other function morality may have, it does not in this case fulfill the function of "keeping genetic material intact."

There are, of course, ways to save sociobiological appearances. Moral arguments may have developed as general rules, perhaps on a pattern of reciprocal benefits, but in certain situations it may be adaptive for the individual to act against them. However, this still leaves us with the question of under what circumstances it is morally permissible to break the rules. The answer cannot be another general rule like "whenever it advances inclusive fitness." Others have faced Mary's problem and have chosen death, and nothing compels us, even with full knowledge of sociobiology, to prefer Mary's choice over theirs.

We can certainly understand the rejection of Mary's conduct by appealing to a biologically based inhibition. However, to say that we can understand biology as a source of morality is rather different from claiming that the promotion of inclusive fitness is the sole function of morality. To satisfy Wilson's claim we would have to be able to show that in an actual conflict of interest moral argument takes the side of sociobiology.

Thus, the moral argument does not always work in the direction of the maximization principle, and the cases where it does not are not merely mistakes. There is no compelling reason to choose inclusive fitness over other moral goods, unless one has already decided that all other goods have to be subordinated to it. Even this is a moral choice, however, which is not automatically justified by reference to evolutionary theory, but has to be defended on its own terms against other possible choices. Since biologically-founded behavior is the object of choice, the argument about the choice itself (i.e., moral argument), cannot itself rest on a biological foundation. Thus, choosing inclusive fitness as the supreme principle can only reinforce the contention that morality is autonomous against genetic control.

The attempt to explain all moral choices on sociobiological principles is counterproductive to our effort to understand human conduct. But before discussing this further we must look at situations that are more common and more complex.

If we look at examples less extreme than the case of Mary, sorting out the genetically determined from the voluntary factors becomes more difficult. That makes it easier to ignore the latter, but if we look more closely, the autonomous character of moral choice does not change. To illustrate the sorting out process I have in mind I will look at adoption, an example that has been much discussed from both sides of the issue.

It is possible to explain adoption in a number of ways without appealing to phenomena beyond the principles of sociobiology. Analogies to adoption in the animal world are not uncommon; cases are documented in at least 36 mammalian species, and many more species of birds and mammals care for unrelated infants in various ways (Riedmann 1982). In humans, childless parents may simply wish to satisfy their parental inclinations; or the practice may have first developed in cases where the adoptees were likely to be close kin, with the practice being eventually stabilized by cultural injunctions (Barash 1977:312-3; Lopreato 1984:221). It is simply kin altruism (with or without reciprocal altruism mixed in) applied to the "wrong" object, and the 'mistake' can be understood in a number of ways. Parents who adopt "deceive," as it were, their own natural inclination of being kind to their biological children, and transfer this affection onto a non-relative.

However, our earlier arguments have suggested to us the autonomy of moral choices over our biological constitution. Once we grant that human parents may consciously choose to adopt, the words in quotation marks in the preceding paragraph begin to look misapplied. No reasonable moral argument would sustain the view of adoption that they suggest.

An adopted child is not the wrong object of altruism; adoption is not a mistake, even when American parents adopt a Korean baby, who is surely genetically unrelated; and no self-deception is required to make it succeed. On the contrary, the transfer of parental love to someone other than biological offspring is in this case entirely conscious and deliberate. Watching adoptive parents, one gets the distinct impression that they are more successful if they are honest and self-critical rather than self-deceptive.

So far I have done no more than to reassert the reality of moral choices. Moral philosophers (who have never denied this) may consider the assertion trivial, but considering the popularity of sociobiology, it is a necessary step. The truly uncharted gulf, however, lies not between genetics and individual choice, but in the way in which culture interacts with both. One view about the effect of culture holds that it is merely a quantitative modification of our genetic impulses: "Culture may intensify, soften, or suppress genetically based tendencies" (Singer 1981:52-3). However, what is characteristic of adoption is not a change in the intensity of genetically based tendencies, but their transference to objects that we can choose. (It should be noted that Singer, in spite of the preceding quotation, would probably agree with this.) Transference of this kind is, in my view, a useful model for the general cultural effects on human behavior. Midgley's formulation of the idea is much more to the point: "In human beings, the complexities of culture can give [the tendency to be altruistic] a much wider range of channels than is possible for other species" (Midgley 1985:127).

The notion that human consciousness merely adds cleverness to instinctive behavior, but sometimes bungles by redirecting this behavior to the wrong object is simply inconsistent with observable facts. Neither is it plausible to shift the blame to culture as a mistake-prone extension of genetically determined behavior. Humans do not "invent" behavior any more than animals do. However, they can choose, at least to a certain extent, the objects of their behavior in a way other animals cannot. Those who regard conscious choice as a priori illusory will deny this, of course. However, we have already seen that the ability to choose is part of the adaptive value of consciousness. Hence a sociobiological account of human behavior must, on its own premise, grant the reality of such choice. Transference of innate behavior patterns from their "natural" objects to culturally or individually defined ones is a constituting element of human consciousness.

We can follow up this assertion in two different ways. First, it can be shown that the ability to voluntarily change social relationships beyond the strictly genetic patterns follows necessarily from the emergence of human faculties. Second, consciousness does not just enable such a choice, but what makes culture possible is an active assertion of this ability.

The first point can be best illustrated by our language faculty. Human language gives us possibilities that no animal (as far as we understand their ways of communication) can express. This is what makes it possible to articulate the transference of behavior, and thus make it an object of conscious choice. We can, for example, say: "treat this child as if you were his mother." It is usually not plausible to say that this is a physical (psychological, biological, genetic) impossibility. We commonly assume that higher animals can, under certain conditions, also make choices; but they lack the level of abstraction that is expressed by the human "as if." The ability to entertain transference of behavior as a possible option is specific to humans.

Other specifically human forms of communication entail similar possibilities. Television shows us the faces of starving children somewhere in the world. This leads us to imagine our own children in this situation, and hence we transfer a part of our parental care, however small, to these children whom otherwise we would have never known. The argument that our response to the television picture may be "purely emotional" is not relevant. We may not always be able to control our emotional response to something we see on television, but whether we act on it, and in what form, is surely subject to moral reflection. Even if it were not, we still have the choice of turning off the set.

The role that imagination plays in the preceding example shows that the conception of morality as it emerges from the sociobiology debate is incomplete in an important sense. Morality is not simply an arbiter that springs into action when conflicts arise (although this is the aspect of most immediate interest for our discussion). At its core, morality is not merely reactive in this way, but purposeful. We do not simply stabilize inherited characteristics by furthering the survival of the appropriate genes. We have moral goals that are shaped by putting our imagination to work. Thus, "[t]he moral life . . . is something that goes on continually, not something that is switched off in between the occurrence of explicit moral choices" (Murdoch 1970:37).

As Singer (1981) argues, moral imagination is the basis for an expanding circle of moral obligations. Although his contention that reason alone is responsible for the expansion is problematic, particularly in view of some of his more controversial moral conclusions, the general idea is surely right.

In cases where it is not straightforward to define an object of our drives, it may be better to talk about a recontextualization of our genetic tendencies. Although in this paper I am mostly concerned with deliberate choice, the human faculty of recontextualizing genetically determined behavior may begin at a deeper level of consciousness, or even in our pre-conscious mind. For example, Konrad Lorenz regarded laughter as a recontextualization of aggression. His comments on this view (Lorenz 1966:293-7) clearly show the complex interplay of genetic and cultural factors.

The second argument concerning the role of moral decisions is that culture originates, in a sense, through an active assertion of the ability to choose the objects of our behavior. We can conclude this from looking at the mythical narratives that expound human origins. The assertion of moral autonomy seems to be an obligatory ingredient of origin narratives. The initial emergence of culture cannot be directly observed. But the study of myths provides us with some insight into the foundational elements of cultures. Whether sociobiology and, as Wilson calls it, the "myth of scientific materialism" are indeed vastly superior to the traditional myths or not, the latter have to be taken seriously in the present context, because they represent the self-understanding of a culture. Since the significance of myths to the origin of culture (discussed, e.g., by Lévi-Strauss 1969) is such a vast topic, I can not do justice to this idea here.

The example of adoption, which so far has served us as an illustration of the deliberate transference of biologically determined behavior, appears in mythology as the narrative genre of the "Foundling Founder." Moses, for example, was adopted and raised by a person who was most emphatically not a close relative (Exodus 2:1-10). As the story is told, this deed of ascetic altruism was a condition for the survival of the Chosen People. If the author of this passage could have traveled forward in time by nearly 3000 years to read the sociobiological literature, he could hardly have been more emphatic about excluding the possibility of genetic altruism, or the likelihood of reciprocal benefits. Clearly, the Pharaoh's daughter is risking death by saving the infant.

The aim of the entire book of Exodus is to establish the identity, the self-understanding of the Hebrew people (Sarna 1986). The story of Moses' birth and "adoption" seems to say that transference of behavior to objects other than the biologically appropriate ones is a prerequisite for our "being who we are." Altruism, the aspect made most prominent by the sociobiological debate, remains in the background throughout the narrative. The important point is that something unusual, something other than what is implied by biological relationships has to be done in order to save the Chosen People.

A noteworthy feature of this particular narrative is that no supernatural events are invoked at all. Adoption narratives are widespread in the creation myths of other cultures as well, although the stories are frequently less naturalistic. In the Navajo creation myth, for example, Changing Woman, who is adopted by First Man and First Woman, plays a redemptive role similar to that of Moses (Zolbrod 1984), and the Moses passage itself has precursors in ancient Middle Eastern mythology (Sarna 1986).

The significance of such narratives in the present context is that they show us a very different view of culture from the one put forward by the sociobiologists. The ubiquity of these stories documents an awareness of the biological constraints of human nature by mythologizing the acts that transcend these constraints. It suggests that the people with whom the stories originated intuitively understood the biological limitations very well – in some ways perhaps better than some modern sociobiologists. But they insist that the culturally decisive event is an act that goes against the biological fabric. The special role of this act shows two things: First, that a violation of the maximization principle is regarded as possible, albeit perhaps only under special circumstances. Second, that such acts are somehow unusual; normally moral behavior does conform to sociobiological expectation. Under ordinary circumstances, acts against our biological interests are probably evil. It is the appeal to a higher level, an autonomous morality, a "good" in Iris Murdoch's sense, that decides the issue when such exceptional acts are morally appropriate. The metaphor of altitude here means that if a conflict arises that cannot be settled on the "lower" level, a "higher" one is invoked to arbitrate. Nothing is implied about how frequently this might happen, nor do the conflicts have to be entirely conscious. The Pharaoh's daughter may have acted on an impulse; nonetheless her act symbolizes the autonomy of choice over biology.

Someone doggedly determined to reduce any selfless act to some kind of reciprocal altruism in the sociobiological sense can, of course, always appeal to some unspecified expectation of reward, if not in this life then in the next (Wilson 1978:164-5). But this amounts to little more than saying that humans usually have reasons for acting the way they do. At this point sociobiological accounts of behavior run into the problem that ". . . very general explanations of motive . . . are notoriously subject to two alternative drawbacks – vagueness and falsehood. Defined very widely, they tend to become analytically true but trivial. Defined more narrowly, they are interesting but have endless exceptions (Midgley 1984:170)."

Sociobiological explanations ought to properly confine themselves to behavior that evolved, or could conceivably have evolved, by natural selection. The usefulness of sociobiology for understanding human conduct is actually enhanced by the admission that it cannot explain everything. A great deal of cultural customs and moral injunctions may indeed turn out under normal circumstances to promote inclusive fitness. But the instances where this is not the case are especially instructive to both biology and morality. They are also, I would argue, critical to our understanding of the origin of culture. Efforts to water down biological causes until they seem to explain all human conduct therefore obscure rather than illuminate the central problem.

The foundational narratives of great cultures show us human prototypes who assert the autonomy of moral choice over biological determination. Cultural self-awareness apparently perceives such acts as constitutive of its own identity. The moral dimension of these narratives becomes apparent when they function to shape the cultural identity of the individual. In this context the ritual role of foundational narratives in initiation ceremonies is highly significant. For example, the story of Changing Woman, whose adoption has been mentioned before, plays a central role in the Kinaaldá, the puberty ceremony of Navajo girls (Frisbee 1967).

As narratives such as the story of Moses and many others like it emphasize, it is the autonomy of choice over biology that makes us truly human. Although many sociobiologists agree in principle with this notion of humanness, many assume that it is their insight that provides us with this autonomy. This is explicitly stated by Dawkins (1976), and implicitly by many others, including such critics of sociobiological excesses as Singer (1981:168–73). However, we have known how to be human long before we have come to know all the mysteries of genetics. Conversely, our modern biological knowledge has not yet improved our behavior to any noticeable extent. When it comes to human conduct, we ought to be much more cautious about exalting the insights of science above everything that has gone before.

We have seen that the autonomy of choice is not a delusion, since in situations of extreme conflict between biological impulses we do not always identify moral goodness with the maximization principle. This makes it plausible that the argument for the reality of ascetic altruism is correct, though perhaps not compelling by itself. Ascetic altruism is possible, not because human behavior is infinitely plastic, but primarily because we can transfer innate behavior patterns from their biologically defined objects to individually chosen ones. This choice is inherent in our capacity for language and imaginative thought, and is explicitly asserted in the foundational myths of world cultures.

In what sense, then, do "the genes hold culture on a leash?" If this simply means that there are natural constraints on cultural behavior, the point is trivial; it has been made long before sociobiology. On the other hand, if the metaphor means that culture is simply an implementation of the maximization principle, there is good reason to reject it. In this sense, the constitutive act of culture is the cutting of the leash by asserting the choice, collectively as well as individually, of the object or context of our genetic tendencies.

Taken together, the ideas presented here suggest that ever since the earliest beginning of human culture there has existed an awareness of the biological limits of human behavior. In the mythological narratives that have survived to our time this

220

awareness has often reached a sophistication that surpasses the parallel reasoning of sociobiology.

On the other hand, sociobiology has been able to formulate some of the constraints with scientific precision. A properly restricted sociobiology which grants that it cannot explain all human actions would not only be more credible scientifically, but could also help us recognize the significance of symbolic narratives such as the mythical adoption stories. On this view, a dialogue between these very different traditions, science and mythology, is necessary to advance our self-understanding as human beings (Kracher 1992). Neither one by itself is likely to improve human conduct.

Acknowledgments. This paper has been significantly shaped by discussions with Michael Bishop, Gary Comstock, and their students at Iowa State University. Comments by James Hurd helped to clarify a number of points. I am grateful to the many friends and adoptive parents whose loving example has led me to think about adoption in terms of actual human families rather than abstract principles.

References

Alexander, R.D.
1987   *The Biology of Moral Systems.* New York: Aldine de Gruyter.

Barash, D.P.
1977   *Sociobiology and Behavior.* New York: Elsevier.

Frisbie, C.J.
1967   *Kinaaldá: A study of the Navaho girl's puberty ceremony.* Middletown, CT: Wesleyan University Press.

Dawkins, R.
1976   *The Selfish Gene.* New York: Oxford University Press.

Kracher, A.
1992   A Scientist's View From Coyote's Rock. *Chrysalis* 7: 73-77.

Lévi-Strauss, C.
1969   *The Raw and the Cooked.* Trans. by John and Doreen Weightman New York: Harper and Row.

Lopreato, J.
1984   *Human Nature and Biocultural Evolution.* Boston, MA: Allen and Unwin.

Lorenz, K.
  1966 *On Aggression*. Trans. by M. K. Wilson New York: Harcourt, Brace and World.

Lumsden, C.J. and E.O. Wilson
  1983 *Promethean Fire*. Cambridge, MA: Harvard University Press.

Midgley, M.
  1984 *Wickedness: A philosophical essay*. London: Routledge and Kegan Paul.
  1985 *Evolution as a Religion*. London: Methuen.

Murdoch, I.
  1970 *The Sovereignty of Good*. New York: Schocken.

Riedmann, M.L.
  1982 The evolution of alloparental care and adoption in mammals and birds, *Quarterly Review of Biology* 57: 405-435.

Sarna, N.M.
  1986 *Exploring Exodus*. New York: Schocken.

Singer, P.
  1981 *The Expanding Circle: Ethics and Sociobiology*. Oxford University Press: Oxford.

Wilson, E.
  1975 *Sociobiology: The new synthesis*. Cambridge, MA: Harvard University Press.
  1978 *On Human Nature*. Cambridge, MA: Harvard University Press.

Zolbrod, P.G.
  1984 *Diné bahane': The Navaho creation story*. Albuquerque, NM: University of New Mexico Press.

Chapter 12   Ethics and Evolution

James H. Fetzer

In a fascinating book, Robert Richards (1987) has suggested that the development of evolutionary theories of mind and behavior confronts at least three fundamental problems, which involve "heritable habits," rationality, and morality, respectively. The solution to the problem of heritable habits thus turns out to be the theory of natural selection, which operates at the level of behavior through a process of selection to yield changes in the frequency of genes across time, whereby combinations of genes which predispose various phenotypes toward adaptive behavior tend to be perpetuated.

The problems of rationality and morality have proven somewhat more difficult to resolve. Lumsden and Wilson (1981, 1983) have advanced their conception of mentality as susceptibility to social learning, which might, in turn, provide at least a partial solution to the problem of rationality. And the conception of an ethics based upon evolution has been widely supposed to supply the basis for a resolution of the problem of morality, as a succession of contemporary authors – from Wilson (1975, 1978), Ruse and Wilson (1985, 1986) to Richards (1987) and Alexander (1987) – have maintained.

The purpose of this inquiry is to review the most general features of their conceptions of evolutionary ethics. The conclusions that emerge here include these: that humans do not always behave morally; that kin selection and reciprocal altruism are not invariably ethical; that social cooperation is not sufficient for morality; that evolutionary ethics requires a commitment to the intrinsic value of the survival of the human species; that positive and negative species of evolutionary ethics are possible; but that any evolutionary approach requires supplementation to be complete.

The basic position

While these authors advance somewhat different views, the basic ideas they advance can be cast into a coherent position, which accents the nature of human beings in light of their biological origins. Ruse and Wilson (1985) for example, observe that humans are animals and that "the social behavior of animals is firmly under the control of the genes, and has been shaped into forms that give reproductive advantages." Ruse and Wilson (1986) reject the is/ought distinction as "debilitating," while suggesting that kin selection and reciprocal altruism afford the foundation for a biologically-based ethics.

Richards (1987) and Alexander (1987), by contrast, accept the is/ought distinction but believe that it can be overcome. Alexander (1987), for example, contends that "those who have tried to analyze morality have failed to treat the human traits that underlie moral behavior as outcomes of evolution," on the one hand, while he "explicitly reject[s] the attitude that whatever biology tells us is so is also what ought to be," on the other. Richards (1987) claims that the distinction succumbs to arguments relating empirical premises about "what is" to normative conclusions about "what ought to be."

Insofar as ethics concerns how we should behave and evolution concerns how we do behave, they might very well stand in direct opposition. If we sometimes do not behave the way we ought to behave toward one another, ethics as a domain of inquiry might transcend the resources that evolution can provide. Ethics could require more than science can supply. But if we always behave the way we ought to behave, then perhaps evolution could provide everything we need to know about moral behavior. Ethics might then require no more than science can provide. That is an open possibility.

Kin selection and reciprocal altruism

The existence of crime, of course, makes this position a rather difficult one to seriously defend. Human beings all too frequently commit murder, robbery, and rape, among their varied offenses against their fellow human. The occurrence of murder, robbery and rape supports the conclusion that we do not always behave the way we ought to behave, however, only provided we have access to normative premises concerning how we ought to behave. In the absence of access to such standards, it does not follow that the existence of crime counts as behavior that humans should not display.

Moreover, similar considerations apply to evolutionary conceptions of ethics. The existence of kin selection, reciprocal altruism and other forms of social cooperation supports the conclusion that kin selection, reciprocal altruism and other forms of social cooperation are moral behavior *only if* we have access to normative standards concerning our behavior. In their absence, it might turn out to be the case that kin selection, reciprocal altruism and social cooperation are *not* behaviors that humans ought to display. They could be evolved forms of behavior that might not qualify as moral.

Consider, for example, favoritism and corruption in businesses and corporations. When marginally qualified applicants are shown preference in hiring over others who are far better qualified because they are close relatives, kin selection may be displayed, but it is not therefore ethical. When close friends are given inside information that enable them to make fantastic profits on the market in the expectation that they will return the favor, reciprocal altruism may be involved, but it is not for that reason any less immoral. Kin selection and reciprocal altruism are not inevitably ethical.

Richards' "community good"

Richards (1987) "bites the bullet" by arguing that evolved behavior is directed toward "the community good." His position is that human beings have evolved to act for the community good and that acts for the community good are "moral acts," as a matter of definition. It presumably follows that human beings are moral beings who act as they ought to act. But the kinds of behavior that he has in mind are kin selection, reciprocal altruism and other forms of social cooperation. We have already discovered forms of kin selection and reciprocal altruism that appear to qualify as immoral.

Moreover, the phrase "the community good" harbors ambiguity. The good of the community can vary with the interests of the community and may or may not be morally praiseworthy. The existence of communities of Nazis suggests that various activities, such as book burning, forcible detention, military invasions or systematic genocide, which require social cooperation, may be for *the community good* but are not therefore moral. If humans had evolved to act for the community

good, that would not be enough to establish the morality of their acts. Cooperation is not morality.

Thus, it is a mistake to assume that behaviors which have evolved are always
moral, as Alexander (1987) seems to understand. In denying the contention that
whatever biology tells us is so is what ought to be, he implies the possibility that
evolved traits may or may not be moral. Insofar as the adaptations that evolution
has produced are not invariably moral, however, the problem remains of establishing which traits and behaviors are moral and why. Richards has not supplied the
missing premise that would provide the foundation for a theory of ethics based
upon evolution.

The descriptive vs. the normative

Other evolutionary thinkers have also emphasized that behaviors that have evolved
are not therefore moral. George Williams, for example, in a recent review of Richards (1987), quotes Thomas Huxley (with approval) when he observes that the
immoral sentiments have evolved no less than the moral sentiments, which means
that "there is, so far, as much natural sanction for the one as the other" (Williams
1989a:387). This, in turn, hints that descriptive solutions to ethical problems are
unlikely to be availing, unless we already know which traits and behavior are moral
and why.

If we already know which traits and behavior are moral and why, however, then
descriptive solutions to ethical problems are no longer required. This recognition
may be more subtle than it appears, since Richards (1987) also finds it seductive to
suppose that societies might be positioned to overcome the is/ought distinction by
appealing to *metaethical inference principles,* such as, "Conclude as sound ethical
injunctions what moral leaders preach" (Richards 1987:616). These principles are
supposed to enable normative conclusions to be drawn from factual premises.

What Richards apparently overlooks, however, is an ancient question raised about
God and His moral laws, namely: are the moral laws right because God commands
them, or does God command them because they are right? Surely we cannot know
that the ethical injunctions preached by moral leaders are right merely because they
preach them. But that means we are still confronted by the necessity of discovering precisely which ethical injunctions are right, *whether or not* moral leaders

preach them. The gap between the descriptive and the normative cannot be resolved by "metaethical inference principles" of the kind he recommends.

Ruse and Wilson's position

Similar considerations apply to other positions as well. When Ruse and Wilson (1985) suggest that the social behavior of animals is firmly under the control of the genes, the conclusion that kin selection, reciprocal altruism and other forms of cooperation are *moral* depends on other premises, such as that social behavior that is firmly under the control of the genes is always moral. If kin selection, reciprocal altruism and other forms of social cooperation can promote behavior that is immoral, however, then even behavior that is firmly under the control of the genes is not always moral.

The "firmness" of "the control of the genes," moreover, requires further contemplation. If human behavior were *completely* "under the control of the genes," the question of morality might not even arise. Our behavior, then, like that of many lower species, would be instinctual and *non*-moral, where the same kinds of social behavior would be displayed across every similar environment. Human behavior is *not* completely "under the control of the genes," since it would be a blunder to overlook the influence of other causal factors, such as social learning, in shaping human behavior.

The position that comes the closest to endorsing the idea of ethics as instinctual behavior, no doubt, is known as *psychological egoism*. According to its tenets, every human being invariably acts in his or her own personal interest, because it is impossible for humans to do otherwise. This is simply part of our nature as humans. Since psychological egoism advances a descriptive hypothesis about human nature, it has to be sharply distinguished from *ethical egoism*, which asserts the normative thesis that every human ought to act in his or her own personal interest, which is a different thing.

Psychological and ethical egoism

Indeed, as ordinarily understood, if psychological egoism is true, then ethical egoism is not merely false but actually meaningless. Such a consequence appears to follow because, if acting in our own personal interest is something that we have to do as a matter of human nature, then it makes no more sense to suggest that we ought to do it than it does in the case of eating, breathing, and sleeping. Ethical egoism would be meaningless and not merely false if psychological egoism were true, therefore, because it is normally assumed that the truth of an ought-statement presupposes that we might or might not behave that way, an issue to which we shall return.

Neither psychological nor ethical egoism, however, should be confused with the position that we always act selfishly because we always act from motives that move us. Such an attitude completely obscures fundamental moral differences between selfish and unselfish behavior. Indeed, psychological egoism turns out to be false (as a descriptive theory) if humans ever act from a sense of duty, out of friendship, for the welfare of society, for the sake of justice or to promote the well-being of others, just as ethical egoism turns out to be false (as a normative theory) if humans ever ought to act from a sense of duty, out of friendship, and so forth – assuming that these are motives that can move us (Facione, Scherer, and Attig 1991:96-98).

A weaker but more defensible version of the connection between ethics and evolution, therefore, would maintain that the trait which evolution has produced is not *moral behavior* as such but *the capacity for moral behavior* instead. Thus, if moral behavior has benefits for reproduction and survival, then when the presence and absence of moral behavior separates different human beings or different human groups, the adaptive benefits that moral behavior provides might afford a selective advantage. Every human could have the same adaptive capacity, even if only some of us ever exercise it.

Evolution and morality

There are cases, however, where ethics and morality would not appear to provide a selective advantage. Consider the Mafia hitman, for example. His success depends upon his ability to perform such acts as murder and mayhem. These seem to be immoral acts, if any acts are immoral. As a consequence, he may lead a comfortable lifestyle, with plenty of money, women, and respect. Yet consider his prospects were he to lose his talent for performing immoral acts. His potential for survival and reproduction appears to depend on his immorality. Similarly for con-artists and pimps.

If humans do not always behave morally, if kin selection and reciprocal altruism are not invariably ethical, and if social cooperation is not enough for morality, then what prospects remain for evolutionary ethics? Traditional theories of morality, which include *consequentialist accounts*, such as ethical egoism, limited utilitarianism and classic utilitarianism, are based upon the conception of something as intrinsically desirable ("the good"), where actions are proper (or "right") whenever they maximize the good. An evolutionary ethic should be based upon a similar value commitment.

The suitable foundation for an evolutionary theory of ethics thus seems to be a commitment to the intrinsic value of the reproduction and survival of the human species. The appropriate stance to adopt, I think, is to maintain that the survival and reproduction of the human species is intrinsically valuable, if anything is. Indeed, even if the existence of intrinsic values might be disputed on various grounds, a commitment of this kind appears to compare favorably with the value commitments that other theories have embraced, which include pleasure, happiness, knowledge, and even power.

Alexander's position

Among the authors under consideration here, perhaps Alexander (1987) comes the closest to adopting this conception. His emphasis upon reproductive success parallels widely-held theories about inclusive fitness as the basic value that human behavior should be expected to maximize. The distinction between "somatic" altruism, which can be adaptive, and "genetic" altruism, which is never adaptive, thus supports the inference that kin selection and reciprocal altruism can be expected to occur more frequently than behavior that sacrifices a person's genetic self-interest.

Alexander's position, however, like those of the others under consideration here, appears to reflect an impoverished conception of morality. When he contends that "moral issues can only be resolved by the collective opinions and decisions of the populace" and that "otherwise what occurs is not a resolution or by definition is not moral" (Alexander 1987:255), he confuses the nature of *ethics* with the nature of *politics*. The collective opinions and decisions of a population may be indispensable to a functional democracy, for example, but they do not define morality.

The debates over the morality of abortion, for example, do not hinge on collective opinions, voting preferences, or even the judicial decisions that determine the law

230

of the land. Traditional moral theories arise instead as a consequence of rational deliberation over general principles as they apply to specific cases in an effort to arrive at recommendations or proposals concerning how human beings ought to act toward each other. They result from *explication* as an activity aimed at clarifying and illuminating language that is vague and imprecise (Hempel 1952, Fetzer 1984).

Philosophical criticism

Consider, for example, classic utilitarianism, which adopts happiness as the nature of the good and happiness maximization as the measure of the right. When everyone is viewed as of equal moral worth, utilitarianism is commonly described by means of the maxim of *the greatest happiness for the greatest number*. But a theory of this kind can be subject to criticism on various grounds. The acute unhappiness of a minority within a population may be compatible with the greatest happiness of that population as a whole, where a slave-based society might thereby be morally justifiable.

If a morally justifiable slave-based society appears to you to be an unacceptable consequence, then you should argue for revision or rejection of any theory that implies it. Thus, ethical egoism, which makes each *person* the arbiter of his own morality, and limited utilitarianism, which makes each *group* the determiner of its own morality, appear to be untenable. The Nazis and the Mafia are two relevant counter-examples. Indeed, my discussion here of kin selection, reciprocal altruism and social cooperation illustrates the kind of reasoning characteristic of theorizing in philosophy.

One of the most persuasive reasons for taking *deontological theories* of morality – such as the categorical imperative of always treating persons as ends and never merely as means – seriously is that they provide an alternative to consequentialist approaches. Murder, robbery and rape, as well as slavery and genocide, are immoral on deontological grounds precisely because they involve treating other humans merely as means. Employers and employees, of course, may still treat one another as means as long as they regard each other with respect, which appears to be the right result.

Morality and methodology

Perhaps the most disturbing aspect of Ruse and Wilson (1986), from this point of view, is their presumption that there are just three possible sources of moral standards, namely: religious sources, especially ones derived from belief in God; genuinely objective moral axioms, which are derived from an abstract domain; and genetically based and empirically testable rules of conduct, which are derived from epigenetic rules (Ruse and Wilson 1986:174 and 186, for example). Even I admit that, if these were our only alternatives, the prospects for genuinely prescriptive, non-religious moral theories would be rather bleak. But that is not the case.

What Ruse and Wilson tend to overlook is that moral theorizing can also be pursued as a form of explication, in which notions that are vague and ambiguous, but nevertheless important, such as *right* and *wrong*, are subjected to critical scrutiny in an effort to clarify and illuminate their meaning. This process involves assessing general principles on the basis of specific cases, and specific cases on the basis of general principles, in order to arrive at tentative recommendations as to how these notions should be understood. This is the method of philosophy. Traditional moral theories, after all, cannot be adequately characterized as derived from belief in God, as derived from an abstract domain, or as derived from epigenetic rules. However, it does not follow that they are either subjective or arbitrary. As recommendations concerning the nature of moral phenomena, they can be subjected to systematic criticism and to empirical test in relation to specific examples that may display the scope and limits of those principles. This is the practice I have followed here in discussing traditional moral theories.

"Ought implies can"

More important than any misconceptions about morality and methodology, however, is Alexander's emphasis (which others share) on the role of evolution in determining human behavior. Most of his efforts appear to be directed toward the goal of securing a conception of morality that is at least consistent with if not exhausted by what evolutionary biology has to say about human nature. In this respect, his work appears to be focused less upon the is/ought distinction than it is upon the principle that "ought implies can." This emphasis accounts for much of the appeal of his work.

The principle that "ought implies can" holds that no one should be held responsible for their behavior when they could not have done otherwise. What this means, however, requires interpretation. The driver who races through an intersection at 80 mph would not be exonerated on the basis of the contention that, because he entered the intersection at 80 mph, it was impossible for him to have done otherwise. A proper rebuttal would note that he could have driven more slowly, not as a matter of historical possibility, but as a matter of physical possibility. The laws of nature permit it.

If the laws of nature made genetic altruism impossible, for example, it would be morally inappropriate to hold anyone morally responsible for his failure to display it, because "ought implies can." In this sense, biology constrains morality, since a theory of morality whose satisfaction contravened the laws of biology would thereby violate this principle. Although compatibility with the laws of biology counts as a necessary condition for morality, however, it does not likewise qualify as a condition sufficient for morality.

Rationality and morality

The strongest case for supposing that adaptations are as they should be, I suspect, emerges from the adaptationist attitude that assumes "the latest is the best" (Dupre 1987). Once we recognize that evolution is not an optimizing process, we should also realize that the way things are is not always the way things ought to be, especially in relation to behavior (Fetzer 1993). Once we recognize that evolution is unfinished and ongoing, we can resist the temptation to identify evolved traits with optimal traits, where there remains room to consider ways in which we and our world could be better.

Moreover, once we recognize that human behavior is not completely under the control of the genes, we must also admit that, to the extent to which our behavior is under the influence of social learning, older forms of biological determinism must yield ground to current conceptions of gene-culture co-evolution, where cultural traditions, customs and practices exercise their own role in shaping social behavior. Our ability to consider and to criticize the strengths and the weaknesses of various methods, processes and procedures further suggests that morality may have originated with criticism.

Our capacity for criticism represents an exercise of imagination and conjecture in thinking about how things might be different (how they could be improved upon or "made better"). Our capacity for criticism – of ourselves, our theories, and our methods – indicates that human minds can contribute to improving their own culture by "bettering" their capacities for communication, cooperation and community. It hints that, by exercising our higher mental faculties, human beings might also contribute to the survival of our species (Fetzer 1991). It thereby implies ways morality transcends biology.

Positive vs. negative ethic

Before discussing Alexander's views further, it should be observed that, given the commitment to the intrinsic value of the survival of the species, there still appear to be at least two approaches to implementing an ethic based on evolution. The first is (let us say) the *positive* ethic of doing anything we can possibly do to advance the survival of the species. The second is (let us also say) the *negative* ethic of not doing anything we can possibly do to inhibit the survival of the species. Though some theoreticians might be inclined to disagree, these principles do not amount to the same thing.

The negative ethic, for example, suggests not reducing any cooperation and communication between the members of the population of human beings to avoid diminishing the well-being of the species. It also implies that global pollution and nuclear warfare are patterns of behavior that ought to be discouraged. The positive ethic, by contrast, could be offered in support of genetic engineering and even infanticide on behalf of doing everything possible to promote the survival of the species. The positive ethic might threaten individual rights. It could even justify forms of genetic fascism.

I therefore believe that theories of morality based upon evolution are ultimately destined to prove to be incomplete. It appears to me as practically inevitable that they have to be supplemented by deontological commitments to the equal worth of every human being. It appears to me as theoretically indispensable to combine the intrinsic value of the survival of the species as a *collective* end (for all of us together) with respect for the intrinsic value of every member of the species as a *distributive* end (for each of us individually). An approach of this kind appears theoretically defensible.

An evolutionary ethics

An approach of this kind not only embraces the necessity for a commitment to the intrinsic value of the species but also concedes the importance of the is/ought distinction. It makes no effort to dispense with the difference between the way things are and the way things should be, but rather views the way things are as a stage in the evolution of the species, where cultural innovations and improvements might yet generate enormous benefits for future generations. Ethics does require more than science can provide. It requires an exercise of rationality of a certain philosophical kind.

The apparent necessity to encompass personal rights within evolutionary ethics suggests that moral behavior may or may not possess an evolutionary advantage. The proper response, I think, is that sometimes it does and sometimes it does not. Virtue, of course, is supposed to be its own reward. While cooperation may frequently provide evolutionary advantages, there is more to morality than cooperation. And as a largely cultural rather than exclusively genetic phenomenon, there can be no "genetic explanation" for morality as a trait of every human. Morality is a normative conception.

Incorporating respect for the individual together with concern for the species does not mean that scientific discoveries and technological innovations cannot be put to work on behalf of human beings. What it means is that, when genetic engineering or other techniques are utilized on behalf of the species, it must be within a context of respecting every person's individual worth. As we confront the problem of over-population, for example, we ought to employ every available method *provided* that it does not violate personal rights. On this account, there is a crucial difference between forced sterilization and voluntary birth control. It is a matter of morality.

Motivation and morality

In the final analysis, the problems of rationality and of morality turn out to be intimately intertwined. Understanding the nature of morality requires the exercise of rationality, where the difference between consequentialist and deontological theories deserves consideration. In the end, a morality based upon evolution implicitly shifts attention from the population to the species, where the long term interests of the species tend to displace the short term interests of the population. But it would be all too easy to misunderstand the nature of this exchange in points of view.

Because individuals are the agents who perform actions, it might be supposed that, since they are the actors, the rightness or wrongness of their actions must be a function of their motives. But, as in the case of other consequentialist theories, the rightness or the wrongness of acts is determined by their contribution to maximizing the survival of the species, provided, of course, that personal rights are respected. Whether an action is right or wrong, therefore, is not determined by whether or not an agent recognizes that fact. Right acts can be done for wrong reasons.

Still, it would be (at least vaguely) reassuring if humans could act on the basis of appropriate motives for morality. If humans could never be motivated by appropriate moral sentiments, then it might be maintained that, even if psychological egoism happens to be false (because we sometimes act on the basis of motives that do not put our own interests first), the principle that ought-implies-can precludes the truth of another moral theory. If the most promising moral theories imply that humans should (at least sometimes) act to benefit the species or to respect the rights of others, for example, their plausibility would be drastically undermined or completely destroyed if humans never act on the basis of such motives.

Recent research results

I have been fascinated to learn that recent empirical studies provide strong support for the existence of moral sentiments of the kinds implied by the conception of evolutionary ethics which I have outlined (Petrinovich, O'Nell and Jorgensen 1993). These studies involved samples of college students who were presented with (hypothetical) choice situations of two kinds, namely: "trolley problems" and "lifeboat problems." In *trolley problems*, a decision must be made whether or not to throw a switch that would determine whether individual-or-group X or individual-or-group Y is killed. In *lifeboat problems*, a decision has to be made to determine which among six members of a lifeboat survive.

The examples that were employed tested the subjects' attitudes toward killing or sacrificing human beings vs. members of other species, unfamiliar persons vs. friends and relatives, ordinary persons vs. Nazis, endangered species vs. non-endangered species, and ordinary persons vs. elite members of society. The results displayed a very strong bias in favor of human beings over members of other species, a very strong bias in favor of friends and relatives, and a strong bias against persons who were Nazis. Mere numbers turned out to be moderately important, while the endangered species factor and the elitist factor were minimal.

These findings suggest that (at least some) humans have motives of the kinds that are appropriate to moral behavior in accordance with the conception of evolutionary ethics described above. Indeed, although no component directly tested the motive of respect for the rights of others, insofar as Nazis represent a group devoted to deliberate and systematic violations of the rights of others, I think it is reasonable to interpret the strong negative bias against Nazis as a strong positive bias in favor of respect for the rights of others. Moreover, since kin selection is not improper when employed as a "tie breaker" within a context of respecting the rights of others, for example, nothing here appears to undermine, much less destroy, the conception of evolutionary ethics which I have defined.

Ultimate value conflicts

If an ultimate commitment to the intrinsic value of the survival of the human species has to be combined with respect for the intrinsic value of every member of the species, then the question arises of whether conflicts between these value commitments can occur and, if so, how they can be resolved. I believe that the influence of mere numbers ought to make more and more of a difference – both in test situations and in daily life – as other factors are balanced out. In other words, when the lives of few innocent human beings are pitted against the lives of many innocent human beings, the importance of numbers should increase proportionately.

Consider, for example, the choice between killing one innocent human being and killing the entire human species. Surely there should be little room for controversy in a case of this kind. This suggests that societies may have important (collective) evolutionary reasons for imposing severe penalties upon those who would (distributively) threaten their existence (by disclosing secrets vital to the national defense, by assassinating their political leaders, and the like). Precisely when cases of these kinds are at hand, of course, can be controversial, since "national security" may at least sometimes be advanced as a rationalization for political purposes.

Another kind of ultimate value conflict, however, may not be resolved quite so easily. It follows from our ultimate commitment to the intrinsic value of the species that the members of other species are equally entitled to an ultimate commitment to the intrinsic value of their species. This consequence has sometimes been labeled "speciesism," precisely because an organism's ultimate values depend upon the species to which it belongs. Nothing about speciesism appears to defeat the prospects for evolutionary ethics, provided that we acknowledge that other species possess the same moral rights to defend themselves against humans as we do against them.

Inclusive fitness

Nothing about an approach of this kind necessarily has to contradict the genetic interest of members of societies in relation to their offspring. Assuming that each parent contributes 50% of their genes to the genetic composition of their children, that their children in turn contribute 50% of their genes to the genetic composition of their offspring, and so forth, each parent would seem to have a genetic representation equal to $1/2\ n$ per offspring in each successive generation, where n is the number of that generation. The consequences of this conception for evolutionary theory itself, of course, were introduced by Hamilton (1964).

As Williams has observed, Hamilton's theory of *inclusive fitness* elaborates the conception that "the survival and reproduction of a relative are partly equivalent, in evolutionary effect, to one's own survival and reproduction" (Williams 1989b:184). When we know who our relatives are and how closely they are related to us, therefore, we can be in an appropriate position to act toward them as manifestations of our own genetic legacy. Even when we have no offspring of our own, we can still retain an interest in the survival and reproduction of the culture of our species, especially if we have made contributions (books, tools, etc.) of our own.

The most difficult case appears to be when we do not know who our relatives are or how closely they are related to us and when we have no cultural contributions of our own. Even then we may still be motivated to act to benefit the survival and reproduction of the species, especially when we have offspring who might have other offspring of their own in unknown and unpredictable numbers across successive generations. The perpetuation of our own personal genetic or cultural representation thus appears to be compatible with an evolutionary ethics of the above kind, because it reinforces our impersonal motives to perpetuate the species.

Is nature immoral?

The position that I have advanced appears to be "moderate" relative to those advanced by other thinkers. While Ruse and Wilson, Richards, and Alexander tend to assume that natural selection operates in favor of morality (when *morality* is properly understood), Williams contends that natural selection operates against morality (when *natural selection* is properly understood). Thus, he maintains that the biological effects of natural selection display "gross immorality" in a sense which goes far beyond mere selfishness of the kind attributed to human beings by psychological or by ethical egoism (Williams 1989b:180-181). For Williams, the conception of an "evolutionary ethics" is virtually a self-contradiction.

The basis of Williams' attitude appears to be that nothing in nature exemplifies conformity to traditional maxims of morality: "Nothing resembling the Golden Rule or other widely preached ethical principles seems to be operating in living nature. It could scarcely be otherwise, when evolution is guided by a force that maximizes genetic selfishness" (Williams 1989b:195). Yet here and elsewhere Williams appears to confound the difference between behavior that is *instinctual* and behavior that is *voluntary*, where it makes no sense to describe instinctual behavior as "moral" or "immoral." He even attacks speciesism by comparing the triumph of one population over another to a form of "systematic genocide" (Williams 1989b:196).

If nature operates on the basis of laws of nature that it cannot violate and it cannot change, however, then it appears to make no more sense to hold nature responsible for its conduct than it would to hold humans responsible for theirs. If the appropriate standard for moral responsibility among humans turns out to be that no laws of nature inhibited us from acting otherwise, then the same standard should apply with respect to nature. The principle that ought-implies-can also holds *between* different species. There is no good reason here for describing nature as "immoral" or for believing that an evolutionary ethics cannot be consistent.

Concluding reflections

The ultimate import of the ought-implies-can connection with which Alexander, especially, has been concerned, therefore, is that, as Scoccia (1990) has observed, we must clearly distinguish *our motives for being moral* from *what makes our actions right*. Acts that were motivated by reciprocal altruism, by kin selection or simply by self-interest may still turn out to be morally proper acts, provided that they maximize the survival of the species without violating personal rights. The existence of a defensible evolutionary ethics in this sense is no longer in doubt. While biology constrains morality, morality cannot be reduced to biology alone.

The existence of a defensible evolutionary ethics, however, does not by itself afford any guarantees that human beings will be smart enough or courageous enough or (even) moral enough *to do the right thing* from an evolutionary point of view. Even if the positive evolutionary ethic advises us to do anything we possibly can do to advance the survival of the species and the negative evolutionary ethic advises us to not do anything we can possibly do that might inhibit the survival of the species (where acts of both kinds are compatible with acknowledging the intrinsic value of every human being), our actions still may or may not qualify as moral.

If the conception of evolutionary ethics that I have proposed amounts to an adequate theory of morality (in its general conception, if not in its specific details), then we have the general normative premises in relation to which the morality or immorality of actions may be suitably assessed. Nevertheless, unless our motives for morality are sufficiently strong that we bring ourselves to the point of acting on the basis of policies that implement those normative standards, our prospects for the future may be just as poor as they have been in the past. We can continue to pollute the world and we can continue to run the risk of nuclear warfare. We must learn to act in ways that will nurture and sustain the reproduction of the human species as a whole. Even when we understand both biology and morality, therefore, our survival ultimately depends upon our rationality.

Postscript

At least three questions might be raised about the position that I have developed here. The first is that the combination of a commitment to the intrinsic worth of each individual with a commitment to the survival and reproduction of the human species appears to mix together deontological and utilitarian conceptions of morality in a fashion that some theoreticians may find unsatisfactory. Even deontological commitments, however, must take *consequences* into account, since it follows that treating persons with respect is morally appropriate, while not doing so is morally inappropriate. Actions that have these consequences are moral or immoral, respectively, apart from any utilitarian framework. I thus maintain that the position I defend here is essentially deontological both distributively and collectively.

The second question concerns how thinking about populations is meant to differ from thinking about species. I envision *populations* as collections of individuals who exist at one time, while a *species* includes the ancestors and the offspring of a population. The underlying conception, therefore, is that a population is a temporal stage in the evolution of a species. Thus, a proper conception of the connection between ethics and evolution dictates that consideration be given to future generations of existing populations in arriving at decisions that may affect their prospects for reproduction and survival. This is the sense in which we owe it to our offspring to provide them with the resources that are essential to their well-being, at least in the sense of the negative ethic, if not also in the sense of the positive ethic.

The third question concerns what may appear to be tacit commitments to *group selection* as a mechanism that affects the course of evolution. As many readers are no doubt aware, there is a very strong aversion to group selection among evolutionary thinkers today. I admit that this issue does not lend itself to easy resolution. So far as I can discern, "group selection" occurs whenever any arrangement (organization or cooperation) between various conspecifics makes a difference to their prospects for survival and reproduction. Insofar as particular arrangements between conspecifics do influence their evolutionary prospects, therefore, group selection appears to make a difference to the course of evolution (cf. Fetzer 1986). I would concede, however, that for other conceptions the matter may be less clear.

Acknowledgments

Special thanks to George C. Williams, Kristin Shrader-Frechette, Lewis Petrinovich, and James P. Hurd, the editor of this volume, for their valuable comments and criticism. In addition to various other revisions, their very pointed queries led me to compose the "Postscript" as a formal response.

References

Alexander, R.
1987   *The Biology of Moral Systems*. New York, NY: Aldine de Gruyter.

Dupre, J., ed.
1987   *The Latest on the Best: Essays on Evolution and Optimality*. Cambridge, MA: MIT Press.

Facione, P., D. Scherer and T. Attig.
1991   *Ethics and Society*, 2nd ed. Englewood Cliffs, NJ: Prentice Hall.

Fetzer, J. H.
1984   Philosophical Reasoning. *In* J. H. Fetzer, ed., *Principles of Philosophical Reasoning*. Totowa, NJ: Rowman and Allanheld. Pp. 3-21.
1986   Methodological Individualism: Singular Causal Systems and Their Population Manifestations. *Synthese* 68: 99-126.
1991   *Philosophy and Cognitive Science*. New York, NY: Paragon House, Chapter 8.
1993   *Philosophy of Science*. New York, NY: Paragon House, Chapter 8.

Hamilton, W. D.
1964   The Genetical Evolution of Social Behavior. *Journal of Theoretical Biology* 7: 1-52.

Hempel, C. G.
1952   *Fundamentals of Concept Formation in Empirical Science*. Chicago, IL: University of Chicago Press.

Huxley, T. H.
1897   *Evolution and Ethics and Other Essays*. New York, NY: D. Appleton and Company.

Lumsden, C. and E. O. Wilson
1981   *Genes, Mind and Culture*. Cambridge, MA: Harvard University Press.
1983   *Promethean Fire: Reflections on the Origin of Mind*. Cambridge, MA: Harvard University Press.

Petrinovich, L., P. O'Neill and M. Jorgensen.
1993   An Empirical Study of Moral Intuitions: Toward an Evolutionary Ethics. *Journal of Personality and Social Psychology* 64: 467-478.

Richards, R.
1987   *Darwin and the Emergence of Evolutionary Theories of Mind and Behavior*. Chicago, IL: University of Chicago Press.

Ruse, M. and E.O. Wilson
1985   The Evolution of Ethics. *New Scientist* 17: 50-52.
1986   Moral Philosophy as Applied Science. *Philosophy* 61: 173-192.

242

Scoccia, D.
    1990   Utilitarianism, Sociobiology, and the Limits of Benevolence. *Journal of Philosophy* LXXXVII: 329-345.

Williams, G. W.
    1989a   Review of Robert Richards, Evolution and the Emergence of Evolutionary Theories of Mind and Behavior. In *Evolutionary Biology* 2: 385-387.
    1989b   A Sociobiological Expansion of *Evolution and Ethics*. In *Evolution and Ethics*. J. Paradis and G. C. Williams, eds. Princeton, NJ: Princeton University Press. Pp. 179-214.

Wilson, E. O.
    1975   *Sociobiology: The New Synthesis*. Cambridge, MA: Harvard University Press.
    1978   *On Human Nature*. Cambridge, MA: Harvard University Press.

Index

—D—

—E—

SYMPOSIUM SERIES